D0132348

Guggenheim Museum: A to Z

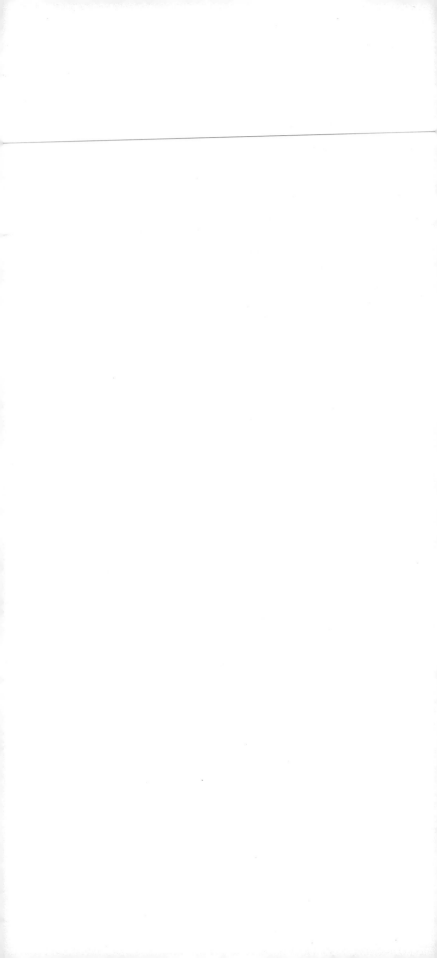

Guggenheim Museum: A to Z

Nancy Spector, General Editor

Preface by Thomas Krens

Entries by Nancy Spector, Jennifer Blessing,
Cornelia Lauf, Jan Avgikos

and Dore Ashton, Germano Celant,
Lisa Dennison, Judi Freeman, Gary Garrels,
Michael Govan, Linda Dalrymple Henderson,
Lysa Hochroth, John Miller, Rose-Carol
Washton Long, Bruce Brooks Pfeiffer,
Mark Rosenthal, Joseph Thompson,
Coosje van Bruggen, Diane Waldman

©The Solomon R. Guggenheim Foundation,
New York, 1992, 1993, 1996
All rights reserved

ISBN: 0–89207–071–4

Guggenheim Museum Publications
1071 Fifth Avenue
New York, New York 10128

All photographs are by David Heald with the exception of: pp. 59 (top), 185 (bottom), 247 by Andrew Frolows; p. 85 by Robert E. Mates; p. 101 by James Franklin; p. 195 (top and middle) © Giorgio Colombo, Milan; p. 217 by Attilio Maranzano; p. 227 courtesy Bernice Steinbaum Gallery, NYC; p. 239 courtesy The Pace Gallery; p. 253 courtesy Sonnabend Gallery

The captions provide English titles and dates for works that are illustrated. Dimensions are given in inches; height precedes width, followed by depth when relevant. The first two digits of the Solomon R. Guggenheim Foundation number indicate the year of acquisition.

Color separations by Color Control, Inc., Redmond, Wash.

Printed in Italy by G. Canale & C. S.p.A, Milan

Contents

Preface

The overall quality and importance of the works of art presented in this book might give the impression that the Guggenheim collection is the realization of a carefully considered and implemented strategy, one that anticipated the major artists and developments of the 20th century with a singular prescience. There is more than a bit of irony in such a conclusion, however, for the museum evolved without benefit of a master plan. That it is now celebrated in this guide is a testimony to the felicitous nature of collecting and the fortuitous circumstances that brought these significant aesthetic objects together.

The story of the Guggenheim Museum in New York is essentially the story of five very different private collections—Solomon R. Guggenheim's collection of non-objective paintings; Justin K. Thannhauser's singular array of Impressionist, Post-Impressionist, and early Modern masterpieces; Karl Nierendorf's holdings in German Expressionism; Katherine S. Dreier's paintings and sculptures of the historic avant-garde; and Count Giuseppe Panza di Biumo's vast holdings of American Minimal Art of the 1960s and 1970s—augmented through the years by the directors and curators of the museum to form one great collection of art dating from the late 19th century through the present.

The metamorphosis from private collection to public museum is an extraordinary transition. For the Guggenheim, this occurred in 1937, when Solomon R. Guggenheim established a foundation empowered to operate a museum that would showcase his impeccable—though narrowly focused—collection. The subsequent addition of private collections has led to the evolution from a museum dedicated solely to non-objective painting to one in which the history of Modern art, albeit with strongly stated preferences, emerges. This dynamic process continues today, an ongoing testimony to the richness of the relationship between private collectors and a public trust.

But the Guggenheim is not merely the sum of its component collections. Like the other great museums of the U. S. and Europe—many of which have at their core personal collections that were formed in a passionate and often idiosyncratic manner—the Guggenheim plays a greater role than as a repository for works of art. Museums perform a vital social function by creating the conditions necessary for the public to encounter objects of material culture. (These conditions include exhibition, conservation, preservation, and interpretation.) Museums secure for current and future generations the opportunity to see and experience cultural history, while ensuring the survival of inherently fragile works of art against the fickleness of taste and the ravages of time.

Guggenheim Museum: A to Z is the first publication marking the reopening of the Guggenheim Museum after a two-year closing for an extensive restoration and expansion project. It is the result of the staff's continued dedication to the never-ending task of researching, evaluating, and presenting each important work in the collection. It also provides the opportunity to highlight several important works that were generously donated to the museum during the last two years.

Under the deft direction of Nancy Spector, Associate Curator, this guide represents an attempt to create a fresh and timely approach to the collection, sensitive to the broad fields of understanding—social and political history, philosophy, psychoanalysis, and critical theory—that have become integral to dialogues about art. The result, we trust, will be both satisfying for the specialist and inviting to the museum's varied visitors.

—Thomas Krens

Introduction and Acknowledgments

The works illustrated and examined in the following pages were selected for their historical and aesthetic significance with an eye toward creating a concise overview of the Guggenheim Museum's exceptional collection of Modern and contemporary art. Although the book is organized alphabetically by artist rather than chronologically or by art-historical movement, the entries propose to situate the artists' works within their historical, social, and cultural climates. This approach represents the application of recent revisionist art-historical methodologies to the analysis of the museum's holdings, thus marking a departure from other publications on the collection that have emphasized documentation over interpretation.

The alphabetical arrangement of the guide—spanning from Albers to Zorio—was adopted to avoid the often arbitrary categorizations that occur when an artist's work is presented exclusively within specific aesthetic movements or chronological periods. The arrangement also serves as a gentle parody of the prevalent notion of the art museum as an encyclopedia, filled with singular examples of myriad objects removed from their cultural contexts. To extend our play on the encyclopedia, we have interspersed texts on various concepts of Modern art—"Action," "Non-Objective," "Spiritual," and the like—throughout the alphabet. Particular art-historical movements referred to in the entries, such as Cubism and Surrealism, are explained in the glossary at the end of the book. This alphabetical array of artists with their art works and various theoretical concepts has produced intriguing juxtapositions and revealed unexpected affinities. Collectively, the entries and concepts form a fragmented, yet coherent, survey of late-19th- and 20th-century artistic thought and vision.

Guggenheim Museum: A to Z reflects the contributions of numerous individuals: My co-authors, Jennifer Blessing, Cornelia Lauf, and Jan Avgikos, brought insightful and provocative perspectives on Modern and contemporary art—as well as a great sensitivity—to the works under discussion. The guidebook is also enhanced by the concepts on art provided by a range of leading scholars, whose unique and distinctive voices demonstrate the diversity of analytical methods in today's art community. Kim Paice compiled the thorough glossary of art-historical terms found at the end of this book. Special thanks are owed to architect Michael Gabellini, whose creative renderings of the Guggenheim Museum were used as the basis for the overlay—a delightful, imaginary tour through the structure. The drawings were brought to life by illustrator Tom Powers, of the Ivy League of Artists. I am indebted to Massimo Vignelli, who not only designed this guidebook but was a key participant in the development of its concept.

A project of this complexity and detail would not have been feasible without the invaluable organizational and editorial skills of our Publications Department. In particular, I want to acknowledge Anthony Calnek, Managing Editor, whose tireless efforts made the realization of this book possible. Laura Morris, Assistant Editor, aided in many stages of the editorial and production process. I also wish to thank the Guggenheim's designer, Cara Galowitz, who took the guidelines set forth by Vignelli Associates and designed each page. David Heald is largely responsible for the high caliber of the reproductions in this book, both through his talent as a photographer and his close involvement in the production process. Pamela Myers, Administrator for Exhibitions and Programming, skillfully coordinated many aspects of design and production.

Thanks are also due to Andrea Feeser, Collections Curatorial Assistant, Sonja Bay, Librarian, and Ward Jackson, Archivist. Clive Phillpot, Director of the Museum of Modern Art's library, also provided invaluable assistance.

At certain stages in the making of this guidebook Gail Harrity, Deputy Director for Finance and Administration, and Judith Cox, General Counsel, provided timely help.

I want to express my personal gratitude to Diane Waldman, Deputy Director and Senior Curator, Michael Govan, Deputy Director, and Lisa Dennison, Collections Curator, for assisting with the selection of the works in this guidebook. And for his support of this endeavor, my deepest appreciation goes to Director Thomas Krens.

Finally, this catalogue was supported in part by a grant from the National Endowment for the Arts, a Federal agency, generously matched by the Stephen C. Swid and Nan G. Swid Foundation. For both of these contributions we are most grateful.

—Nancy Spector

Solomon R. Guggenheim Museum
1071 Fifth Avenue

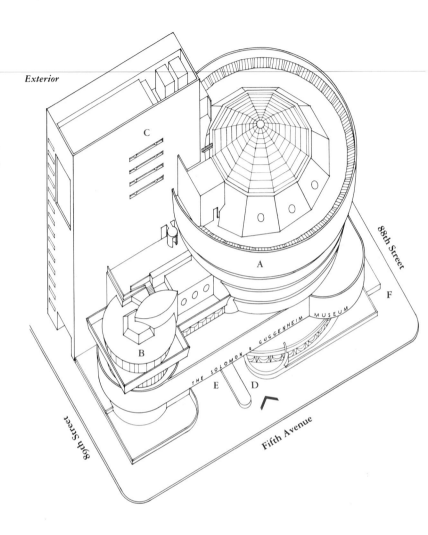

Exterior

Architects:
Frank Lloyd Wright: original museum, completed in 1959.
Gwathmey Siegel and Associates Architects: Tower, completed in 1992.

Solomon R. Guggenheim Museum designated a New York City Landmark in 1990.

Drawings by Peter Sweeny based on Gwathmey Siegel and Associates Architects' drawings.

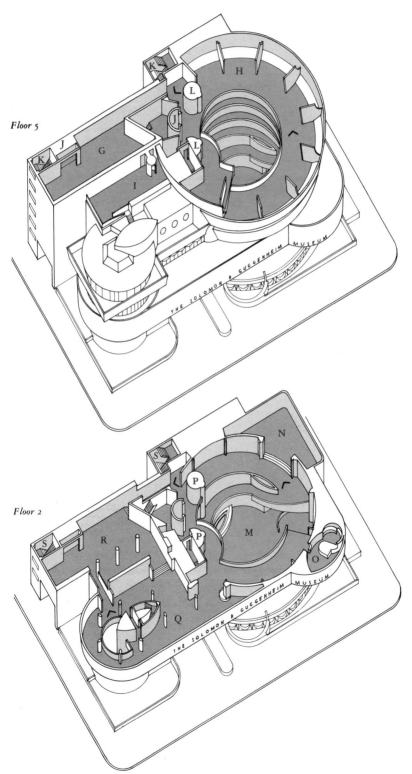

Floor 5

Floor 2

THE SOLOMON R. GUGGENHEIM MUSEUM

13

Guggenheim Museum SoHo
575 Broadway

Second floor
A   Second-floor
    galleries
B   Rest rooms

First floor
C   Main entrance
D   Guggenheim
    Museum Store
E   Main lobby
F   Admissions/
    membership desk
G   Information desk
H   Coatroom
I   First-floor galleries
J   Stairs
K   Elevator
L   Entrance

Basement
M   Café
N   Rest rooms

Architects:
Thomas Stent: 575 Broadway, completed 1882.
Arata Isozaki: Guggenheim Museum SoHo, completed 1992.

*Exterior of building designated a New York City Landmark within
the SoHo Cast-Iron Historic District in 1973.*

Drawings by Peter Sweeny based on Arata Isozaki's drawings.

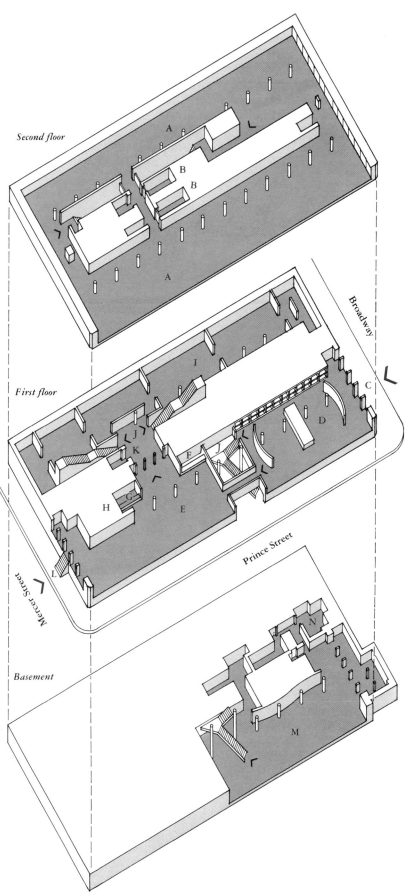

Second floor

A

B

B

A

Broadway

First floor

I

C

D

J

K

E

J

H

G

E

Mercer Street

L

Prince Street

N

Basement

M

15

Solomon R. Guggenheim Museum

The commission to design a gallery for Solomon R. Guggenheim's Museum of Non-Objective Painting came to Frank Lloyd Wright by way of a letter from its director, Baroness Hilla Rebay von Ehrenwiesen, on June 1, 1943. "I want a temple of spirit, a monument!" she wrote.

Wright's first sketch showed a museum of six levels in a hexagonal plan around an open, central court. Each level contained a band of high windows, bringing diffused light in through horizontal glass tubes, much as in his S. C. Johnson and Son administration building of 1936–39. Additional light came from a central glass dome at the sixth level. On the plan of this first proposal, the architect wrote "continuous ramp," and the idea of a spiral-ramped building was born. Later studies portrayed the spiral getting either smaller or larger as it rose; the latter solution was eventually settled upon by Wright.

The architect described his scheme as one in which the visitor would enter the building on the ground level, take an elevator to the top, and descend the gradually pitched ramp until returning to the entrance. At any point during the descent one could look over the parapet of the central court and see where one was. Each complete circle brought one around to the elevator.

The rising costs of building materials as well as changes in the museum's own program brought on a series of steady delays, each demanding new plans and working drawings from Wright's office. But finally in August of 1956 ground was broken and construction launched. Wright last visited the job site in January 1959, by which time the basic form of the building was in place. He died on April 9 of the same year, and the completed museum, by now renamed the Solomon R. Guggenheim Museum, opened to the public in October.

The greatest change that has occurred in the last 33 years is an addition designed by Gwathmey Siegel and Associates Architects, which provides four additional floors of exhibition space and two floors of office space. This addition engages the Frank Lloyd Wright rotunda behind the triangular stair tower at the second, fifth, and seventh floors, but does so in such a way that the drama and completeness of the main ramp is not impaired or disturbed.

—Bruce Brooks Pfeiffer

Solomon R. Guggenheim Museum
1071 Fifth Avenue, New York City

Architects:
Frank Lloyd Wright: original museum, completed in 1959.
Gwathmey Siegel and Associates Architects: Tower, completed in 1992.

A   Main entrance
B   Café entrance
C   Guggenheim
    Museum Store
D   Thannhauser
    Collection
E   Thannhauser
    galleries
F   Sculpture Terrace
G   High Gallery
H   Staff offices
I   Auditorium
J   Tower galleries
K   Rotunda

Drawings by Michael Gabellini based on Gwathmey Siegel and Associates Architects' drawings. Illustrated by Tom Powers, Ivy League of Artists.

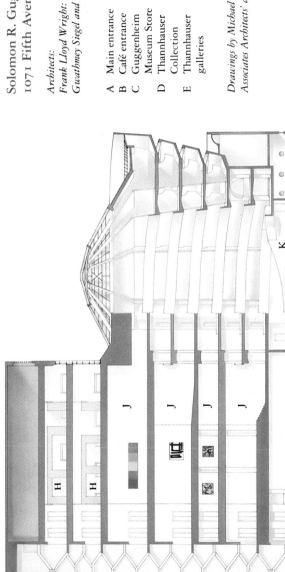

A to Z:
Guggenheim Museum Collection and
Concepts in 20th-Century Art

A

Action

The concept of action forcefully entered visual-arts commentary in 1952, when Harold Rosenberg articulated it in a celebrated essay, *The American Action Painters*. "At a certain moment," he wrote, "the canvas began to appear to one American painter after another as an arena in which to act. . . . His act-painting is of the same metaphysical substance as the artist's existence." Rosenberg drew his image from his impression of American Abstract Expressionist painters such as Willem de Kooning and Jackson Pollock, but comparable diction was also used in Europe, where terms such as Art Informel, Art Autre, and Tachisme were used to discuss works by Hans Hartung, Wols, and Matta, among others. The theories behind these terms also identified the gesture—or act—of painting as the most significant aspect of the painter's process.

Such postwar thoughts were drawn from several prewar sources. The emphasis on gesture as a self-mirroring process was derived from Surrealist doctrine, in which "pure psychic automatism" was thought to free the artist from stylistic convention and rationalist construction. In the process of automatist drawing, the artist would, in André Breton's phrase, heed "thought's dictation" without mental preconceptions and interference, and, ideally, in full freedom.

The issue of freedom loomed large after the cataclysmic war, and action was fused with ethical and philosophical concerns. The notion that an individual can be defined by his acts was implicit in existentialism. Sartre declared that "a man is not other than a series of undertakings." Other philosophers stressed the "lived" experience in aesthetics, as opposed to theoretical doctrine. In the phenomenology of Heidegger and Husserl and the writings of William James and John Dewey, the concept of the lived experience was applied to a dynamic aesthetic in which the whole being of the viewer is in action as a work of art is contemplated.

—Dore Ashton

Willem de Kooning, Composition *(detail).*

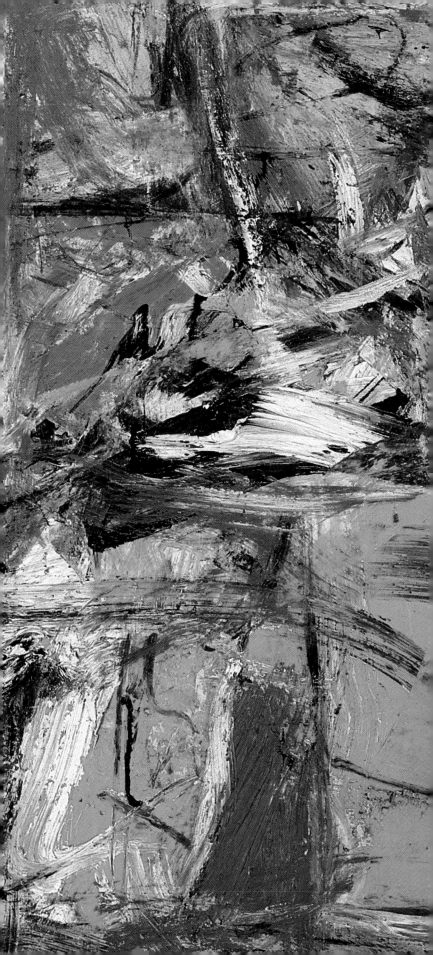

"No smock, no skylight, no studio, no palette, no easel, no brushes, no medium, no canvas. No variation in texture, or 'matière', no personal handwriting, no stylization, no tricks, no 'twinkling of the eyes.' I want to make my work as neutral as possible."

Josef Albers

b. 1888, Bottrop, Germany; d. 1976, New Haven

Josef Albers was a professor at the Bauhaus before leaving his native Germany in 1933 for America, where he taught at Yale University and Black Mountain College, among other art schools. As a teacher, his influence in this country was enormous, and may be detected in the works of a diverse range of artists, including Robert Rauschenberg, Michael Loew, Donald Judd, and, more recently, Peter Halley.

Impossibles dates from Albers's years at the Bauhaus and represents his experiments with nontraditional materials and techniques. The mechanical means of producing such glass pieces allowed him to achieve the discipline and detachment that he considered necessary to create nonrepresentational forms. Like other artists of his generation, Albers moved from a figurative style of picture-making to geometrically based abstraction. *Homage to the Square: Apparition*, painted in 1959, is a disarmingly simple work, composed of four superimposed squares of oil color applied with a palette knife directly from the tube onto a white, primed Masonite panel. It is part of a series that Albers began in 1950 and that occupied him for 25 years. The series is defined by an unmitigating adherence to one pictorial formula: the square. The optical effects Albers created—shimmering color contrasts and the illusion of receding and advancing planes—were meant not so much to deceive the eye as to challenge the viewer's faculties of visual reception. This shift in emphasis from perception willed by the artist to reception engineered by the viewer is the philosophical root of the *Homage to the Square* series. Albers tried to teach the mechanics of vision and show even the uninformed viewer *how* to see. He was always proud that many non-art students took his classes at Yale.

The *Homage to the Square* series is also distinguished by the carefully recorded inscriptions of technical details on the back of each panel. This codification of the making of the painting, along with the reductively systematic application of colors, anticipated much of the art of the mid-1960s, when painting was stripped of the transcendental, and (in the case of Conceptual Art) the paint was often left out altogether.

—C. L.

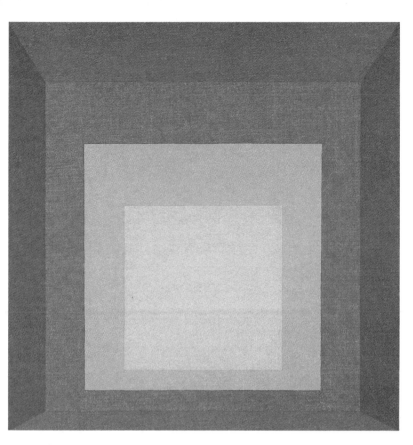

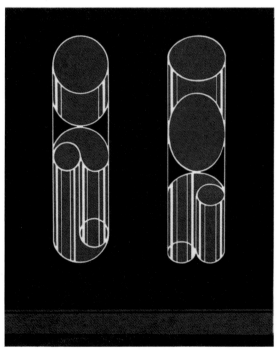

Homage to
the Square:
Apparition,
1959. *Oil on
Masonite*, 47 1/2 x
47 1/2 *inches*.
61.1590

Impossibles,
1931. *Sand-
blasted flashed
glass*, 17 11/16 x
14 7/8 x 13/16 *inches*.
*Gift, The Josef
Albers Foundation,
Inc*. 91.3878

*"My works are
not the embodiments
of ideas or
conceptions."*

Carl Andre

b. 1935, Quincy, Mass.

The work of Carl Andre occupies an essential transitional position in contemporary art. The artist himself places it in a tradition spanning Constantin Brancusi to Henry Moore, yet historically it rests within the more recent context of ideational gestures, starting with the early paintings of Frank Stella. The Guggenheim Museum's collection covers a wide range of Andre's oeuvre, including the viewer-interactive *10 x 10 Altstadt Copper Square*, in which space is defined by both the work and the spectator who is free to walk across it; *Fall*, an angle of hot-rolled steel; and *Trabum*, a cube made of nine interlocking beams of Douglas fir.

These examples embody the characteristic features of Andre's sculpture, such as the use of ready-made materials, the employment of modular units, and the articulation of three-dimensionality through a consideration of its negative as well as positive space. Andre has sought to reduce the vocabulary of 20th-century sculpture to basic phonemes such as squares, cubes, lines, and diagrams. In his avowed transition from the exploration of form to that of structure and of place, Andre has placed significant emphasis on the relation between site and viewer. His pseudoindustrial, untheatrical arrangements hover between being ideas and testing the limits of physical presence.

Poetics play an important role in Andre's work, manifested most literally by his experiments with linguistic equivalents to his sculpture. Since the 1960s he has created poems and, in the tradition of concrete poetry, situated the words on the page as if they were working drawings. He has often reached to ancient languages for titles in his attempt to craft a primordial language of form; for example, the title *Trabum* is derived from the Latin for log or timber. Andre's consistent search for the simplest, most rational models embodies a moral philosophy as well as an artistic practice.

—C. L.

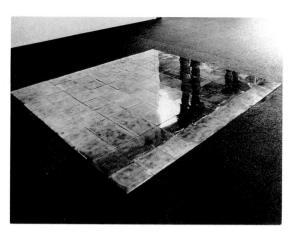

10 x 10 Altstadt
Copper Square,
1967. *Copper;
100 pieces, each
³/₁₆ x 19 ¹¹/₁₆ x
19 ¹¹/₁₆ inches.
Panza Collection.
91.3673*

Fall, 1968. *Hot-
rolled steel; 21
pieces, each 71 ⁷/₈ x
28 x 72 ¹¹/₁₆
inches. Panza
Collection.
91.3670.a-.u*

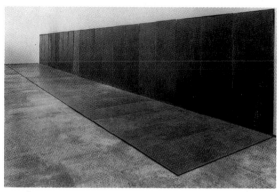

Trabum, 1977.
*Douglas fir, nine
sections, 36 x 36 x
36 inches.
Purchased with the
aid of funds from
the National
Endowment for the
Arts in Washing-
ton, D.C., a
Federal Agency;
matching funds
contributed by Mr.
and Mrs. Donald
Jonas.
78.2519.a-.i*

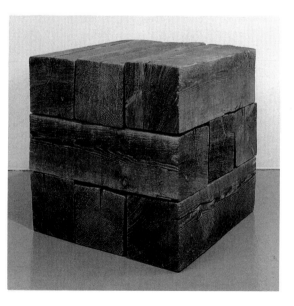

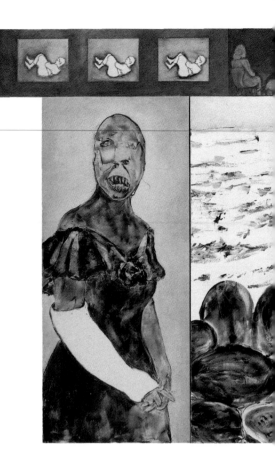

*"Push Low Comedy
to Its Extreme /
Take a series of
skits and routines /
If you push hard
enough it becomes
tragedy."*

Ida Applebroog
b. 1929, Bronx, N.Y.

During the 1970s Ida Applebroog, like other
artists such as Neil Jenney and Jonathan
Borofsky, sought to return content—including
political commentary and humor—to painting,
which seemed to have become hermetic and self-
referential. They often relied on narrative styles
and the interaction of image and text, borrowing
freely from any visual form that served their
purposes. Applebroog has called on such diverse
sources as Renaissance altarpieces and the
techniques of modern cinematography to create
her multipanel paintings. Her subject matter is a
mixture of people engaged in mundane activities
and enigmatic moments of horror or implied
violence, resulting in a highly nuanced nonlinear
narrative of human experience.

Applebroog's cartoonlike characters enact
legacies of domination and dependency. In *Noble
Fields*, the apparently innocent child eating a
watermelon (which gives him a giant smile)
seems threatened by the toothy, monster-masked
mother figure in the left panel. Yet the cast on
the woman's arm renders her threat of ferocity
dubious, and the strange echo between the flat
oval of her face and the watermelons leaves one to

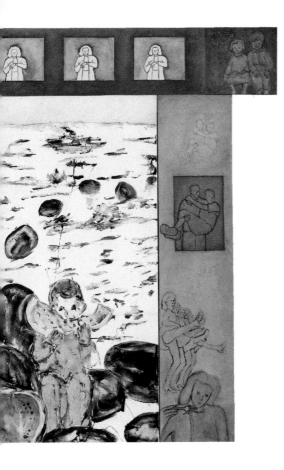

Noble Fields,
1987. *Oil on
canvas, five panels,
86 x 132 inches
overall. Gift,
Stewart and Judy
Colton.
87.3560.a-.e*

wonder if the child is in a field of beheaded
monster-mothers. Although much of
Applebroog's imagery suggests the socially
sanctioned abuse of power, it is often difficult to
separate the victim from the victimizer. This kind
of ambiguity, typical of late-20th-century art, has
a precedent in Goya's work, which has inspired
many politically conscious contemporary artists.
Through pictures combined with words, Goya
criticized human evils and foibles, setting his
sights in particular on the hypocrites who might
deny their own complicity.

The disjunctive relationship between the two
large panels reverberates in the juxtaposed stop-
action scenes. Although the vignettes often
suggest literalizations of figures of speech, it is
rarely possible to assert any single reading—all
interpretations are valid. There is no clear
beginning and end here, but on many levels we
recognize these moments and fill in the blanks
between them with our own experiences: that
signal event in childhood that dogs us, moments
of terror, loneliness, and guilt, and the
melancholy of life gone by.

—J. B.

Alexander Archipenko
b. 1887, Kiev; d. 1964, New York City

No doubt it was a sense of pride and more than an inkling of historical place that prompted the young Alexander Archipenko to inscribe these two works with his name and "1913 Paris." Soon after arriving in Paris at the age of 20, the Ukrainian artist could claim membership in the prestigious Section d'Or group, putting him in the company of the Duchamp brothers, Pablo Picasso, and Guillaume Apollinaire. *Carrousel Pierrot* and *Médrano II* are souvenirs of this heady time.

None of Archipenko's colleagues would have missed the allusions in these works to the Cirque Médrano (which many artists frequented), the vogue for puppetry, or the jesters in Picasso's paintings. Harlequins and saltimbanques were traditional stand-ins for the artistic persona; they also offered a unique package of shapes and colors for formal resolution.

Carrousel Pierrot fits into Archipenko's lifelong fascination with the possibilities of polychromy and the abstract figure in the round. Reminiscing about the origin of *Carrousel Pierrot*, Archipenko later recalled that he was inspired by a festival where "dozens of carrousels with horses, swings, gondolas and airplanes imitate the rotation of the earth." *Médrano II* is almost anomalous within Archipenko's oeuvre. Although it relates to the later "sculpto-paintings" for its crossover between two disciplines, the work is the only extant example of the theme of a figure in motion, with which Archipenko experimented in two other works (*Médrano I* and *Woman in Front of Mirror*, both destroyed). In this investigation, he was keeping pace with Marcel Duchamp, who had explored this theme in his 1912 painting *Nude Descending a Staircase*. Also aware of the advances of Synthetic Cubism, Archipenko incorporated reflective glass, wood, and metal into *Médrano II*. In two early poems, Archipenko's friend and supporter Apollinaire had featured saltimbanques and a protagonist named Columbine, who "disrobes and / Admires her reflection in the pool." Perhaps this was the inspiration for the dancer in *Médrano II,* who seems to gaze at her own image in a mirror.

—C. L.

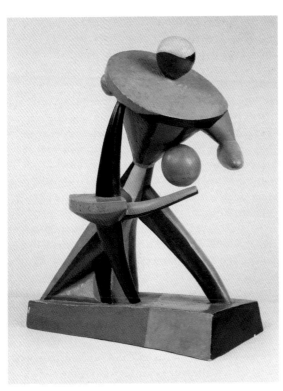

Carrousel Pierrot,
1913. *Painted
plaster, 24 x
19 $^1/_8$ x 13 $^3/_8$
inches.* 57.1483

Médrano II,
1913–14?
*Painted tin, wood,
glass, and painted
oilcloth,* 49 $^7/_8$ x
20 $^1/_4$ x 12 $^1/_2$
inches. 56.1445

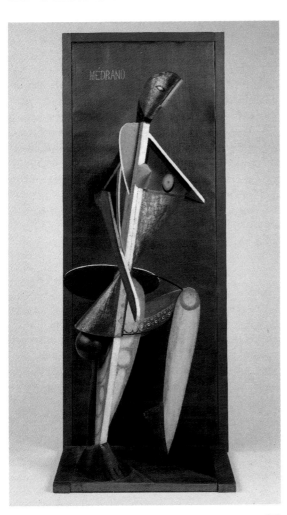

"These works, like nature, were ordered 'according to the law of chance.'"

Jean Arp

b. 1886, Strasbourg, Alsace-Lorraine; d. 1966, Basel

As a founding member of Dada, Jean Arp was among those artists who espoused a rejection of traditional bourgeois values and taste. Arp's response to illusionistic art, which he saw as a bogus reproduction of reality, was to create an abstract one, which would ultimately be a truer indication of reality because its generative principles would echo nature's. His method included the expression of chance, informed by the Dadaists' desire for liberation from the so-called rationality that led to World War I. For Arp, chance also represented a fundamental law of the organic realm, and his first reliefs, made during the war, are colorful and witty evocations of plant and animal forms on layered wooden panels.

In the early 1930s Arp developed the principle of the "constellation," employing it in both his writings and art works. As applied to poetry, the principle involved using a fixed group of words and focusing on the various ways of combining them, a technique that he compared to "the inconceivable multiplicity with which nature arranges a flower species in a field." In making his *Constellation* reliefs, Arp would first identify a theme—for example, five white biomorphic shapes and two smaller black ones on a white ground—then recombine these elements into different configurations. *Constellation with Five White Forms and Two Black, Variation III* is the last of three versions of this theme. Rather than doggedly copying nature, Arp's variations are poetic evocations of the metamorphosis and change inherent to the cycle of life.

While Arp worked on his reliefs through the 1920s and early 1930s he was actively engaged with both Surrealism and the approach to pure abstraction associated with Neo-Plasticism. Membership in these movements was usually mutually exclusive, but Arp's diplomacy enabled him to maintain contact with both. His work, like Joan Miró's, engaged Surrealism at the level of process, for he used automatist strategies to get beyond the constrictions of rational thought. Yet, like Piet Mondrian, he believed in the Neo-platonic goal of representing a higher plane of reality through abstraction.

—J. B.

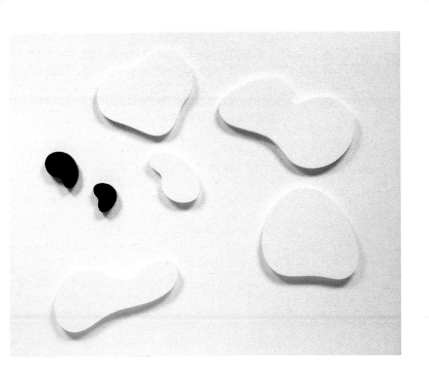

Constellation
with Five White
Forms and Two
Black, Variation
III, *1932. Oil on
wood, 23 ⁵/₈ x
29 ⁵/₈ inches.*
55.1437

Avant-Garde

The term "avant-garde" is usually used to describe the engine of thrust and forward motion that aids art in its progression from one stage to another. It is closely aligned with the term "Modernism," and both concepts have been used as analytical springboards for discussions of art produced roughly between 1860 and 1960. This period, the "machine age," coincided with European and American dominance of the world militarily, politically, and economically. Following World War II, this balance of power began to break down. The 1960s saw an acceleration of the process, and by the 1970s only the shell of the old order remained intact.

The shifting postwar situation coincided with a sense of the failure of progress both as a historical condition and as a legitimate concept. Belief in the avant-garde necessarily was attenuated, if not lost, within this analysis. But the redefinition of art is an ongoing issue. The question is whether the term avant-garde itself should be attached to what is now a different set of conditions from that of the previous epoch or if it might be better to let it fall into disuse.

As we move toward the end of the century, it becomes clearer that a redefinition of progress and of the nature of the avant-garde *is* possible. We may find a new way to look forward, to engage the future, to challenge the present. One striking possibility is that the avant-garde may no longer bear a direct lineage to the traditions of European painting and sculpture, even as transformed by the great Modern artists of the early 20th century. A different continuum of cultural precedents and influences is possible, as is a new balance between Europe and America, within Europe, and between the West and Japan, the Arab world, Latin America, Africa, or elsewhere.

A vitally diverse cultural expression is now emerging, even under economic duress, from various regions, countries, and groupings of people. If avant-garde can be equated with radical challenge and formative synthesis and creativity, then the concept remains alive, even if we let the term itself go. Its validity is assured if we acknowledge its achievements by in turn expanding our own terms of evaluation and understanding. In this sense the vanguard functions to push us toward the recognition of the new against the historical claims of the past.

—Gary Garrels

Max Beckmann, Paris Society *(detail).*

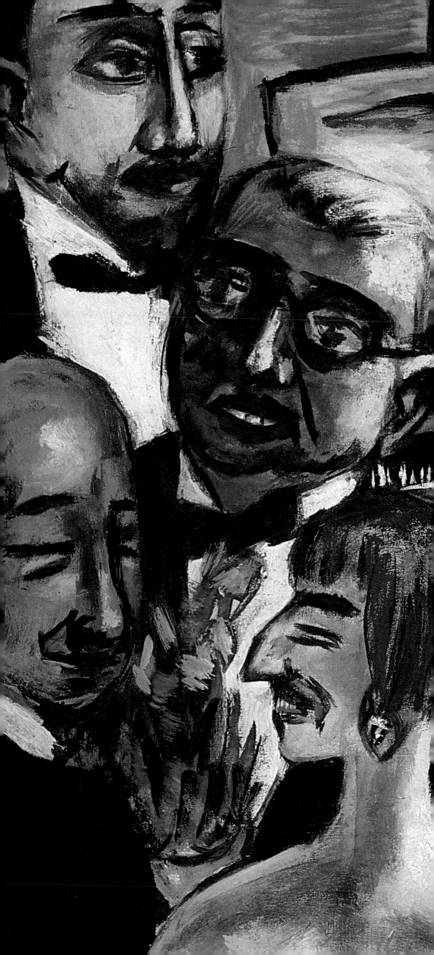

B

"The greatest art
always returns you
to the vulnerability
of the human
situation."

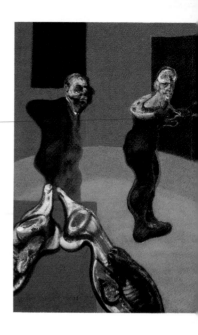

Francis Bacon
b. 1909, Dublin; d. 1992, Madrid

In 1944, one of the most devastating years of
World War II, Francis Bacon painted *Three Studies
for Figures at the Base of a Crucifixion.* With this
horrific triptych depicting vaguely anthropomorphic creatures writhing in anguish, Bacon
established his reputation as one of England's
foremost figurative painters and a ruthless
chronicler of the human condition. During the
ensuing years, certain disturbing subjects
recurred in Bacon's oeuvre: disembodied, almost
faceless portraits; mangled bodies resembling
animal carcasses; images of screaming figures; and
idiosyncratic versions of the Crucifixion.

One of the most frequently represented
subjects in Western art, the Crucifixion has come
to symbolize far more than the historical and
religious event itself. Rendered in modern times
by artists such as Paul Gauguin, Pablo Picasso,
and Barnett Newman, this theme bespeaks
human suffering on a universal scale while also
addressing individual pain. The Crucifixion
appeared in Bacon's work as early as 1933. Even
though he was an avowedly irreligious man,
Bacon viewed the Crucifixion as a "magnificent
armature" from which to suspend "all types of
feeling and sensation." It provided the artist with
a predetermined format on which to inscribe his
own interpretive renderings, allowing him to
evade narrative content—he disdained painting as
illustration—and to concentrate, instead, on
emotional and perceptual evocation. His
persistent use of the triptych format (also
traditionally associated with religious painting)

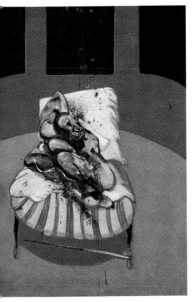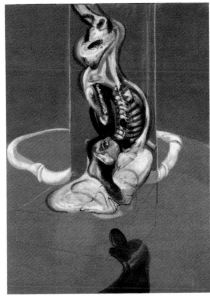

furthered the narrative disjunction in the works through the physical separation of the elements that comprise them.

That Bacon saw a connection between the brutality of slaughterhouses and the Crucifixion is particularly evident in the Guggenheim's painting. The crucified figure slithering down the cross in the right panel, a form derived from the sinuous body of Christ in Cimabue's renowned 13th-century *Crucifixion*, is splayed open like the butchered carcass of an animal. Slabs of meat in the left panel corroborate this reading. Bacon believed that animals in slaughterhouses suspect their ultimate fate. Seeing a parallel current in the human experience—as symbolized by the Crucifixion in that it represents the inevitability of death—he has explained, "we are meat, we are potential carcasses." The bulbous, bloodied man lying on the divan in the center further expresses this notion by embodying human mortality.

—N. S.

Three Studies for a Crucifixion, March 1962. Oil with sand on canvas; three panels, each 78 x 57 inches.
64.1700

Georg Baselitz

b. 1938, Deutschbaselitz, Germany

The dark of night laps at the edges of *The Gleaner*, a fire burns on the upper left, and a sunlike shape hovers beneath the lone figure. Yet Georg Baselitz's monumental, somber work was painted during a decade of well-being in Germany, when the generation of the *wirtschaftswunder*—the economic miracle—was only interrupted in its relentless quest for stable prosperity by the occasional political scandal or terrorist attack. How does this image, so clearly a representation of an existentialist condition, address the complex issues facing postwar German art and society?

The key lies in the orientation of the gleaner, searching for sustenance in a barren landscape: the figure is depicted upside down. Baselitz has used this device consistently since 1969–70, his intention being, in part, to subvert the criteria for viewing paintings. To this end, Baselitz inverts, and thus negates, the subjects of his work. He cites but does not pay homage to the mythic protagonists that, as in Wagner's epic operas, have so often been the focus of German art and culture. For Baselitz, the individual is the locus of redemption and the cause for despair. He has painted a great number of his anti-heroes in guises ranging from military costumes to stark nudity.

Baselitz once termed his technique a non-style. The upside-down figure, brutality of gesture, and emotive yet distanced strokes have, however, long since become highly recognizable trademarks. Ironically, Baselitz, who 30 years ago sought to replace the congealed expressionism sweeping Europe with a fresh, aggressive style and comparably controversial subjects, is now regarded as one of the foremost artists of Germany and has been accorded retrospective exhibitions internationally. His work strongly influenced the generation of painters that came of age during the early 1980s. But unlike the Neo-Expressionists he inspired, Baselitz does not rehash past styles, nor is his milieu truly international. Baselitz's painting remains a deeply felt and authentic engagement with the spiritual depletion of the postwar period.

—C. L.

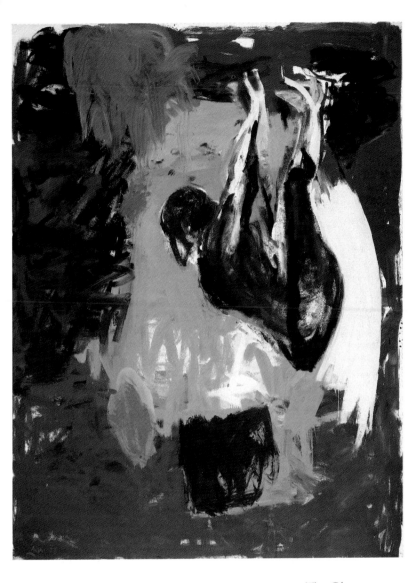

The Gleaner,
*Aug. 1978. Oil
and tempera on
canvas,* 129⁷/₈ *x*
98³/₈ *inches.
Purchased with
funds contributed by
Robert and Meryl
Meltzer.* 87.3508

"The things in my painting are intended to strike something that is an emotional involvement—that has to do with the human personality and all the mysteries of life, not simply colors or abstract balances."

William Baziotes

b. 1912, Pittsburgh; d. 1963, New York City

William Baziotes's paintings are freely improvised, intuitive affairs created in the spirit of Surrealist automatism. Each canvas, he claimed in 1947, "has its own way of evolving. . . . Each beginning suggests something. . . . The suggestion then becomes a phantom that must be caught and made real." For Baziotes, the "reality" he aspired to exists only in a poetic realm, one in which color and form serve as analogues for psychological and emotional states. This use of visual metaphor was inspired by the artist's love for poetry, particularly that of Charles Baudelaire, whose theory of "correspondences" proclaimed the fundamental equivalence of all things in nature and the capacity of any designated thing to symbolize something beyond itself. By the late 1940s Baziotes achieved his signature formal motif—delicate, semitranslucent, biomorphic shapes suspended within aqueous fields of muted color—which invokes the Baudelarian world of allusion and association. "The emphasis on flora, fauna and beings," explained the artist about his painting, "brings forth those strange memories and psychic feelings that mystify and fascinate all of us."

Baziotes shared his keen interest in nature with other artists of the New York School, who were motivated simultaneously by their search for primordial truths and their fascination with scientific inquiry. What bridged these two utopian investigations was the microscope; the invisible world of protean forms it revealed promised to disclose the origins of life. This preoccupation with identifying metaphysical features of the organic realm may illuminate Baziotes's predilection for marine imagery, as demonstrated in *Aquatic*, a painting of serpentine forms swimming through a calm, watery world. The symbolic possibilities of the ocean are vast and Baziotes drew on many of its meanings. *Aquatic* has been interpreted as an expression of the artist's romantic vision of the sea as a domain of symbiotic relationships. The artist was captivated by the mating practice of eels, which swim through the ocean, rarely touching but always together. The delicately intertwined lines in the picture have been thought to represent these faithful eels on their course through the watery depths. *Dusk*, one of many pictures relating to nocturnal themes, is a lyrical evocation of a contemplative moment, the nuanced ebb of time between day and night, the half-light of evening.

—N. S.

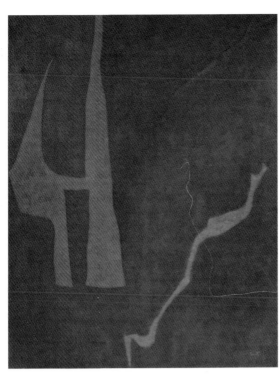

Dusk, *1958. Oil
on canvas, 60 ³/₈ x
48 ¹/₄ inches.
59.1544*

Aquatic, *1961.
Oil on canvas, 66 x
78 ¹/₈ inches.
Collective
anonymous gift.
63.1630*

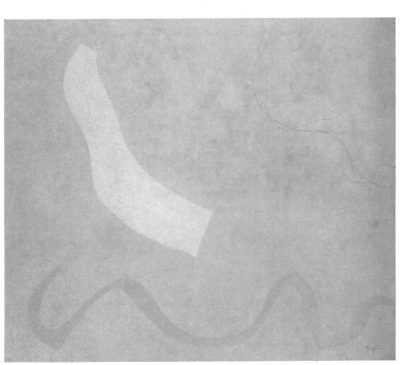

"We wanted to provide a viewpoint or rather a grammar for people to understand and compare different structures."
—Bernd Becher

Bernd and Hilla Becher

Bernd Becher, b. 1931, Siegen district, Germany
Hilla Becher, b. 1934, Berlin

In 1990 Bernd and Hilla Becher, a husband-and-wife team, received an award at the Venice Biennale. Although photography is their exclusive medium, the prize was granted in another category—sculpture. This ingenious gesture by the Biennale jury testifies to the artists' success in creating an art form that falls beyond existing aesthetic parameters.

Since 1957 the Bechers have traveled throughout Europe and North America taking black-and-white photographs of industrial architecture: water towers, coal silos, blast furnaces, lime kilns, grain elevators, preparation plants, pithead gears, oil refineries, and the like. They organize their photographs into series based exclusively on functional typologies and arrange them into grids or rows. This serves both to invoke and reinforce the sculptural properties of the architecture—they have called the subjects of their photographs "anonymous sculptures"—the forms of which are primarily determined by function. Through this method the artists reveal the diverse structural and material variations found within specific kinds of edifices. The water towers comprising the sequence presented here, for example, are all constructed of metal, yet they differ vastly in form. Such differences are underscored by constants that prevail from series to series: the photographs are usually taken from the same angle, the light is evenly distributed, and the prints are identical in size.

The photographs, particularly those of now-demolished structures, refer to specific historical periods, particularly the late-19th-century shift to industry. When contemplated in our post-industrial society, these images can be interpreted as nostalgic ruminations on a lost era. But they do not lack a critical edge. The intense and obsessive nature of the Bechers' project mirrors and discloses the relentless order of industrial production, a phenomenon that has had monumental implications for the economy and the environment.

The serial repetition of the Bechers' work, coupled with its focus on industrialization, has inspired comparisons to Minimalism. The artists, who avoid any form of categorization, would not necessarily condone such an analogy. It is telling, however, that one of the finest appreciations of the Bechers to have been written is by Minimalist sculptor Carl Andre.

—N. S.

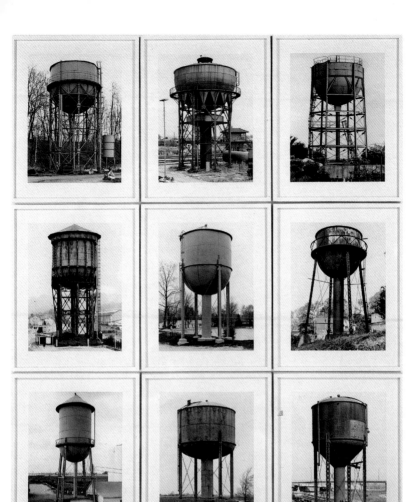

Watertowers,
1980. Nine black-
and-white
photographs
mounted on board,
each 15 7/8 x 12
inches. Purchased
with funds
contributed by
Donald Jonas.
81.2793.1-.9

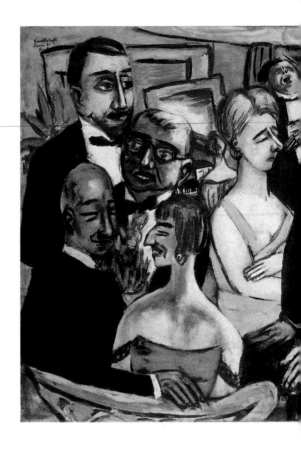

"Everywhere I find deep lines of beauty in the suffering and endurance of this terrible fate."

Max Beckmann

b. 1884, Leipzig, Germany; d. 1950, New York City
Paris Society is Max Beckmann's portrait of émigrés, aristocrats, businessmen, and intellectuals engaged in disjointed festivity on the eve of the Third Reich. Beckmann painted the work on an invitation from the German embassy in Paris. A series of sketches shows that Beckmann had conceived of the composition as early as 1925. By 1931, when he completed it, accusations and slander against the free-thinking artist had begun to mount in Germany, and the somber character of *Paris Society* seems to reflect his sense of foreboding. Beckmann spent much of his time in Paris, although financial hardship stemming from his persecution led him to give up his studio there one year later. He eventually emigrated to Amsterdam and then to the U.S.

Paris Society is rife with ambiguities. The event depicted is a black-tie party, although the socialites gathered there seem strangely depressed. Some of the figures in the composition were identified by the artist's widow, Mathilde Beckmann. They include the central figure, Beckmann's friend Prince Karl Anton Rohan; the Frankfurt banker Albert Hahn at the far right; the music historian Paul Hirsch seated at the left; the German ambassador Leopold von Hoesch, at

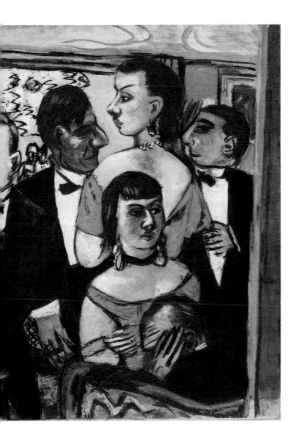

Paris Society, *1931. Oil on canvas, 43 x 69 ⅛ inches.* 70.1927

the lower right, with his head in his hands; and possibly Paul Poiret, the French couturier, standing at the left. But why they are together in this scene and what their peculiar postures denote remain a matter of speculation.

In café, hotel, and beach scenes, Beckmann had proven himself to be a mordant painter of modern life, and some German critics counted him among the artists of the Neue Sachlichkeit (New Objectivity). The universalizing tendency of his moral allegories, however, diverged from the political satire of his colleagues, such as Otto Dix and George Grosz. Beckmann's paintings do not succumb to precise interpretation. In spite of their period detail, they seem to represent a condition rather than a historical moment.

—C. L.

"My personal history is of interest only in so far as I have attempted to use my life and person as a tool, and I think this was so from a very early age."

Joseph Beuys
b. 1921, Krefeld, Germany; d. 1986, Düsseldorf

These works by Joseph Beuys may be said to reflect three distinct phases in the artist's career. *Animal Woman*, an example of Beuys's early work, is closely tied to his years in the workshop of his teacher, Ewald Mataré. Beuys accentuated the fetishistic character of the work by finishing the various casts of the statue (there are seven casts and one artist's proof) with different patinas. The grossly enhanced sexual characteristics of *Animal Woman*, notably the hips and breasts, are in keeping with the type of nature imagery that Mataré and he favored during the late 1940s; a primordial female nude was a recurring subject of Beuys's work at this time.

By 1962 Beuys had ceased creating objects, turning his attention to performance art and sculptural experiments with nontraditional materials. *F. I. U.: The Defense of Nature* exemplifies the way Beuys's life came to merge with his art. The work refers to an ecological campaign that Beuys and his dealer, Lucrezia de Domizio, waged in the 1980s with the help of his students at the art academy he had founded to encourage creativity—the Free International University (hence the F. I. U. of the title). The campaign required the use of a car, pamphlets, copper tubing, and spades that were meant to be plunged vigorously into the Italian countryside. Beuys sold the car, its contents, and two blackboards as part of his routine transformation of performance materials into art works that would in turn fund other projects.

Encounter with Beuys (a title probably given by de Domizio) consists of a vitrine containing felt, fat, copper pieces, and cord, the materials he used repeatedly to describe significant events in his life. The first two materials refer to the pivotal incident in his life, a wartime plane crash in which mountain people saved his life by wrapping him in felt and fat; copper was used by Beuys to represent spiritual conduction, while cord as a ready-made has fascinated artists from Piero Manzoni to Dorothea Rockburne. The placement of autobiographical objects in a vitrine relates particularly to his major 1985 exhibition in Naples, where he installed a series of golden plates and vitrines, suggesting the burial hall of a king. Beuys favored the vitrine for its ready association to ethnographic installations. As part of his fusion of rituals and their fetishes, he believed that art and artifacts could not always be distinguished from one another.

—C. L.

42

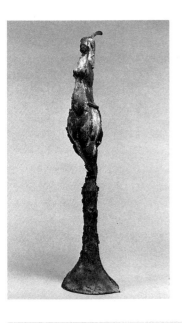

Animal Woman,
1949, cast 1984.
Bronze, 18 ³/₈ x
5 ¹/₄ x 4 inches.
85.3256

Encounter with
Beuys, *1974–84.*
Vitrine containing
felt, copper, fat, and
cord, 75 x 78 ⁵/₈ x
23 ¹/₂ inches.
Purchase, The
Gerald E. Scofield
Bequest.
87.3522.a-.h

F. I. U.:
The Defense
of Nature,
1983–85.
Automobile, 13
shovels, 21 copper
pieces, 159
pamphlets, and 2
slate blackboards;
installation area
approx. 50 x 210 x
70 inches.
85.3315.a,
.b.1-.13,
.c.1-.21,
.d.1-.159,
.e.1,.2

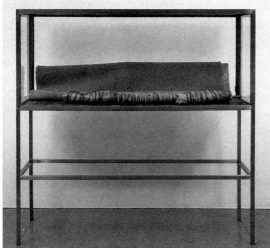

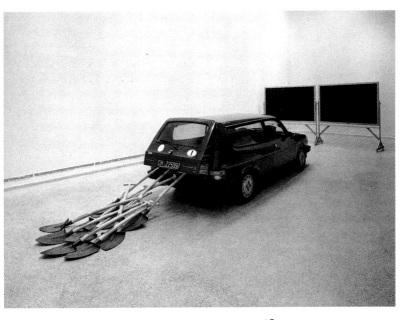

Joseph Beuys

Terremoto means earthquake in Italian; more specifically, on November 23, 1980, it meant the destruction of a small city on the volcanic heights above Naples. At the invitation of a Neapolitan cultural center, Beuys and several other artists made works to commemorate the lost lives and other effects of the disaster. The Guggenheim Museum's *Terremoto*, constructed in Rome at roughly the same time, is a pendant to the Neapolitan work. Although its title and date tie it specifically to the Neapolitan earthquake, it also refers to a contemporary political situation.

This installation reiterates Beuys's public support of independence for this region of Italy. An Italian flag, wrapped in felt, is draped against an ancient typesetting machine that was once used in the production of the newsletter of a leftist political party, Lotta Continua (The Fight Continues). Grease has been smeared on the keys of the machine, rendering them dysfunctional. A blackboard on the floor leans against a small oil drum, as if elemental lessons would suffice to educate people to the inequities of capitalism. More blackboards form an altar around the printing machine. They bear alchemical symbols and chalk drawings of skulls, which might represent the victims of the quake.

The manifestos glued to the printing machine refer to the Action Third Way, a theory of political activism that Beuys helped to develop in the late 1970s; it argues for an economic system based neither on the values of Western capitalism nor on the monopolies of the state created by 20th-century interpretations of Marxism. One important element of the Third Way is an emphasis on ecology. Beuys alludes to this in *Terremoto* by opposing technology with organic substances, and printed texts with handwritten ones. He developed this further in the larger environmental installations dating from the last years of his career, which are among his most far-reaching works, enormous in scope, magnificent in their intention, and involving hundreds of participants. They center around a single theme: his call for a change in thinking that develops out of personal understanding rather than from technological advances.

—C. L.

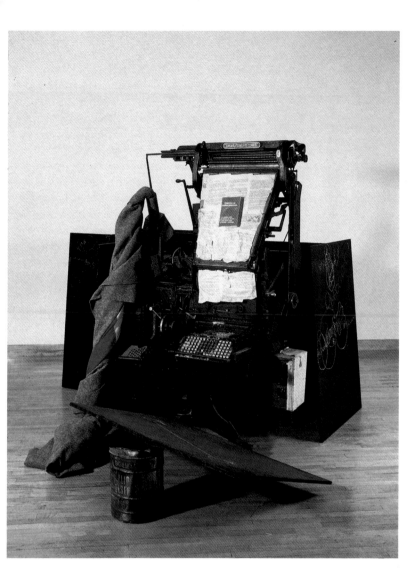

Terremoto, 1981.
*Room installation
consisting of a
typesetting machine,
an Italian flag,
felt, 9 blackboards
with chalk
drawings and
diagrams, a metal
container with fat
and lead type, a
cassette recorder
with tape, and a
brochure, 80 x
137 3/4 x 193
inches.*
91.3960.*a-.n*

Pierre Bonnard

b. 1867, Fontenay-aux-Roses, France; d. 1947, Le Cannet, France

At the time Bonnard was painting this summer breakfast scene, Rockefeller Center stood half built and Europe was gearing itself for war. Yet the modern world seems all but ignored in Bonnard's painting, which harks back to the artistic tenets of the late 19th century, its vibrant colors conjuring up the canvases and theories of Paul Gauguin's circle. Around 1890 Bonnard belonged to the Nabis (from the Hebrew word for prophet), a group that tended to paint mystical or occult scenes in order to invoke extraordinary psychic states. As this painting shows, Bonnard still lent a hallucinatory aura to the everyday some 40 years later.

Bonnard resolutely painted subjects such as *Dining Room on the Garden* for most of his life, being called an "intimiste" and "très japonard" for his attempts to create a charged psychological moment in a virtually nonperspectival domestic space. This painting, one of more than 60 dining-room scenes he made between 1927 and 1947, is neither decorative (as these works have often been called) nor is its subject truly his first concern. *Dining Room on the Garden* sets out to capture the moment and the intrinsically ungraspable play of mood and light. On close inspection, the colored areas within the flattened picture plane lose their relation to the objects depicted: a chair melds into the window frame; the window echoes the painting's borders, becoming a view within a view; and Marthe, the painter's oft-depicted wife, merges passively into her surroundings. It is in his ability to create a timeless microcosm while laying bare the gesture of applying paint to canvas that Bonnard's Modernism is revealed.

—C. L.

46

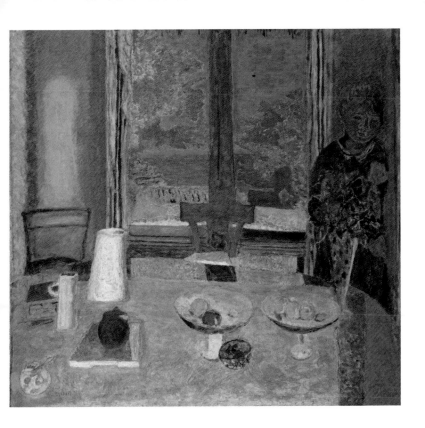

Dining Room on
the Garden,
*1934–35. Oil on
canvas, 50 x 53 ¹/₄
inches. Gift,
Solomon R.
Guggenheim.
38.432*

"The subject of pain
is the business I am
in. To give meaning
and shape to
frustration and
suffering. What
happens to my body
has to be given a
formal aspect. So
you might say, pain
is the ransom of
formalism."

Louise Bourgeois
b. 1911, Paris

The designation of an artist's "late work"—as in the case of Paul Cézanne or Pablo Picasso—often implies a slackening of formal criteria and an introspective, if not nostalgic, attitude that results, ultimately, in a clarity of vision. For Louise Bourgeois, these qualities have held true for an aesthetic production spanning five decades, during which she has created a rich and ever-changing body of work that oscillates between abstraction and the visceral representation of psychic states. What unifies Bourgeois's myriad drawings, installations, and sculptural essays in marble, wood, metal, plaster, or latex is an intense emotional substance that at once exposes facets of her own personal history and confronts the bittersweet ordeal of being human. Present throughout the oeuvre is a fusion of seeming opposites, a deliberate dismantling of Western dualistic thought, which rends male from female, order from chaos, good from evil, pleasure from pain. In many of her anthropomorphic sculptures, Bourgeois merges images of breasts and vaginas with representations of penises to create ambiguous but, nevertheless, complete entities. The tension between diametrically opposed emotional states—aggression and impotence, desire and rejection, terror and fortitude—is explored in her most recent work.

In haunting assemblages of collected objects that trigger memory and association, Bourgeois contemplates the various permutations of pain. According to the artist, the elegant sculpture *Defiance* symbolizes self-preservation in the face of adversity and anguish. Composed of delicately, but tenaciously, balanced shelves supporting manifold glass containers and mirrors, all of which have belonged to Bourgeois, *Defiance* suggests the strength achieved by acknowledging, even embracing, vulnerability. Whereas her carved stone sculptures represent defense against pain through rigidity—a resistance under pressure—the open, transparent vessels in this work signify, for Bourgeois, the courage to reveal feelings of inadequacy, fear, and loneliness. The soft light that shines through them from a hidden source of illumination expresses the will to adopt this particular strategy of defense, in which one is utterly exposed yet self-possessed and thus secure. Fragile yet resilient, ephemeral yet exceedingly tangible, *Defiance* is essentially a three-dimensional poem that bespeaks the emotional struggles at the core of Bourgeois's art.

—N. S.

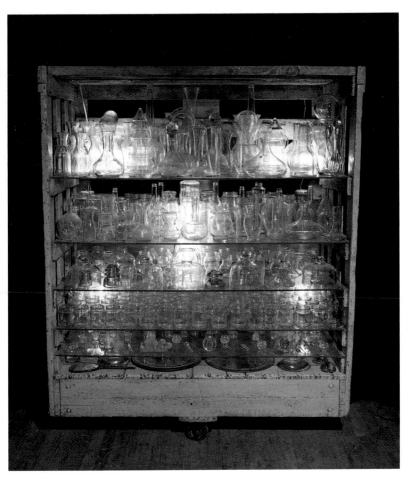

Defiance, 1991.
Painted wood,
glass, and electrical
light, 67 ¹/₂ x 58 x
26 inches.
91.3903

"Simplicity is not an objective in art, but one achieves simplicity despite oneself by entering into the real sense of the thing."

Constantin Brancusi
b. 1876, Hobitza, Romania; d. 1957, Paris

When Constantin Brancusi moved to Paris from his native Romania in 1904, he was introduced to Auguste Rodin, the French master sculptor who was then at the height of his career. He invited Brancusi to join his atelier as an apprentice, but the younger artist—with the confidence, stubbornness, and independence of youth—declined, claiming that "nothing grows in the shade of a tall tree." Brancusi rejected Rodin's 19th-century emphasis on theatricality and accumulation of detail in favor of radical simplification and abbreviation; he suppressed all decoration and all explicit narrative referents in an effort to create pure and resonant forms. His goal was to capture the essence of his subjects—which included birds in flight, fish, penguins, and a kissing couple—and render them visible with minimal formal means.

Brancusi often depicted the human head, another favorite subject, as a unitary ovoid shape separate from the body. When placed on its side, it evokes images of repose. Some of Brancusi's streamlined oval heads, whose forms recall Indian fertility sculptures in their fusion of egglike and phallic shapes, suggest the miracle of creation.

Brancusi's marble *Muse* is a subtle monument to the aesthetic act and to the myth that Woman is its inspiration. The finely chiseled and smoothly honed head is poised atop a sinuous neck, the curve of which is counterbalanced by a fragmentary arm pressed against the ear. The facial features, although barely articulated, embody the proportions of classical beauty. As in the sculptor's *Mlle Pogany*, also of 1912, the subject's hair is coiffed in a bun at the base of the neck. But while *Mlle Pogany* is the image of a particular woman, *The Muse* is the embodiment of an ideal.

—N. S.

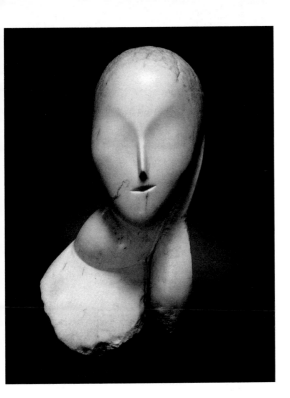

The Muse, *1912.*
Marble, 17 ¹/₂ x
9 ¹/₂ x 8 inches.
85.3317

"Only the Africans and the Romanians know how to carve wood."

Constantin Brancusi

The monumental oak *King of Kings* was originally intended to stand in Brancusi's *Temple of Meditation*, a private sanctuary commissioned in 1933 by the Maharaja Yeshwant Rao Holkar of Indore. Although never realized, the temple—conceived as a windowless chamber (save for a ceiling aperture) with interior reflecting pool, frescoes of birds, and an underground entrance—would have embodied the concerns most essential to Brancusi's art: the idealization of aesthetic form; the integration of architecture, sculpture, and furniture; and the poetic evocation of spiritual thought.

Wood elicited from Brancusi a tendency toward expressionism, resulting in unique carved objects. While his sculptures executed in stone or metal represent archetypal forms, such as birds in flight and sleeping figures, individual works in wood suggest specific characters or spiritual entities. For example, *King of Kings* may be interpreted as Brancusi's attempt to translate the power of Eastern religion into sculptural form. The work's original title was *Spirit of Buddha*, and Brancusi is known to have been familiar with Buddhism through the writings of the Tibetan

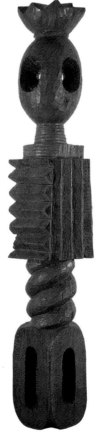
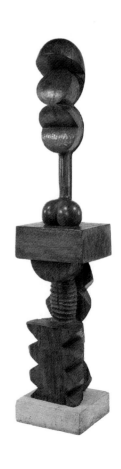

philosopher Milarepa.

Although the extent to which Brancusi's work was inspired by African sculpture and Romanian folk carvings has been widely debated among scholars, it is clear that he was acutely responsive to "primitivizing" influences early in his career. Paul Gauguin's technique of direct carving to emulate the raw quality of native Tahitian art inspired Brancusi to experiment with more daring approaches to sculpture than his academic training had previously allowed. Gauguin's aesthetic most likely prompted Brancusi to study tribal art, evident in the serrated patterns typical of African carvings on the bottom portion of *Adam and Eve* as well as on the sides of *King of Kings*. The overt sexual references in the former work may also have been inspired by "primitive" fetishes.

Sculptural sources from Brancusi's native country are also abundant: prototypes for the sequential designs of *King of Kings* have been found in Romanian vernacular architecture such as wooden gate posts and chiseled ornamental pillars. *The Sorceress* has been interpreted as the flying witch described in Romanian peasant tales. Brancusi never clarified the visual sources for his designs, preferring instead to promote an air of mystery surrounding the origins of his vision.

—N. S.

King of Kings,
*early 1930s. Oak,
118 1/8 inches high.
56.1449*

Adam and Eve,
*1916–24. Eve:
oak, 46 1/4 inches
high; Adam:
chestnut, 34 7/8
inches high; on
limestone base.
53.1329.a-.d*

The Sorceress,
*1916–24. Wood,
39 3/8 inches high;
on limestone base.
56.1448
Shown on* Oak
Base, *1920. Oak,
38 3/8 inches high.
58.1516*

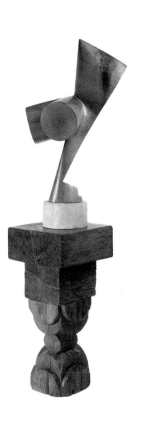

"At this period I painted musical instruments, in the first place because I was surrounded by them, secondly because by their very nature they appertained to my conception of a still life and lastly because I was already working toward a tactile *space."*

Georges Braque

b. 1882, Argenteuil-sur-Seine, France; d. 1963, Paris

When Georges Braque abandoned a bright Fauve palette and traditional perspective in 1908, it was the inspiration of Paul Cézanne's geometrized compositions that led him to simplified faceted forms, flattened spatial planes, and muted colors. By the end of that year, Braque and Pablo Picasso, who first met in 1907, began to compare the results of their techniques and it became obvious to both artists that they had simultaneously and independently invented a revolutionary style of painting, later dubbed "Cubism" by Guillaume Apollinaire. During the next few years the new style blossomed with stunning rapidity from its initial formative stage to high Analytic Cubism. The hallmarks of this advanced phase, so-called for the "breaking down" or "analysis" of form and space, are seen in an extraordinary pair of pendant works, *Violin and Palette* and *Piano and Mandola*.

Objects are still recognizable in the paintings, but are fractured into multiple facets, as is the surrounding space with which they merge. The compositions are set into motion as the eye moves from one faceted plane to the next, seeking to differentiate forms and to accommodate shifting sources of light and orientation. In *Violin and Palette*, the segmented parts of the violin, the sheets of music, and the artist's palette are vertically arranged, heightening their correspondence to the two-dimensional surface. Ironically, Braque depicted the nail at the top of the canvas in an illusionistic manner, down to the very shadow it cast, thus emphasizing the contrast between traditional and Cubist modes of representation. The same applies to the naturalistic candle in *Piano and Mandola*, which serves as a beacon of stability in an otherwise energized composition of exploding crystalline forms: the black-and-white piano keys all but disembodied; the sheets of music virtually disintegrated; the mandola essentially decomposed.

"When fragmented objects appeared in my painting around 1909," Braque later explained, "it was a way for me to get as close as possible to the object as painting allowed." If the appeal of still life was its implied tactile qualities, as Braque noted, then musical instruments held even more significance in that they are animated by one's touch. Like the rhythms and harmonies that are the life of musical instruments, dynamic spatial movement is the essence of Braque's lyrical, Cubist paintings.

—J. A.

54

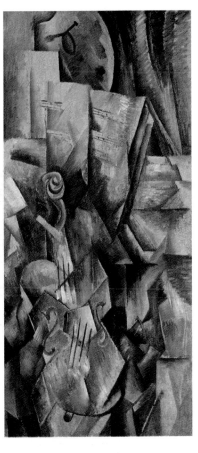

Violin and Palette, *autumn* 1909. *Oil on canvas, 36¹/₈ x 16⁷/₈ inches.* 54.1412

Piano and Mandola, *winter* 1909–10. *Oil on canvas, 36¹/₈ x 16⁷/₈ inches.* 54.1411

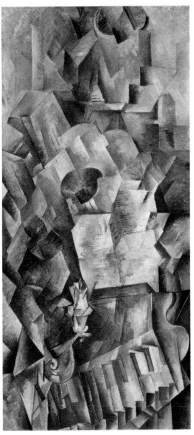

*"Words are no help
to me when I try to
speak about my
painting. It is an
irreducible presence
that refuses to be
converted into any
other form of
expression. It is a
presence both
imminent and
active."*

Alberto Burri

b. 1915, Città di Castello, Umbria, Italy

In 1943 Alberto Burri, a doctor in the Italian army, was captured by the British and sat out the remainder of World War II in a Texas P.O.W. camp. He began to paint there, covering his stretchers with burlap when other materials were unavailable. Upon his return to Italy in 1946 Burri renounced his original profession and dedicated himself to making art.

Composition is one of his *Sacchi* (sacks), a group of collage constructions made from burlap bags mounted on stretchers, which the artist began making in 1949. One of Burri's first series employing nontraditional mediums, the *Sacchi* were initially considered assaults against the established aesthetic canon. His use of the humble bags may be seen as a declaration of the inherent beauty of natural, ephemeral materials, in contradistinction to traditional "high" art mediums, which are respected for their ostentation and permanence. Early commentators suggested that the patchwork surfaces of the *Sacchi* metaphorically signified living flesh violated during warfare—the stitching was linked to the artist's practice as a physician. Others suggested that the hardships of life in postwar Italy predicated the artist's redeployment of the sacks in which relief supplies were sent to the country.

Yet Burri maintained that his use of materials was determined purely by the formal demands of his constructions. "If I don't have one material, I use another. It is all the same," he said in 1976. "I choose to use poor materials to prove that they could still be useful. The poorness of a medium is not a symbol: it is a device for painting." The title *Composition* emphasizes the artist's professed concern with issues of construction, not metaphor. Underlying the work is a rigorous compositional structure that belies the mundane impermanence of his chosen mediums and points to art-historical influences. The *Sacchi* rely on lessons learned from the Cubist- and Dada-inspired constructions of Paul Klee and Kurt Schwitters.

Despite Burri's cool public stance, the *Sacchi* are examples of the expressionism widely practiced in postwar Europe, where such work was called Art Informel (in the U.S. it was called Abstract Expressionism). Artists used powerfully rendered gesture and accommodated chance occurrences to express the existential angst characteristic of the period.

—J. B.

Composition,
1953. Oil, gold
paint, and glue on
burlap and canvas,
33 ⁷/₈ x 39 ¹/₂
inches. 53.1364

Alexander Calder
b. 1898, Lawnton, Pa.; d. 1976, New York City

One fortuitous event associated with Alexander Calder's 1964–65 retrospective at the Guggenheim was the rediscovery of two wire sculptures made in 1928: *Romulus and Remus* and *Spring* (both are now in the museum's collection).

"I think best in wire."

A few years after he constructed these witty, figurative works, Calder stored them away in a closet. On retrieving them he commented, "I'd always thought these particularly humorous, but now they look like good sculpture." *Romulus and Remus* represents the mythological founders of Rome being suckled by a protective she-wolf. This scene, often depicted in Western art, is rendered here in a most whimsical manner: both the boys' genitals and the wolf's nipples are represented by wooden doorstops. The sculpture's armature consists of a single wire that is twisted and bent to suggest both volume and void. *Romulus and Remus* is a drawing executed in space; its calligraphic outline is the equivalent of Calder's rapid, abbreviated pencil-and-pen sketches of acrobats and animals. Although entertaining and uncomplicated in execution, it explores issues critical to 20th-century sculpture: the interchangeability of space and mass, translucency, and the relation of two- to three-dimensionality. While Calder experimented with other unusual materials, his favorite medium was wire. Its flexibility and capacity to vibrate may have inspired his kinetic sculptures.

Dating from 1932, Calder's first hanging sculptures of discrete moveable parts powered by the wind were christened "mobiles" by Marcel Duchamp. It is now a vernacular art form, but when Calder invented it the mobile was viewed as an avant-garde achievement, a sculptural counterpart to Joan Miró's paintings of buoyant, biomorphic figures and Jean Arp's abstract reliefs. Although they are nonfigurative, Calder's hanging mobiles, particularly the monumental yet delicate *Red Lily Pads*, retain references to the natural world: the dancing and spinning of the disks evoke the intangible qualities of the air that propels them. According to art historian Rosalind Krauss, the mobiles—as interconnected vertical structures in space—create a sense of volume analogous to that of the human body. In their surrender to the pull of gravity and their displacement of space through motion, the mobiles become anthropomorphic metaphors.

—N. S.

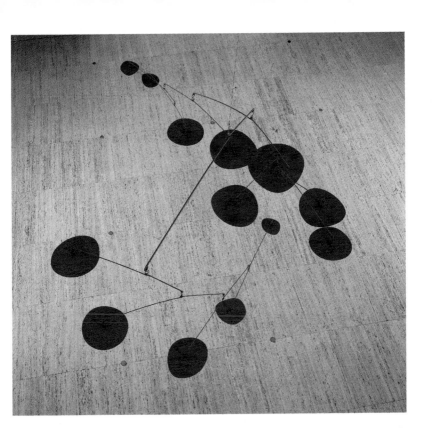

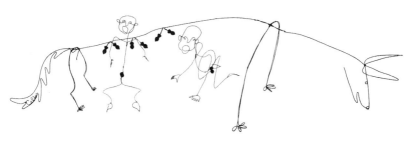

Red Lily Pads,
1956. *Painted
sheet metal, metal
rods, and wire,
42 x 201 x 109
inches. 65.1737*

Romulus and
Remus, *1928.
Wire and wood,
30 1/2 x 124 1/2 x
26 inches.
65.1738.a-.c*

*"I think of art as
personal
apperception. I place
this perception in
sensation, and I
require that the
intelligence organize
it into a work of
art."*

Paul Cézanne

b. 1839, Aix-en-Provence; d. 1906, Aix-en-Provence

Paul Cézanne's shimmering landscapes, searching portraits, and complex still lifes may be viewed as the culmination of Impressionism's quest for empirical truth in painting. His work was motivated by a desire to give sculptural weight and volume to the instantaneity of vision achieved by the Impressionists, who painted from nature. Relying on his perception of objects in space as visually interrelated entities—as forms locked into a greater compositional structure—Cézanne developed a style premised on the oscillation of surface and depth. Each tiny dab of color, as demonstrated on the mottled apples in *Still Life: Flask, Glass, and Jug*, indicates a spatial shift while simultaneously calling attention to the two-dimensional canvas on which it rests. This play of illusion, along with the conceptual fusion of time and space, has led Cézanne to be considered the foremost precursor of Cubism.

The artist's late work, created in relative isolation in the south of France, is marked by an intensification of his perceptual analysis coupled with an increasingly introspective sensibility. In *Man with Crossed Arms*, the strangely distorted, proto-Cubist view of the sitter—his right eye is depicted as if glimpsed from below and the left as if seen from above—contributes an enigmatic, contemplative air to the painting. This portrait of an anonymous sitter has come to be seen as a psychological study of quiet resignation and reserve—characteristics often attributed to Cézanne during the last decade of his life.

The artist's obsession with the nuances of spatial construction and optical effect is evinced in the numerous landscapes painted during this late period. In the abandoned and overgrown quarries known as Bibémus, east of the town of Aix-en-Provence, Cézanne discovered a rough, partially man-made, and intensely chromatic landscape that suited his geometrizing style. Between 1895 and 1899 he proceeded to visually explore the geographic and tonal variations that occurred in this remote, deserted area. In the Guggenheim's canvas, Cézanne's restless strokes and intermittent patches of complementary colors form passages of flatness and volume that create at once a diaphanous surface pattern and an illusion of great depth. The artist's unique sensations of the terrain are manifest in this picture as a radiant tapestry that heralds the imminent advent of abstract painting.

—N. S.

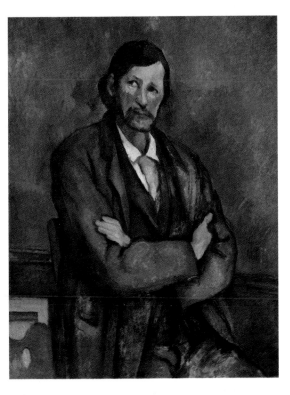

Man with Crossed
Arms, *ca. 1899.
Oil on canvas,
36 1/4 x 28 5/8
inches. 54.1387*

Still Life: Flask,
Glass, and Jug,
*ca. 1877. Oil on
canvas, 18 x 21 3/4
inches.
Thannhauser
Collection, Gift,
Justin K.
Thannhauser.
78.2514 T3*

Bibémus, *ca.
1894–95. Oil on
canvas, 28 1/8 x
35 3/8 inches.
Thannhauser
Collection, Gift,
Justin K.
Thannhauser.
78.2514 T6*

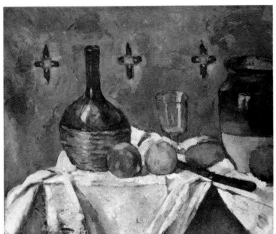

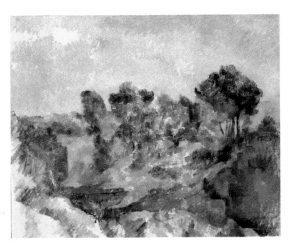

*"Oh! If astride the
stone chimera of
Notre Dame I
could manage with
my arms and my
legs to trace my
way in the sky!
There it is! Paris,
you are my second
Vitebsk!"*

Marc Chagall

*b. 1887, Vitebsk, Russia; d. 1985, St. Paul de Vence,
France*

After Marc Chagall moved to Paris from Russia in
1910, his paintings quickly came to reflect the
latest avant-garde styles. In *Paris Through the
Window* Chagall's debt to the Orphic Cubism of
his colleague Robert Delaunay is clear in the
semitransparent overlapping planes of vivid color
in the sky above the city. The Eiffel Tower, which
appears in the cityscape, was also a frequent
subject in Delaunay's work. For both artists it
served as a metaphor for Paris and perhaps
modernity itself. Chagall's parachutist might also
refer to contemporary experience, since the first
successful jump occurred in 1912. Other motifs
suggest the artist's native Vitebsk. This painting
is an enlarged version of a window view in a self-
portrait painted one year earlier, in which the
artist contrasted his birthplace with Paris. The
Janus figure in *Paris Through the Window* has been
read as the artist looking at once westward to his
new home in France and eastward to Russia.
Chagall, however, refused literal interpretations of
his paintings, and it is perhaps best to think of
them as lyrical evocations, similar to the allusive
plastic poetry of the artist's friends Blaise
Cendrars (who named this canvas) and Guillaume
Apollinaire.

Years after Chagall painted *The Soldier Drinks*
he stated that it developed from his memory of
tsarist soldiers who were billeted with families
during the 1904–5 Russo-Japanese war. The
enlisted man in the picture, with his right thumb
pointing out the window and his left index finger
pointing to the cup, is similar to the two-faced
man in *Paris Through the Window* in that both
figuratively mediate between dual worlds—
interior versus exterior space, past and present,
the imaginary and the real. In paintings such as
these it is clear that the artist preferred the life of
the mind, memory, and magical symbolism over
realistic representation.

In *Green Violinist* Chagall evoked his
homeland. The artist's nostalgia for his own work
was another impetus in creating this painting,
which is based on earlier versions of the same
subject. His cultural and religious legacy is
illuminated by the figure of the violinist dancing
in a rustic village. The Habad Hasidim of
Chagall's childhood believed it possible to achieve
communion with God through music and dance,
and the fiddler was a vital presence in ceremonies
and festivals.

—J. B.

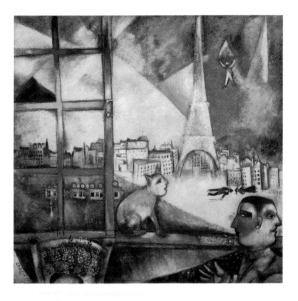

Paris Through the Window, *1913. Oil on canvas, 53 ½ x 55 ¾ inches. Gift, Solomon R. Guggenheim. 37.438*

Green Violinist, *1923–24. Oil on canvas, 78 x 42 ¾ inches. Gift, Solomon R. Guggenheim. 37.446*

The Soldier Drinks, *1911–12. Oil on canvas, 43 x 37 ¼ inches. 49.1211*

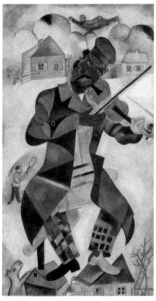

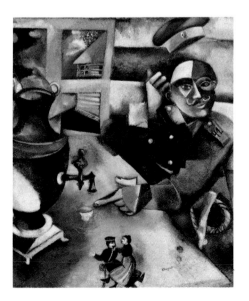

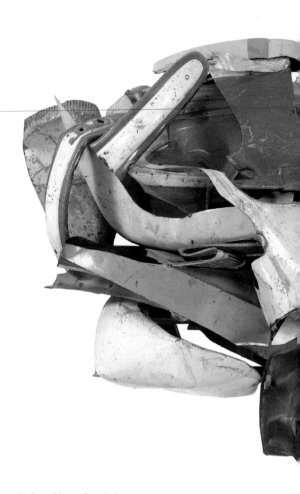

"I'm a collagist. A collagist fits things together."

John Chamberlain
b. 1927, Rochester, Ind.

John Chamberlain's dynamic agglomerations of scrap metal and used automobile bodies have been admired for translating the achievements of Abstract Expressionist painting into three-dimensional form. The whirling arabesques of color in wall reliefs such as *Dolores James* echo the energy and expressive power of paintings by Willem de Kooning; the heroic scale and animated diagonals suggest the canvases of Franz Kline. Like the Abstract Expressionists before him, Chamberlain revels in the potential of his mediums. In a 1972 interview with critic Phyllis Tuchman he remarked, "I'm sort of intrigued with the idea of what I can do with material and I work *with* the material as opposed to enforcing some kind of will upon it." Chamberlain emphasizes the importance of "fit," or the marriage of parts, in his sculpture. As in other early works, the various elements of *Dolores James* stayed in place by virtue of careful balances when the sculpture was first assembled; later, the work was spot-welded to insure its preservation.

Chamberlain's oeuvre appeared in the context

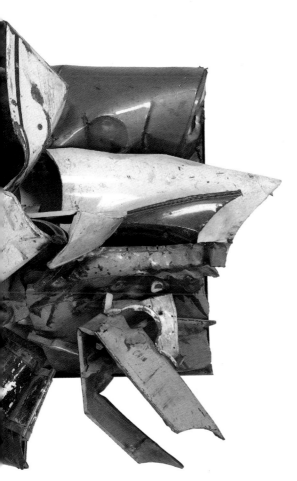

Dolores James,
1962. *Welded and
painted automobile
parts,* 76 x 97 x
39 *inches.*
70.1925

of late-1950s assemblage or Junk Art, in which
the detritus of our culture was critiqued and
revitalized as fine art. On some level, his
conglomerations of automobile carcasses must
inevitably be perceived as witnesses of the car
culture from which they were born, and for which
they serve as memorials. There is a threatening air
about the jagged-edged protuberances in
Chamberlain's sculptures, and the dirty, dented
automobile components suggest car crashes; the
artist, however, prefers to focus on the poetic
evocations that his sculptures elicit.

—J. B.

Collaboration

Collaboration has both positive and negative connotations. It means working jointly, either in a partnership with varying degrees of equality, or in a communal effort that enriches the self. At the same time it implies sacrificing part of one's individuality in order to adapt to the personality of the other, which may lead to a loss of identity, with irreversible consequences. And since World War II, especially in France, a collaborator is also someone who sides with the enemy.

As an alternative to the predominant tradition of light-footed immortal muses descending from their pedestals to bestow genius upon artists, poets, and scientists, collaboration posits the model of the twins Castor and Pollux, who in living and dying alternately share immortality between one another. The non-hierarchical attitude of mutual give-and-take is perfectly embodied in the artists Gilbert and George, who since 1967 have presented themselves side by side as "living sculptures." Both artists have fused their twoness into one consciousness, a united we-form.

There are as many different collaborations as there are collaborators. One of the most moving was the eight-year-long partnership between the young Polish student of mathematics and physics Marie Sklodowska and the brilliant French physicist Dr. Pierre Curie. Their leap into the unknown was a joint adventure; they cooperated inseparably as one mind. In their notebooks they referred to one another only in terms of "we found" and "we observed."

One of the most desirable forms of collaboration occured between the choreographer Merce Cunningham and the composer John Cage, who worked both cooperatively and independently. Like two electrodes forming an arc, the two artists have never stopped being involved in one another's experiments. At the same time they have respected one another's individuality, such as when the dancers do not rely on the sound or when the music varies rhythmically from performance to performance while the total length of the dance is the same.

If a collaboration succeeds, it always appears inevitable in retrospect. When Stan Laurel was asked how Oliver Hardy and he first met and how they developed into a team, Stan's casual answer summed up that of most successful teammates: "I always explained we just sort of came together—naturally."

—Coosje van Bruggen

Gilbert and George, Dream *(detail).*

66

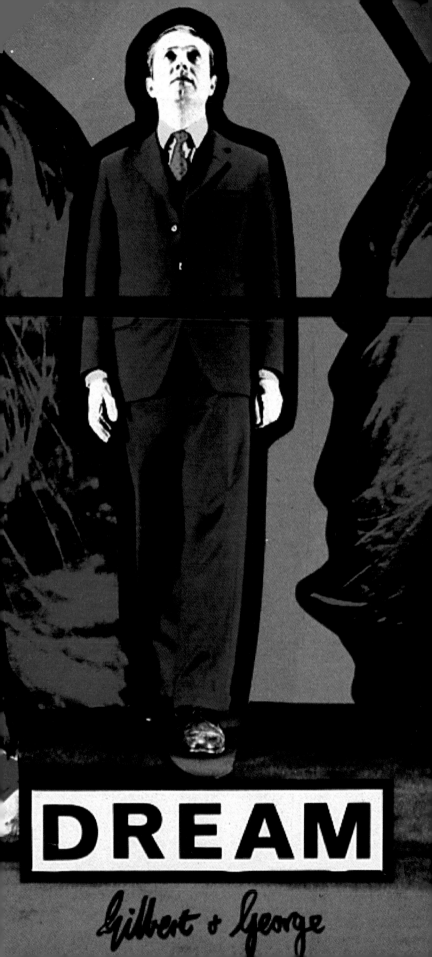

DREAM

Gilbert & George

Collage

In their experiments with Cubism, Pablo Picasso and Georges Braque proposed a new art form in which the subject of the café collided with the surface plane of the painting. At once serious and tongue-in-cheek, they methodically reexamined painting and sculpture and gave each medium some of the characteristics of the other. In the process they invented collage.

It was Braque who purchased a roll of simulated oak-grain wallpaper and began cutting out pieces of the paper and attaching them to his charcoal drawings. Picasso immediately began to make his own experiments in the new medium. Their use of *papier collé* (a term used to distinguish cut and pasted papers from the more inclusive term collage) signaled the beginning of a new approach to art. Picasso and Braque placed great value on commonplace materials and objects and on subjects drawn from the everyday world: a newspaper, a bottle of ale, or a pipe are redolent with meaning. References to current events, such as the war in the Balkans, and to popular culture enriched the content of their art. The artists also extended their experiments to include sculpture constructed out of found objects and flimsy two-dimensional materials such as cardboard.

The Futurists and the Dadaists employed collage to protest entrenched values, while the artists of the Russian avant-garde used photomontage, an outgrowth of collage, to demonstrate their support for a progressive world order. For the Surrealists, collage served as a surrogate for the subconscious. Pop artists recognized it as a means of directly incorporating elements of popular culture into their work. Robert Rauschenberg expanded collage in his own way by creating "combines," assemblages of paintings and found objects that were intended, he said, to act in the gap between art and life.

Emphasizing concept and process over end product, collage has brought the incongruous into meaningful congress with the ordinary. With its capacity for change, speed, immediacy, and ephemerality, collage is ideally suited to the demands of this century. It is a medium of materiality, a record of our civilization, a document of the timely and the transitory. It is no wonder that today's artists continue to use collage as a way of giving expression to the unorthodox, both in art and life.

—Diane Waldman

Kurt Schwitters, Merz 199 *(detail).*

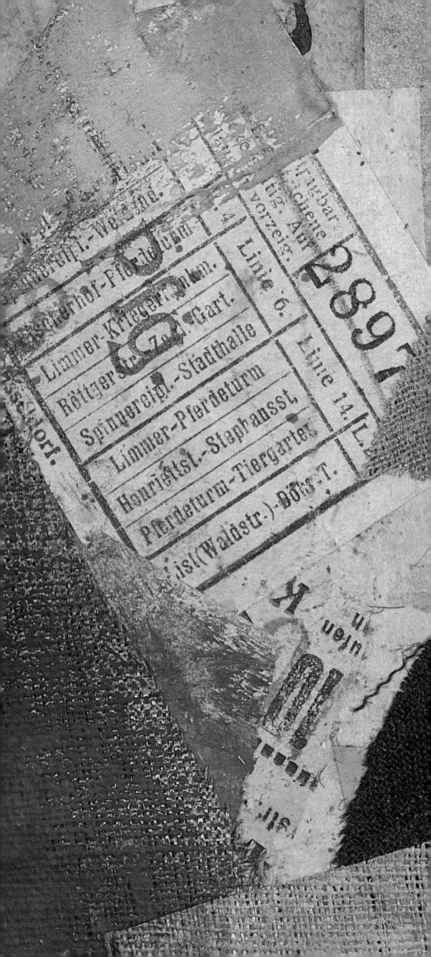

"It all looks as
though it came from
a sailor's sea chest
and just 'happened'
rather than being
made in these
times."

Joseph Cornell

b. 1903, Nyack, N.Y.; d. 1972, Flushing, N.Y.

After his first exposure to Surrealist collage in 1931, Joseph Cornell began to work in that format, eventually extending it into three-dimensional box structures. Unlike many European Surrealists, however, he was less interested in disturbing the viewer than in evoking enchanted worlds past and yet to come. Cornell incorporated printed images and found objects into his boxes, which were often conceived in series. *Space Object Box: "Little Bear, etc." motif* is part of the *Winter Night Skies* series, which includes fragments of celestial maps of the northern sky. The focus of the map fragment in *Space Object Box* is the constellation Ursa Minor— the "Little Bear" of the title. The "etc." refers to the other personifications of stars that the artist has colored, including Cameleopardalis, the giraffe, and Draco, the dragon. The blue cork ball and the ring suggest the moon and its orbit; their movement along the two metal rods alludes to the unending cycle of celestial change. The toy block with a horse on its face is probably a punning reference to Pegasus, a square constellation.

Andromeda appears in a box from the *Hotel* series, *Untitled (Grand Hôtel de L'Observatoire)*, which also contains an image of the head of Draco on a small cylinder hanging from a rod along the roof of the box; the cascading chain could refer to the long trail of stars called the Dragon's Tail. Mottled royal-blue pigment in the glistening white paint evokes the sparkling of stars in the sky. By incorporating the names of Grand Hotels, cut and pasted like hotel stationery in a scrapbook, Cornell nostalgically recalled the souvenirs of travelers. This box seems to promote the heavens as a place of respite, a view that may reflect the artist's education as a Christian Scientist. Mary Baker Eddy, the charismatic founder of the religion, believed that modern scientific theory holds a key to understanding our world. In a book that Cornell called the most important to him after the Bible, she wrote, "The astronomer will no longer look up to the stars— he will look out from them upon the universe." Cornell, who lived most of his life on Utopia Parkway in Queens, never went to Europe, although his boxes are often filled with tokens of European culture. He could no more visit the 19th-century Old World of his imagination than he could visit the stars, but he could dream about these places and invoke them in his boxes.

—J. B.

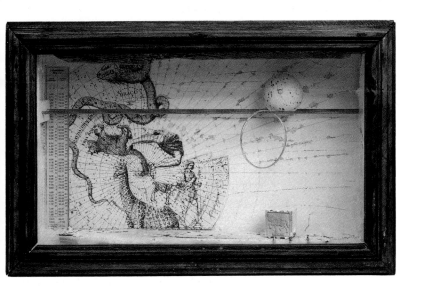

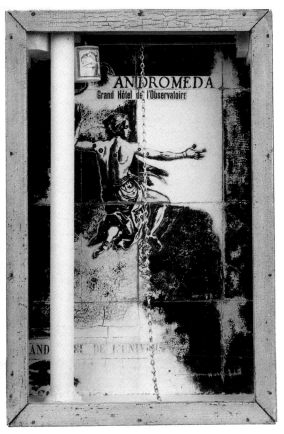

Space Object Box: "Little Bear, etc." motif, *mid-1950s–early 1960s. Box construction and collage, 11 x 17 1/2 x 5 1/4 inches. 68.1878*

Untitled (Grand Hôtel de l'Observatoire), *1954. Box construction and collage, 18 5/16 x 12 15/16 x 3 7/8 inches. Partial gift, C. and B. Foundation, by exchange. 80.2734*

D

"Content, if you want to say, is a glimpse of something, an encounter, you know, like a flash. It's very tiny—very tiny, content."

Willem de Kooning
b. 1904, Rotterdam, The Netherlands

In response to Willem de Kooning's first solo exhibition, in 1948, the art critic Clement Greenberg acclaimed him "an outright 'abstract' painter"; of the gestural black-and-white paintings on display he noted that "there does not seem to be an identifiable image in any of the ten pictures in his show." However, in 1950 de Kooning began a series of gruesomely expressive paintings of women that, when they were exhibited in 1953, brought accusations of betrayal by advocates of pure abstraction and stirred a major controversy: in which style did de Kooning intend to paint, figurative or nonrepresentational? A fusion of the two, it seemed at the time, was untenable.

Composition, completed in 1955, exemplifies the issues at the heart of this controversy. In *Composition*, like his other contemporaneous works that blend aspects of figurative, landscape, and abstract painting, various components that characterized the *Women* can be detected, such as fragmented and scrambled references to female anatomy, a palette of florid reds, pinks, turquoise-blue, and rancid yellow, and de Kooning's signature agitated brushstrokes. Although it shares these elements with the paintings in the *Women* series, *Composition* is far more abstract. Its underlying structure is composed of side-by-side rectangles, obscured by a thick, active paint surface characterized by its slashing gestures, heavy, rasping textures, and a proliferation of suggestive images, such as the red-and-yellow bralike form at the upper right. Ambiguities abound in the painting, brought about by its multiple focuses, visual rhythms, and abrupt breaks and discontinuities. In this manner, de Kooning's *Composition* can be said to lack a final incisiveness—and that is its strength. In reference to the critical debate surrounding abstract and figurative painting—a debate that still surrounds Abstract Expressionism—de Kooning once remarked, "What's the problem? This is all about freedom."

—J. A.

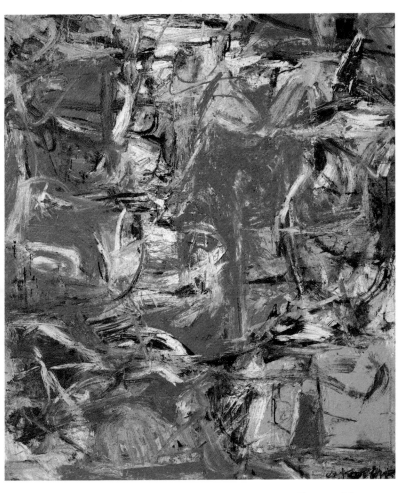

Composition,
1955. *Oil, enamel,*
and charcoal on
canvas, 79 ¹/₈ x
69 ¹/₈ *inches.*
55.1419

*"What is of great
importance to me is
observation of the
movement of colors.
Only in this way
have I found the
laws of complemen-
tary and simul-
taneous contrasts of
colors which sustain
the very rhythm of
my vision."*

Robert Delaunay

b. 1885, Paris; d. 1941, Montpellier, France

Robert Delaunay chose the view into the
ambulatory of the Parisian Gothic church Saint-
Séverin as the subject of his first series of
paintings, in which he charted the modulations of
light streaming through the stained-glass
windows and the resulting perceptual distortion
of the architecture. The subdued palette and the
patches of color that fracture the smooth surface
of the floor point to the influence of Paul Cézanne
as well as to the stylistic elements of Georges
Braque's early Cubist landscapes. Delaunay said
that the Saint-Séverin theme in his work marked
"a period of transition from Cézanne to Cubism."

Delaunay explored the developments of Cubist
fragmentation more explicitly in his series of
paintings of the Eiffel Tower. In these canvases,
characteristic of his self-designated "destructive"
phase, the artist presented the tower and
surrounding buildings from various perspectives.
Delaunay chose a subject that allowed him to
indulge his preference for a sense of vast space,
atmosphere, and light, while evoking a sign of
modernity and progress. Like the soaring vaults of
Gothic cathedrals, the Eiffel Tower is a uniquely
French symbol of invention and aspiration. Many
of Delaunay's images of this structure and the
surrounding city are views from a window framed
by curtains. In *Eiffel Tower* (painted in 1911,
although it bears the date 1910) the buildings
bracketing the tower curve like drapery.

The artist's attraction to windows and window
views, linked to the Symbolists' use of glass panes
as metaphors for the transition from internal to
external states, culminated in his *Simultaneous
Windows* series. (The series derives its name from
the French scientist Michel-Eugène Chevreul's
theory of simultaneous contrasts of color, which
explores how divergent hues are perceived at
once.) Delaunay stated that these works began his
"constructive" phase, in which he juxtaposed and
overlaid translucent contrasting complementary
colors to create a synthetic, harmonic composition. Guillaume Apollinaire wrote a poem about
these paintings and coined the word Orphism to
describe Delaunay's endeavor, which he believed
was as independent of descriptive reality as was
music (the name derives from Orpheus, the
mythological lyre player). Although *Simultaneous
Windows (2nd Motif, 1st Part)* contains a vestigial
green profile of the Eiffel Tower, it is one of the
artist's last salutes to representation before his
leap to complete abstraction.

—J. B.

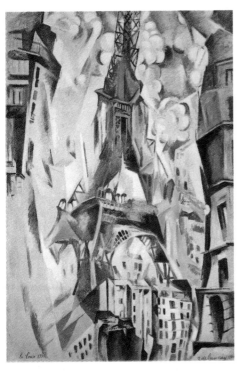

Eiffel Tower,
*1911. Oil on
canvas, 79 ¹/₂ x
54 ¹/₂ inches. Gift,
Solomon R.
Guggenheim.
37.463*

Simultaneous
Windows (2nd
Motif, 1st Part),
*1912. Oil on
canvas, 21 ⁵/₈ x
18 ¹/₄ inches. Gift,
Solomon R.
Guggenheim.
41.464A*

Saint-Séverin
No. 3, *1909–10.
Oil on canvas, 45 x
34 ⁷/₈ inches. Gift,
Solomon R.
Guggenheim.
41.462*

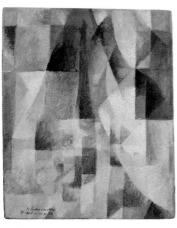

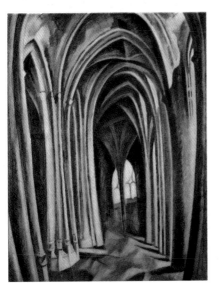

Walter De Maria
b. 1935, Albany, Calif.
Walter De Maria is best known for his 1977
Lightning Field. A rectangular grid in New
Mexico measuring one mile by one kilometer and
containing 400 stainless-steel lightning rods, it
serves as an arena for observing meteorological
activity. The artist has also brought such ordered
experiences of the landscape into the gallery,
translating distance, measure, and nature into
abstract tableaux known as Earthrooms, in which
accretions of soil, rocks, gravel, or peat fill the
floors of architectural structures. De Maria's
reputation as an Environmental artist—linking
him with Robert Smithson, Nancy Holt, and
Michael Heizer—acknowledges only one facet of
his challenging oeuvre. Less appreciated is De
Maria's early association with Fluxus and
performance in San Francisco prior to his arrival
in New York in 1960. From his exposure to the
work of composer La Monte Young and dancer
Simone Forti, among others, De Maria developed
an interest in task-oriented, gamelike projects
that resulted in viewer-interactive sculptures. For
example, his *Boxes for Meaningless Work* (1961) is
inscribed with the instructions, "Transfer things
from one box to the next box back and forth, back
and forth, etc. Be aware that what you are doing
is meaningless." This participative component
was retained, but only metaphorically, in the
artist's small-scale, polished-aluminum floor
sculptures in shapes that possess significant iconic
impact—the cross, the six-pointed star, and the
swastika. The hollow interiors of the sculptures
form narrow channels containing metal spheres.
By including these seemingly movable balls, De
Maria again evoked the notion of game-playing,
but given the narrative association of the symbols,
it seems an ironic gesture.

Conceived of separately, but now often
exhibited together, *Cross*, *Star*, and *Museum Piece*
manifest how ancient symbolic configurations
have undergone various interpretive
transmutations: the cross, mark of Christianity,
has also been discovered on Egyptian tombs; the
six-pointed star, sign of Judaism, first appeared
on Bronze and Iron Age relics; and the swastika,
emblem of Nazism, was once representative of
prosperity, regeneration, and goodwill. By titling
the swastika *Museum Piece*, De Maria seems also to
have been commenting on the neutralizing effects
of the museum environment, in which cultural
artifacts, removed from their original contexts,
are reduced to visual equivalences.

—N. S.

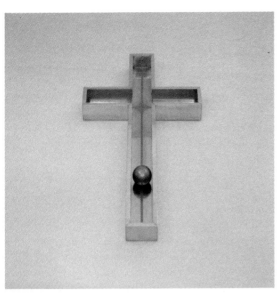

Cross, 1965–66.
*Aluminum, 4 x
42 x 22 inches.*
73.2033

Museum Piece,
1966. *Aluminum,
4 x 36 x 36 inches.*
73.2034

Star, 1972.
*Aluminum, 4 x
44 x 50 inches.*
73.2035

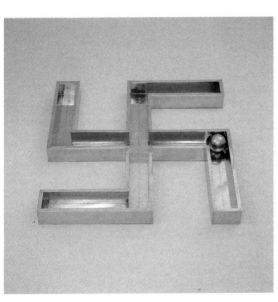

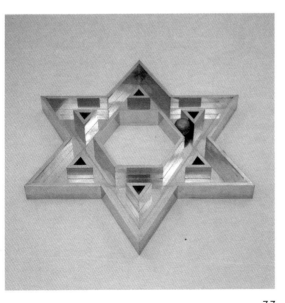

*"The object is used
to make art, just
like paint is used to
make art."*

Jim Dine

b. 1935, Cincinnati

During the early 1960s Jim Dine was part of a loosely affiliated group of artists—including Claes Oldenburg, Lucas Samaras, and Red Grooms—who extended the gestural and subjective implications of Abstract Expressionist painting into outrageous performances, subsequently known as Happenings. Inspired by John Cage's radical approach to musical composition, which involved chance, indeterminacy, and an emphatic disregard for all artistic boundaries, they sought to transgress preexisting aesthetic values. Dine and Oldenburg brought this sensibility to bear on a two-artist exhibition called *Ray-Gun*, held at the Judson Gallery in New York in February and March 1960. For the show, each artist made an installation consisting of a chaotic configuration of found and manipulated objects. In Dine's jumbled environment, *The House*, the walls and ceiling of the gallery were effaced by an agglomeration of painted cloth, fragmented domestic objects, scrawled slogans, crumbled paper, and suspended metal bedsprings. Scattered throughout were cardboard signs spelling out various household platitudes, such as BREAKFAST IS READY and GO TO WORK. Dine claimed that the juxtaposition of these and other banal phrases with the surrounding domestic wreckage revealed the potential violence inherent to a home. His critique of the myth of the happy home was amplified by anthropomorphic references—painted eyes, faces, and other body parts—that were hidden or lost amid the detritus. This accretion of fragmented figures, discarded articles, and tattered elements is present, albeit in abbreviated form, in Dine's sculpture *Bedspring*, which may have been a part of (or at least inspired by) *The House*.

A year later Dine began making paintings of discrete items—a hat, a necktie, and the necklace in *Pearls*, composed of rubber ball halves covered with metallic paint. Although often construed as Pop art emblems, these paintings, which include the names of the depicted objects and, in some cases, collage elements, are more conceptually oriented than the playful and bold appropriations of popular imagery made by Roy Lichtenstein, James Rosenquist, and Andy Warhol. By so blatantly and provocatively combining word, image, and object, Dine invited an investigation into the presumed difference between representation and reality, the construction of meaning, and the arbitrary nature of language.

—N. S.

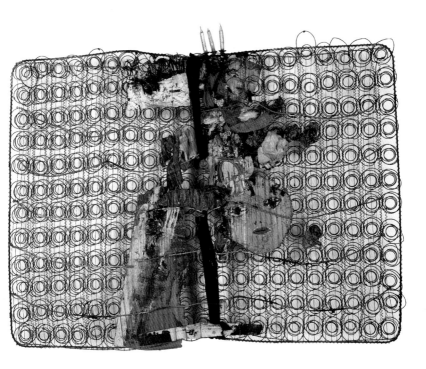

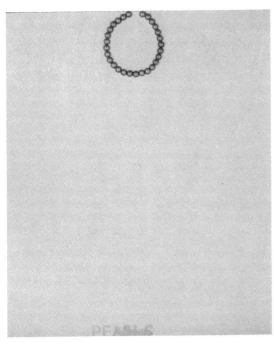

Bedspring, 1960.
*Mixed-media
assemblage on wire
bedspring, 52 ¹/₄ x
72 x 11 inches.
Purchased with
funds contributed by
the Louis and
Bessie Adler
Foundation, Inc.,
Seymour M. Klein,
President. 85.3258*

Pearls, 1961. *Oil
and collage on
canvas, 70 x 60
inches. Gift, Leon
A. Mnuchin.
63.1681*

"I would like people to look at my work as an enterprise for the rehabilitation of scorned values, and, in any case, make no mistake, a work of ardent celebration."

Jean Dubuffet

b. 1901, Le Havre, France; d. 1985, Paris

A grotesque male nude dominates *Will to Power*, his gritty roughness, burly proportions, inlaid stone teeth, and glass fragments for eyes giving him a fierce and threatening air. But the figure's aggressive machismo is itself threatened by the very stance he assumes: hands held behind the back, his gesture is either one of unexpected receptivity or of helpless captivity. The title refers to a central tenet of Nazi ideology, taken from the philosophy of Friedrich Nietzsche. But in a single deft stroke, Dubuffet's caricature mocks Fascism's claims to authority as it emasculates romanticized male aggression.

Dubuffet's painting style, which he called Art Brut (raw art), was contrary to everything expected of a painter in the French tradition and dealt a serious blow to the usual aesthetic assumptions. Inspired by graffiti and art made by the mentally ill, Dubuffet insisted that his protest was against specious notions of beauty "inherited from the Greeks and cultivated by magazine covers." In *Triumph and Glory*, the female nude—treated by most artists with veneration—receives no more charitable treatment than her male counterpart in *Will to Power*. One of 36 female nudes known as the *Corps de dames* series, she lacks psychological presence and personal identity, and could easily be perceived as an abomination.

While the art of "primitive" cultures and unschooled practitioners was of special importance to Dubuffet, he was also interested in a disparate array of found objects and materials. *Door with Couch Grass*, an assemblage of several paintings that he cut down and pieced together to represent a wall, doorstep, and the ground, typifies his insatiable interest in found patterns, textures, and materials. The extraordinary range of techniques that Dubuffet employed in this work includes creating successive layers of paint by shaking a brush over the painting and covering it with a spray of tiny droplets, scattering sand over the surface, and scratching it with the tines of a fork. In his attempt to rehabilitate values and materials dismissed by Western aesthetics, what mattered to Dubuffet was unbridled energy, spontaneity, and truth to self—and with them, a spirit of insubordination and impertinence.

—J. A.

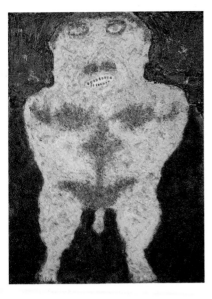

Will to Power, *Jan. 1946. Oil, pebbles, sand, and glass on canvas, 45 ³/₄ x 35 inches.* 74.2076

Triumph and Glory, *Dec. 1950. Oil on canvas, 51 x 38 inches.* 71.1973

Door with Couch Grass, *Oct. 31, 1957. Oil on canvas with assemblage, 74 ¹/₂ x 57 ¹/₂ inches.* 59.1549

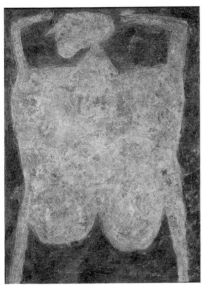

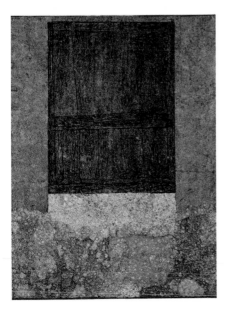

F

Flatness

Starting with Edouard Manet, artists progressively abandoned the illusion of depth achieved through linear perspective. They exchanged the Renaissance concept of mimesis for an ideated notion of flatness in which figure and ground, shape and field seem to merge indissolubly on the canvas. This affirmation of the flatness of the picture plane became a distinguishing characteristic of Modernist painting.

In the formalist tradition of art criticism, flatness is inseparable from aesthetic value, or what Clement Greenberg—formalism's leading voice—defined as "quality." This aspect of Greenberg's doctrine has been the most polemical in recent critical reevaluations of his work, but nonetheless his definition of painting's reduction to flatness is still the most complete. Greenberg applied the Kantian model of self-definition to support his view that each art must isolate and make explicit that which is unique to the nature of its medium. The "irreducible essence" of pictorial art, he wrote in his 1965 essay *Modernist Painting*, is the coincidence of flattened color with its material support: "Flatness, two-dimensionality, was the only condition painting shared with no other art, and so Modernist painting oriented itself to flatness as it did to nothing else."

Greenberg championed a narrow lineage of artists who insistently asserted two-dimensionality. He credited Manet with creating the first Modernist paintings because they declared the restricted space of the picture plane so frankly. Greenberg included Paul Cézanne because the placement and shape of the flat brushmarks in his paintings recall the shape of the flat rectangle on which they were placed. Cézanne, and the Cubists after him, also solved the passage from the contour of an object to its inhabited space without violating the integrity of the flat continuum of the picture surface. He described Piet Mondrian as the flattest of all easel painters, while he identified Jackson Pollock's strength as deriving from the tension inherent in the constructed, *recreated* flatness of the surface or the depicted three-dimensionality of the object. Greenberg concluded his retrospective account with the Color Field painters, whose technique of staining the weave of the canvas visibly weds figure and ground. His list stops short of Frank Stella's *Black Paintings* on the grounds that they pushed painting so far into the third dimension that they verged on becoming "arbitrary objects"—and therefore sacrificed their "quality."

—Lisa Dennison

Paul Cézanne, Bibémus *(detail).*

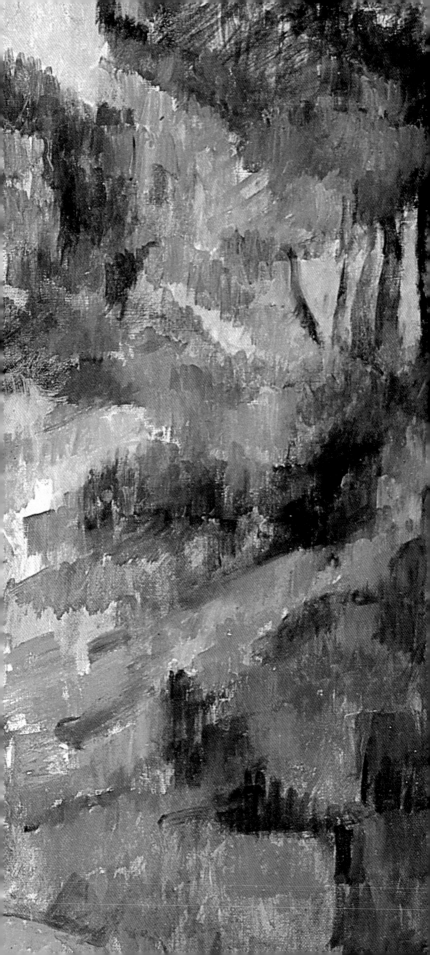

> "My own proposal has become mainly an indoor routine of placing strips of fluorescent light. It has been mislabeled sculpture by people who should know better."

Dan Flavin

b. 1933, Jamaica, N.Y.

In addition to his mistrust of art-historical categories, Dan Flavin has rejected terms such as "sculpture" or "environment" to describe his work. The fixtures he employs to generate his sequences of colored light are not sculpture, but common objects that are mass-produced, may be reinstalled by non-artists, and should be replaced if they burn out. Flavin refers to his installations as "situations," and the looseness of this term functions remarkably well in elucidating his 1971 project for the Guggenheim.

The work is composed of 16 white bulbs, four pink bulbs, four yellow bulbs, four green bulbs, and four blue bulbs. In a letter to Thomas Messer, a former director of the museum, Flavin noted that the installation of his work was "critically fitted to the inconsistent dimensions of the available architecture. There was no other choice that I could sense." The idea of site-specificity is crucial to Flavin's piece, although the light creates perceptual and not actual changes. The artist chose the sixth ramp of the museum for his initial installation in 1971, suffusing nine bays with five colors and their prismatic overlappings. His amplification of Frank Lloyd Wright's building suggests that ephemeral sensory changes can become just as tactile as architectural units.

Characteristically, the work is untitled, for to *name* this type of work, Flavin implies, would be to individualize and thus delimit its generic quality. The *dedication* (to Ward Jackson, an artist who is also the archivist of the Guggenheim), however, indicates that the art work is specific to its designated location. Flavin knew the building well, having worked as an assistant at the Guggenheim in the late 1950s, shortly before it was completed. His light "situations," begun in 1961 and initially called "icons," present an important American corollary to European notions of context-based art, paralleling the work of the Situationists and predating the striped interventions of Daniel Buren and André Cadere.

—C. L.

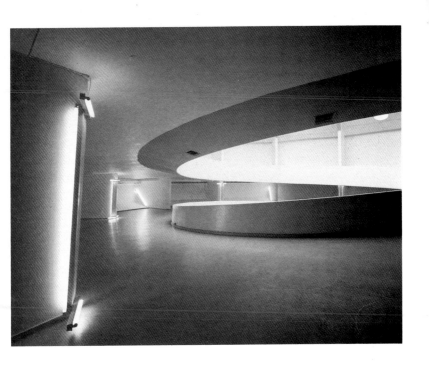

Untitled
(to Ward Jackson,
an old friend and
colleague who,
during the Fall of
1957 when I
finally returned
to New York
from Washington
and joined him to
work together in
this museum,
kindly communi-
cated). *1971. A
system of two
alternating
modular units in
fluorescent light: 16
white bulbs. each
24 inches long: four
each of pink.
yellow. green. and
blue bulbs. each 96
inches long. Partial
gift of the artist in
honor of Ward
Jackson. 72.1985*

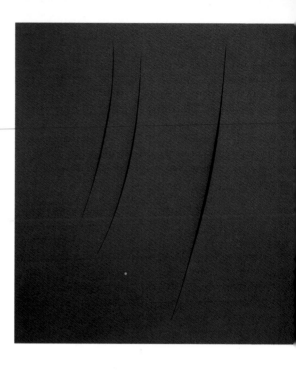

> *"There is a new consciousness in formation in humanity, and so much so that it is no longer necessary to represent a man, a house, or nature. What is necessary is to create spatial sensations with one's own imagination."*

Lucio Fontana
b. 1899, Rosario de Santa Fé, Argentina;
d. 1968, Commabio, Italy

Lucio Fontana's respect for the advancements of science and technology during the 20th century led him to approach his art as a series of investigations into a wide variety of mediums and methods. As a sculptor, he experimented with stone, metals, ceramics, and neon; as a painter he attempted to transcend the confines of the two-dimensional surface. In a series of manifestos originating with the *Manifiesto blanco* (*White Manifesto*) of 1946, Fontana announced his goals for a "spatialist" art, one that could engage technology to achieve an expression of the fourth dimension. He wanted to meld the categories of architecture, sculpture, and painting to create a groundbreaking new aesthetic idiom.

From 1947 on Fontana's experiments were often entitled *Concetti spaziali* (*Spatial Concepts*), among which a progression of categories unfolds. The artist's polychrome sculptures brought color, considered the dominion of painting, into the realm of the three-dimensional. With his *Pietre* (stones) series, begun in 1952, he fused the sculptural with painting by encrusting the surfaces of his canvases with heavy impasto and colored glass. In his *Buchi* (holes) cycle he punctured the surface of his canvases, breaking the membrane of two-dimensionality in order to highlight the space behind the picture. From 1958, Fontana purified his paintings by creating matte, monochrome surfaces, thus focusing the

Spatial Concept, Expectations, 1959. Water-based paint on canvas, 49 ⁵/₈ x 98 ³/₄ inches. Gift, Mrs. Teresita Fontana, Milan. 77.2322

viewer's attention on the slices that rend the skin of the canvas. Paintings such as *Spatial Concept, Expectations* are among these *Tagli* (cuts), whose violent jags enforce the idea that the painting is an object, not solely a surface.

Many of Fontana's proclamations echo Futurist declarations made before World War I. The artist's wish that his materials be integrated with space, his need to express movement through gesture, and his interest in states of being (exemplified in his use of the word "expectations" in the title of this work), suggest the artist's familiarity with the work of Umberto Boccioni, a leading Futurist sculptor, painter, and theorist whom Fontana cited as an inspiration.

—J. B.

"Beyond the three dimensions of Euclid we have added another, the fourth dimension, which is to say the figuration of space, the measure of the infinite."
—Albert Gleizes

Fourth Dimension

The fourth dimension was a highly popular concept in the early 20th century and figured in the theoretical underpinnings of nearly every Modern art movement. The statement by the Cubist painter and theorist Albert Gleizes quoted here brings together the two major characteristics of the fourth dimension in early Modern art theory: its primary, geometric orientation as a higher spatial dimension, as well as its metaphorical association with infinity and resultant function as a new code name for the sublime.

The idea that space might have additional dimensions had developed during the 19th century with the emergence of n-dimensional geometries (geometries of more than three dimensions). Both n-dimensional geometries and the curved spaces of non-Euclidean geometry encouraged recognition of the relativity of human perception. The theme of the inadequacy of sense perception was already present in popular literature by the 1880s. Beyond the general resurgence of idealist philosophy in the late 19th century, which augmented this distrust of visual reality, discoveries such as the X-ray (1895) provided scientific proof of the limited range of visual perception, further encouraging speculation about alternative kinds of spaces. However, it was not until the years around 1910 in Paris that expressions of artistic interest in the fourth dimension occurred.

With its roots in geometry, the fourth dimension was not thought of as time itself—a view that would become dominant only after 1919 with the popularization of Einstein's theory of relativity. Instead, it signified a higher geometric dimension, of which our three-dimensional world might be merely a section. The fourth dimension could thus serve as a rationale for Cubist artists to reject such three-dimensionally oriented techniques as one-point perspective and the traditional modeling of figures. If the Cubists sought to depict forms as they might appear in four dimensions, other artists such as Kazimir Malevich, Piet Mondrian, and František Kupka interpreted the notion in more mystical terms and found in the existence of an invisible, higher-dimensional reality support for the creation of totally abstract art works. Often associated with the evolution of "cosmic consciousness," the fourth dimension in this view also embodied belief in humankind's potential to transcend present limitations and in the need for new forms of language in art, music, and literature.

—Linda Dalrymple Henderson

Georges Braque, Violin and Palette *(detail).*

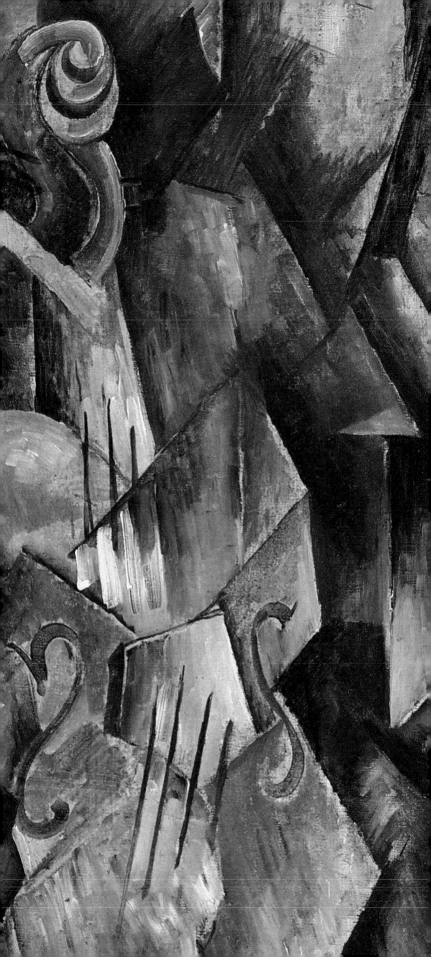

Fragmentation

By their nature, fragments indicate the existence of some previously complete entity. Be they the broken remains of a classical Greek sculpture or stanzas from a lost poem, fragments inspire contemplation of the passage of time and thereby induce memory and nostalgia. During the 19th century museums began collecting relics and ruins from other eras, their value increasing in direct proportion to their age. Decontextualized and displayed in this somewhat obsessive manner, vestiges of previous cultures became highly romantic emblems of the past. Charles Baudelaire located the spirit of modernity in such poeticized artifacts, recognizing that at every historical juncture there exists a fleeting consciousness of the present. By "modernity" he referred to "the ephemeral, the fugitive, the contingent, the half of art whose other half is the eternal and the immutable." Toward the fin-de-siècle, artists embraced the fragmentary as a formal strategy with which to capture the transitory moment. Impressionist paintings often suggest a study or an unfinished sketch, as do Auguste Rodin's abbreviated anatomical sculptures, which appear as if in eternal formation.

Such aesthetic fragmentation of perceived experience reflected the vast economic, social, and cultural disruptions of society initiated toward the end of the 19th century with the advent of industrialization. In Marxist terms, this phenomenon inaugurated a radical disjunction between labor and its products. In the psychological realm, the notion of subjective reality as a seamless construct was suspended when Sigmund Freud construed the human psyche as a tripartite, and not necessarily integrated, entity. The art created during the first part of the 20th century—the splintered planes of Cubist and Futurist art, the disjointed figures in German Expressionist painting, and the strange juxtapositions found in Surrealist imagery—may be read as visual analogues to the social and psychic fragmentation of reality. Those artists involved with Dada, Pop, Nouveau Réalisme, Neo-Dada, and Neo-Conceptual strategies have increasingly utilized the flotsam of everyday existence by drawing formal elements and subject matter from mass culture, often emulating cinematic montage and advertising techniques. As a critical mirror to our postmodern society and its representations—mediated imagery, movie trailers, MTV, and video dating—contemporary art has embraced the fragment as an end in itself.

—N. S.

Robert Delaunay, Simultaneous Windows (2nd Motif, 1st Part) *(detail).*

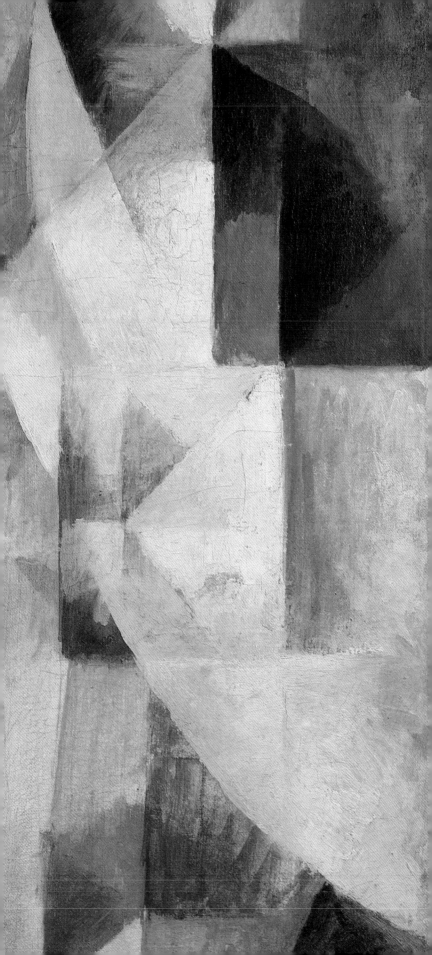

G

"You will always find vital sap coursing through the primitive arts. In the arts of an elaborate civilization, I doubt it!"

Paul Gauguin
b. 1848, Paris; d. 1903, Marquesas Islands

Prior to his first voyage to Tahiti in 1891, Paul Gauguin claimed that he was fleeing France in order "to immerse myself in virgin nature, see no one but savages, live their life, with no other thoughts in mind but to render the way a child would . . . and to do this with nothing but the primitive means of art, the only means that are good and true." Gauguin's desire to reject Western culture and merge with a naive society for the sake of aesthetic and spiritual inspiration reflects the complex and problematic nature of European "primitivism." A concept that emerged at the end of the 19th century, "primitivism" was motivated by the romantic desire to discover an unsullied paradise hidden within the "uncivilized" world, as well as by a fascination with what was perceived as the raw, unmediated sensuality of cultural artifacts. This voyeuristic engagement with underdeveloped societies by artists, writers, and philosophers corresponded to French imperialistic practices—Tahiti, for example, was annexed as a colony in 1881.

The artist's idyllic Tahitian landscapes *In the Vanilla Grove, Man and Horse* and *Haere Mai* reveal the contradictions between myth and reality that are inherent to "primitivism." Both canvases probably depict the area surrounding Mataiea, the small village in which Gauguin settled during the fall of 1891. As richly hued tapestries of flattened forms, they are, however, only evocations of the lush Tahitian terrain, reflecting the simplicity of form sought by the artist during his first visit to the island. Gauguin derived the pose of the man and horse in *In the Vanilla Grove* not from a scene he found in Tahiti but from a frieze on the quintessential monument of Western culture, the Parthenon. Gauguin painted the phrase *"Haere Mai,"* which means "Come here!" in Tahitian, onto the other canvas in the lower-right corner, but it does not appear to coincide with the content of the painting. The artist, who spoke little of the native language at that time, often combined disparate Tahitian phrases with images in an effort to evoke the foreign and the mystical. Evidently, this practice was designed to make the paintings more enticing to the Parisian public, who craved intimations of the distant and the exotic.

—N. S.

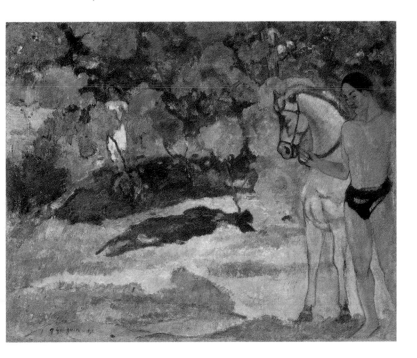

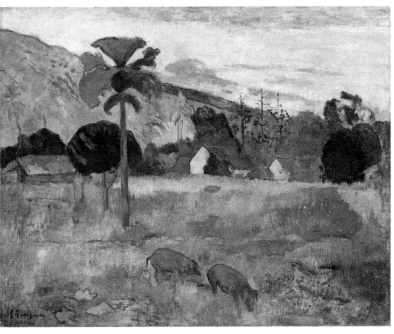

In the Vanilla
Grove, Man and
Horse, *1891. Oil
on burlap, 28 ³/₄ x
36 ¹/₄ inches.
Thannhauser
Collection, Gift,
Justin K.
Thannhauser.
78.2514 T15*

Haere Mai, *1891.
Oil on burlap,
28 ¹/₂ x 36 inches.
Thannhauser
Collection, Gift,
Justin K.
Thannhauser.
78.2514 T16*

Alberto Giacometti

b. 1901, Borgonovo, Switzerland; d. 1966, Chur, Switzerland

Alberto Giacometti was 20 years old when he settled in Paris in order to pursue the career of a sculptor. He studied classical sculpture and the predominant Cubist idioms, but it was not until he began to interpret "primitive" objects that he was able to liberate himself from the influence of his teachers. *Spoon Woman*, one of the artist's first mature works, explores the metaphor employed in ceremonial spoons of the African Dan culture, in which the bowl of the utensil can be equated with a woman's womb. But Giacometti's life-size sculpture reverses the equivalence. As the art historian and theorist Rosalind Krauss has noted, "By taking the metaphor and inverting it, so that 'a spoon is like a woman' becomes 'a woman is like a spoon,' Giacometti was able to intensify the idea and to make it universal by generalizing the forms of the sometimes rather naturalistic African carvings toward a more prismatic abstraction."

Giacometti joined the ranks of the Surrealists in 1929, only to break with them acrimoniously six years later, when he decided to work from models rather than strictly from his imagination. Yet even in *Nose* there is something of the Surrealist tendency toward the fantastic in the incredible proboscis. In this work, Giacometti suspended a head from a cross bar in a rectangular cage, thus implying that the pendant head could be prodded to swing, the nose further extending beyond the confines of its prison. There is a vague threat in the shape of the head: the configuration of nose, skull, and neck recalls the barrel, chassis, and handle of a gun. However, the wide-open mouth suggests a scream of anguish, and the cord attaching it to its cage evokes the gallows. *Nose* should be seen within the context of postwar existential angst that was voiced by Jean-Paul Sartre, a friend of the artist.

In *Diego*, a painting of his brother, Giacometti continued in this vein, insinuating the loneliness caused by each individual's isolation within his own existence. Like the head in *Nose*, the solitary Diego is presented in the confines of a cagelike structure of lines denoting the architecture of the room. The atmosphere of melancholy is further suggested both by the artist's muted palette that seems to drain life from the sitter, and the figure's near-transparency in a haze of reworked paint.

—J. B.

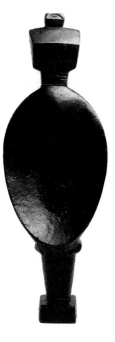

Spoon Woman,
1926. Bronze,
56 ⅝ x 20 ¼ x
8 ½ inches.
55.1414

Diego, 1953. Oil
on canvas, 39 ½ x
31 ¾ inches.
55.1431

Nose, 1947.
Bronze, wire, rope,
and steel; cage:
31 ⅞ x 15 ⅜ x 19
inches; head: 17 x
3 3/16 x 27 ¼
inches. 66.1807

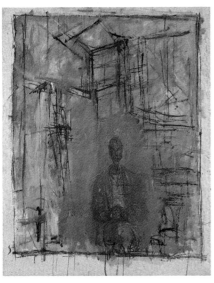

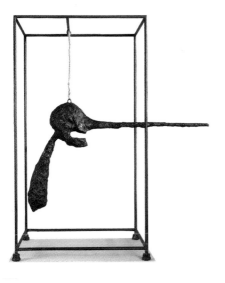

"We want people to bring their life to our exhibitions, not their knowledge of art. True art has to overcome and speak across the barriers of knowledge. We are opposed to art that is about art. A load of string stuck on a wall isn't art—it's a trick. We believe that art has a real function to advance civilization."

Gilbert and George

Gilbert, b. 1943, Dolomites, Italy
George, b. 1942, Devon, England

Since 1965, when Gilbert and George met and began working and living together, they have merged their identities so completely that we never think of one without the other; no surnames, individual biographies, or separate bodies of work hinder their unique twinship. Furthermore, they make no distinction between their life and their art; they *are* their own works of art. In 1967 they began public appearances in the guise of "living sculptures": identically attired in proper business suits, their faces and hands covered with a metallic patina, they paraded themselves at cultural events (they later toured to museums and galleries) playing the game of robotized bronze statues that mirrored the spectacle of art in popular culture. The range of their art has grown to include photography, drawing, painting, written texts, film, and performance. Their presence is clearly felt in their work, which often includes self-portraits.

In the large photo-piece *Dream*, the two artists appear with a beautiful young man from London's East End (where Gilbert and George live and where they find many of their male models) who poses as an archetype of youth and innocence. In their roles as both patrons and worshippers they playfully exploit the tradition of ecclesiastical stained-glass window imagery, which their photographic works have mimicked since the early 1970s. Their technique—collaging black-and-white photographs that are dyed with lurid colors and overlaid with a Modernist grid—synthesizes religious, popular-culture, and high-art motifs in order to render their message as directly as possible. In *Dream* and many related works, Gilbert and George use the particulars of East End society and the British urban homosexual experience, filtered through their own personal experiences, to create contemporary allegories. They include their own images in order to cast themselves as symbolic stand-ins for a larger group.

—J. A.

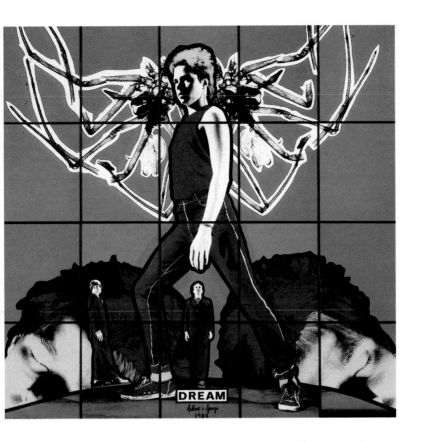

Dream, *1984.*
Photo-piece, 96 x
100 inches. Gift,
C.E.D.E.F., S.A.,
Geneva. 86.3412

*"The principle of
movement in a
machine and in a
living being is the
same, and the whole
joy of my work is to
reveal the balance of
movement."*

Natalia Goncharova

b. 1881, Nechaevo, Russia; d. 1962, Paris

Natalia Goncharova and Mikhail Larionov, her collaborator and companion for more than 60 years, experimented with contemporary French stylistic trends before developing a Neo-primitive vocabulary inspired by indigenous Russian folk art. In late 1912 the two artists fashioned a fusion of Cubo-Futurism and Orphism known as Rayism. *Cats*, painted shortly thereafter, exemplifies the new style.

Using intersecting vectors of color to depict refracted light rays, Rayist works recreate the surface play of light on objects. This perceptual approach to painting was based on scientific discoveries concerning the nature of vision, advances that had also influenced Neo-Impressionist color theories, the Cubist analysis of form, and the Futurist emphasis on dynamic lines. The nationalistic strain apparent in Italian Futurist manifestos also pervades Rayist tracts, in which the Russian theory is posited as a unique synthetic achievement of the East. In the preface to the catalogue of her 1913 Moscow retrospective exhibition, Goncharova wrote: "For me the East means the creation of new forms, an extending and deepening of the problems of color. This will help me to express contemporaneity—its living beauty—better and more vividly."

Cats, which appears to represent two black felines with a tabby in between, illustrates the Rayist view that objects may serve as points of departure for explorations on the canvas. Goncharova used darts of color to suggest the effects of light on the cats' shiny coats and the way that adjacent surfaces reflect neighboring hues. The dynamic slashes of black and white evoke the energized, machine-inspired compositions of the Futurists.

The artist's brilliant color recalls Robert Delaunay's exuberant depictions of the Eiffel Tower as well as Russian woodblock prints and painted trays. *Cats* also suggests the richly hued integration of animals and their environment that Franz Marc was developing contemporaneously in his own synthesis of Cubism and Futurism. Yet unlike Marc and other German Expressionist painters, Rayist painters did not seek to express spiritual goals through their art.

—J. B.

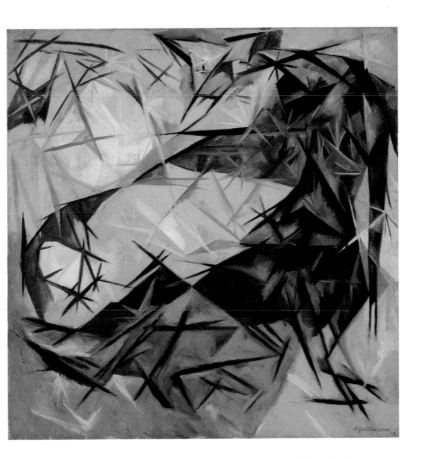

Cats (rayist percep.[tion] in rose, black, and yellow), *1913. Oil on canvas, 33 1/4 x 33 inches.* *57.1484*

*"This {type of}
work is mostly
personal. It is
about those very
early hours in the
morning, while
still half asleep,
when I tend to
visualize
information, to see
panoramas in
which the fictional,
the important, the
banal, and the
historical are
collapsed into a
single caption."*

Félix González-Torres

b. 1957, Guáimaro, Cuba; d. 1996, Miami

Félix González-Torres's pristine stacks of
imprinted paper and eccentric candy spills—
which he has arranged in corners and across floors
since 1990—are subversive rearticulations of
Minimalism's nonrepresentational aesthetic.
While recalling Carl Andre's metal carpets,
Donald Judd's sequenced boxes, and Robert
Morris's seminal Corner Piece of 1964, they
undermine the supposed neutrality of such work.
He reintroduces what has been sublimated in
much Modernist art—desire, loss, vulnerability,
and anger—with a potent but quiet poignancy
through texts inscribed on giveaway paper sheets
and subtitles appended to "untitled" works. Free
for the taking and replaceable, González-Torres's
perpetually shrinking and swelling sculptures
defy the macho solidity of Minimalist form, while
playfully expanding upon the seriality of the
genre and the quotidian nature of its materials.

His early text pieces are lists of seemingly
random historical incidents followed by the dates
of their occurrence, for example, *Pol Pot 1975
Prague 1968 Robocop 1987 H Bomb 1954 Wheel of
Fortune 1968 Spud*. Concurrently, he created
similar inventories of gay-rights events and the
AIDS crisis, culminating in the 1989 Greenwich
Village billboard on which he commemorated in
list form a history of oppression, illness, and
activism. A self-acknowledged gay man who
recently suffered the death of his longtime
companion, González-Torres has expressed his
grief and love for this man—as well as his outrage
at a social system that marginalizes
homosexuals—in much of his recent work. A
stack piece bearing the simple message "Memorial
Day" gives a new, haunting meaning to this
generally trivialized American holiday; the festive
and seductive spill of silver-wrapped candies
subtitled *Placebo* ironically invokes the
controversial and discriminatory modes of drug-
testing in AIDS research. *Untitled (Public Opinion)*,
a 700-pound spill of black rod licorice pieces,
displayable as either a corner piece or a carpet, is a
dark, aggressive work. The missilelike shape of
the candy and its brooding, almost sinister,
appearance alludes to our culture's pervasive
militaristic outlook and hostile hegemonic stance.
As an art work produced in the current
conservative political climate, the sculpture also
refers to the encroaching censorship in America
and suggests that public opinion is not as
informed as it once was.

—N. S.

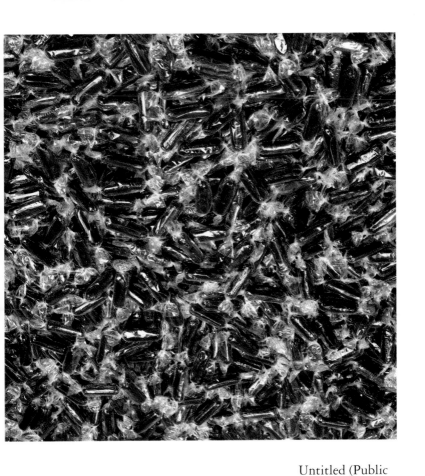

Untitled (Public
Opinion), *1991
(detail). 700
pounds of
cellophane-wrapped
black rod licorice
candy, size
variable. Purchased
with funds
contributed by the
Louis and Bessie
Adler Foundation,
Inc., and the
National
Endowment for the
Arts Museum
Purchase Program.
91.3969*

Grid

The Egyptians constructed their pyramids on a perfect square representing the four corners of the world, the supports of the heavens, and the four winds; they designed their figurative sculptures using a grid based on the measure of a human handbreadth. In the present, grids underlie the design of most Modern architecture—even the terrazzo floor of Frank Lloyd Wright's spiral Guggenheim Museum reflects a pattern of circles inscribed in a squared grid.

The squared grid was the key to the Renaissance invention of linear perspective, a conceptual tool by which painters could represent an abstract model of the world. Persisting through the 19th century as an essential instrument of pictorial representation, the Renaissance grid was a means of objective measurement of the real, and at the same time, in its pure optical geometry, a reflection of spiritual order and human perfection—of man made in God's image.

The grid has been a dominant motif of Modern art, used both to explore the real and what is beyond and behind that reality. With horizontal and vertical brushstrokes that mimic the gridlike weave of the canvas, Paul Cézanne fused the foreground, middleground, and background of his painted landscapes to the concrete reality of the picture plane and the rectangular boundary of its frame. Piet Mondrian utilized the linear horizontal and vertical elements of the grid to develop an entirely abstract painting embodying essential structures that underlie both a spiritual and a material world.

The historic origins and uses of the grid are tied as much to the physical reality of architecture as to the illusionist optics of painting. The modern grid also conveys the modularity of time and mechanization of the machine age—it can be seen in film frames, for example, and boxes on an assembly line—epitomized by Andy Warhol's grid of silkscreened Mona Lisas, electric chairs, and Campbell's soup cans. In Warhol's works the images themselves break down into a photographic grid of dots for mechanical printing.

Marcel Duchamp, the great conceptual artist of this century, publicly gave up making art in order to devote himself to playing chess. In doing so, he recast the Renaissance grid in the form of the 64 squares of a chessboard—a fixed platform, with fixed rules, accommodating any variation of moves and an infinity of expressive possibilities.

—Michael Govan

Piet Mondrian, Composition 2 *(detail).*

H

"The 'stucco' texture is a reminiscence of motel ceilings. . . . The Day-Glo paint is a signifier of 'low budget mysticism.' It is the afterglow of radiation."

Peter Halley
b. 1953, New York City

Two Cells with Conduit resembles the Hard-edge paintings of Brice Marden, Kenneth Noland, and Ellsworth Kelly, but while the work of those artists may be described as "abstract," Peter Halley prefers the designation "diagrammatic" for his precise, austere arrangements. He conceives of his vocabulary of squares, bars, and rectangles as coded referents to the way in which geometry pervades our world. Life in late-capitalist culture, according to Halley's own critical writing, has been inscribed and circumscribed by geometric networks: think of the urban grid, the office tower, the high-rise apartment building, the correctional institution, the parking lot. Halley's morphological investigations also focus on the traditional manner in which geometric abstraction has been perceived. By invoking the formal attributes of Minimalist art—rigid planes of color, unitary shapes, and nonhierarchical compositions—and mapping a narrative sensibility onto them, Halley calls the supposed neutrality of such art into question.

As both author and artist, Halley has drawn upon the writings of the French theoreticians Michel Foucault and Jean Baudrillard to articulate and substantiate his dual critique of culture and art. Foucault's analysis of the geometric organization of industrial society, particularly institutional modes of confinement, inspired Halley to transform a Minimalist square into a prison cell by adding three vertical bars to

Two Cells with Conduit, *1987. Day-Glo, acrylic, and Roll-a-Tex on canvas; top section: 66 1/8 x 155 1/8 inches; bottom section: 12 1/2 x 155 1/8 inches; total 78 5/8 x 155 1/8 inches. Purchased with funds contributed by Denise and Andrew Saul and Ellyn and Saul Dennison. 87.3550.1-.2*

the form. In response to Baudrillard's exploration of postindustrial culture—its reliance on information systems, media representation, and an economy that privileges image over product—Halley shifted to schematized depictions of enclosed spaces, linked to the world through a network of electronic, telephonic, and fiber-optic conduits. The division of *Two Cells with Conduit* into two discrete portions suggests an architectural section; the squares above represent prototypical urban dwellings while the line below indicates the hidden, technological underworld of pipes, cables, and wires connecting them. Begun in 1981, the cell-and-conduit paintings demonstrate what Halley has described as the "seductive" geometry of 1980s culture, epitomized by the irreal space of the video game. The Day-Glo colors and ersatz stucco paint— known as Roll-a-Tex—make these canvases into emblems of current social reality, in which artifice replaces empirical experience.

—N. S.

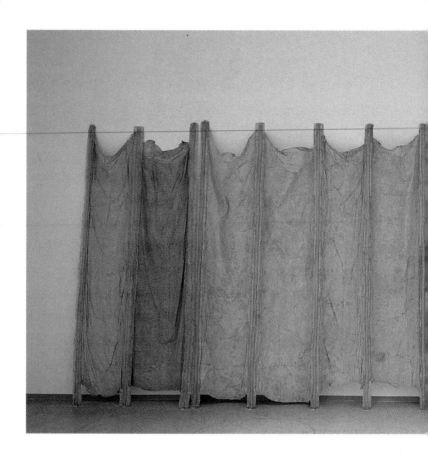

"This piece does have an option."

Eva Hesse

b. 1936, Hamburg; d. 1970, New York City

When Eva Hesse came to maturity as an artist during the mid-1960s, the women's movement and the sexual revolution were emerging as powerful, liberating forces in the U.S. It was a time when voices of the counterculture gained widespread recognition. The urge toward radical reappraisal and reform was manifest in the art world as well—Pop art and Minimalism displaced Abstract Expressionism through their categorical dismissal of artistic subjectivity and the heroic gesture. Almost immediately, however, artists questioned the geometric rigidity of Minimalism and the limitations of the Pop idiom. Finding inspiration in the human body, the random occurrence, the process of improvisation, and the liberating qualities of nontraditional materials such as industrial felt, molten lead, wax, and rubber, these artists mined a new aesthetic sensibility variously known as Anti-Form, Post-Minimalism, or Process Art.

During her brief career Hesse contributed to this radical undermining of artistic convention with her abstract yet sensual sculptural works. She rejected the standard attributes of monumental sculpture—volume, mass, and verticality—in favor of eccentric forms made from

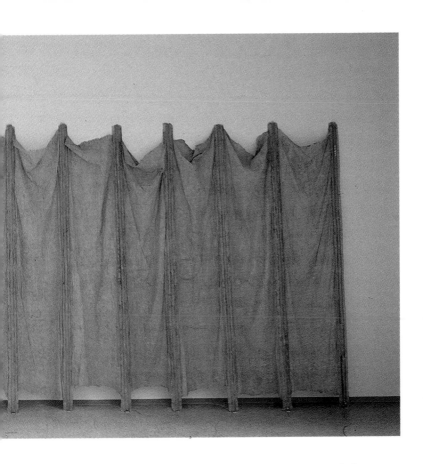

rope, latex, and cheesecloth, all of which decompose with time. Her goal, she explained, was to portray the essential absurdity of life. In formal terms, this theme was realized through a wedding of contradictions: "order versus chaos, stringy versus mass, huge versus small," in the artist's words. Acutely aware of the challenges faced by a female artist in a predominantly male environment, Hesse may have utilized such formal opposites as a metaphor for her own position in the art world and to emphasize the inherent strength of flexibility and vulnerability.

Expanded Expansion is a sculptural embodiment of opposites united. Both permanence and deterioration operate in the piece: fiberglass poles—rigid, durable entities—are juxtaposed with fragile, rubber-covered cheesecloth. While its height is determined by the poles, the width of the piece varies with each installation; like an accordion or curtain, it can be compressed or extended. Its repetitive units echo the programmatic seriality of Minimalism, but here they accentuate Hesse's desire to illuminate her view that "if something is absurd, it's much more exaggerated, more absurd if it's repeated." The very redundancy of the title reinforces this idea.

—N. S.

Expanded Expansion, 1969. Fiberglass and rubberized cheesecloth in three units; three-pole unit, 122 x 60 inches; five-pole unit, 122 x 120 inches; eight-pole unit, 122 x 180 inches. Gift, Family of Eva Hesse, 1975. 75.2138.a-.c

"Pure must not mean poor."

Hans Hofmann

b. 1880, Weissenburg, Bavaria; d. 1966, New York City

Hans Hofmann's life affirms the importance of art as an essential activity of society. "Providing leadership by teachers and support of developing artists is a national duty, an insurance of spiritual solidarity," wrote Hofmann in 1931. "What we do for art, we do for ourselves and for our children and the future."

Hofmann's greatness lay in the consistency and uncompromising rigor of the artistic standards he devised and his aptitude for teaching those principles to a devoted and diverse body of students. Hofmann founded and taught at art schools from 1915 until 1958, and he inspired a wide range of artists, from Lee Krasner and Burgoyne Diller to Irene Rice Pereira. He is best remembered for teaching the fundamental issues of postwar abstraction: the employment of non-representational forms and of color, and the artist's ability to weave sophisticated relationships between them. As one student, the painter Wolf Kahn, reports: "We were like a religious order . . . in the search for formal perfection." For many of Hofmann's students, this search consisted solely of formal innovation. Hofmann's own work as a painter does not center on original discoveries; rather, Hofmann synthesized other movements into his own glowing combination of Expressionism and De Stijl. This forces us to reexamine the definition of artistic "invention" and question the assumption that art must be seen in terms of discrete meaningful objects. In Hofmann's case, it might better be judged as a model from which to teach.

The Gate was painted in 1959–60 as part of a series of works loosely devoted to architectonic volumes. Hofmann used rectangles of color to reinforce the shape of his essentially unvarying easel-painting format. Although *The Gate* is subjectless, Hofmann insisted that, even in abstraction, students should always work from some form of nature. With determination, a viewer can see that the complex spatial relationship established by the floating planes of color begins to resemble the gate of the title.

—C. L.

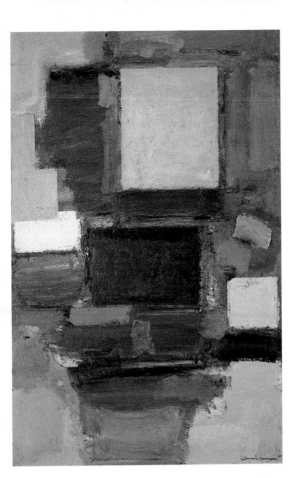

The Gate,
1959–60. *Oil on
canvas, 75 $^1/_8$ x
48 $^1/_2$ inches.*
62.1620

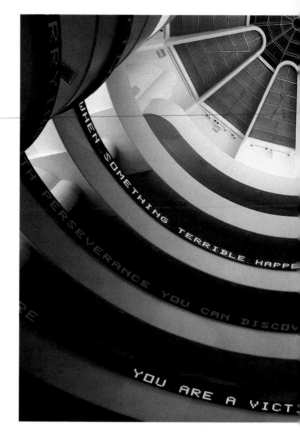

"*The* Truisms were, or at least were as close as I could make them to, genuine clichés. . . . They were unequivocal individually, but as a series, because they came from a zillion different points of view, you had to sort things out for yourself and figure out what it meant."

Jenny Holzer

b. 1950, Gallipolis, Ohio

Jenny Holzer began the *Truisms* series in 1977 as a distillation of an erudite reading list from the Whitney Independent Study Program, where she was a student; by 1979 she had written several hundred one-liners. Beginning with A LITTLE KNOWLEDGE GOES A LONG WAY and ending with YOUR OLDEST FEARS ARE THE WORST ONES, the *Truisms* employ a variety of voices and express a wide spectrum of biases and beliefs. If any consistent viewpoint emerges in the edgy, stream-of-consciousness provocations it is that truth is relative and that each viewer must become an active participant in determining what is legitimate and what is not. Since the *Truisms*, Holzer has used language exclusively and has employed myriad ways to convey her messages. Selections from her *Inflammatory Essays* series, for example, appeared on unsigned, commercially printed posters, which were wheatpasted on buildings and walls around Manhattan.

When such Holzer phrases as ABUSE OF POWER COMES AS NO SURPRISE and MONEY CREATES TASTE flashed from the Spectacolor board above Times Square in 1982, it marked her first appropriation of electronic signage. In doing so, she brought her disquieting messages to a new height of subver-

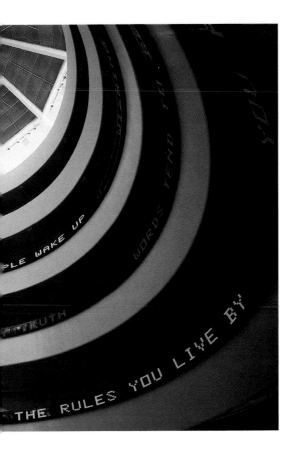

Untitled (Selections from Truisms, Inflammatory Essays, The Living Series, The Survival Series, Under a Rock, Laments, and Child Text), 1990. *Extended helical tricolor L.E.D. electronic-display signboard, 16 ¹/₂ inches x 162 feet x 6 inches (subject to change with installation). Partial gift of the artist, 1989. 89.3626*

sive social engagement. Her strategy—placing surprising texts where normal signage is expected—gives Holzer direct access to a large public that might not give "art" any consideration, while allowing her to undermine forms of power and control that often go unnoticed.

In Holzer's 1989 retrospective installation at the Guggenheim Museum, blinking messages from her various series, programmed to an insistent but silent beat, raced the length of an L.E.D. display board installed along the winding inner wall of Frank Lloyd Wright's famous spiral ramp. The museum's rotunda was transformed into a dazzling electronic arcade. In bringing her art from the street to the museum, Holzer focused on an audience that differed markedly from the unsuspecting passerby. The Guggenheim visitors who stood beneath the revolving ribbons of red, green, and yellow aphorisms were more likely to be aware that this installation brought up such issues as the viability of public art, the commodification and consumption of art, and the conflation of the personal and the political—in short, the pressing issues of American art in the 1980s.

—J. A.

Imaginary

In the desert the mirage is imaginary while the oasis is real and life-sustaining. Plato conceived of painting as a mirage, "a man-made dream for waking eyes," but because it artificially imitates reality without truly *being* what it represents he considered it ethically deficient. Truth to nature has been reasserted in different guises, from the Renaissance ideal of the painting as a window onto the world to the mid-19th-century Realism of Gustave Courbet, who contended, "Show me an angel and I'll paint it."

The concept of the imaginary as a fundamental value of art is rooted in the Enlightenment's privileging of the individual creative genius. Artists have pursued various methods of liberating the mind in order to access the marvelous, such as looking to children, "primitives," and the insane for inspiration or using psychoanalytic techniques and mind-altering substances to stimulate the unconscious. As the individual became the source of originality, the Western male artist was driven to construct himself in opposition to a non-self. The oneiric realms explored by the Symbolists and Surrealists, for example, were based on projections of an exotic and erotic imaginary world implicitly opposed to a reality envisioned as Western, mundane, and masculine.

In the 20th century the difference between the real and the imaginary has been problematized by the latter's usurpation of the former. Since Marcel Duchamp chose his first ready-made in the teens, a strain of literal realism has been evident in art, but it carries conceptual baggage. Is a Hoover that is used to clean simply a vacuum cleaner, and the one in Jeff Koons's *Hoover Convertible* art? The vacuum cleaner on the pedestal really *is* what it represents, but it doesn't yield Truth as Plato supposed. Today, cinematic fables like *E.T.* make the marvelous seem more ordinary by featuring familiar brand-name products, while the real is reenacted—and thereby fictionalized—in T.V. programs like *America's Most Wanted*. The synthetic realism of advertising is the most persistent and pervasive visual mapping of the postmodern imagination. When Clairol displays a blonde and asks, "Does she or doesn't she?" a universe of values and desires—and the issue of authenticity—is invoked. Nowadays, the imaginary masquerades as the real, reflecting a world where the most "real" object is the commodity, be it a Campbell's soup can or the Breck girl.

—J. B.

Joan Miró, Landscape (The Hare) *(detail).*

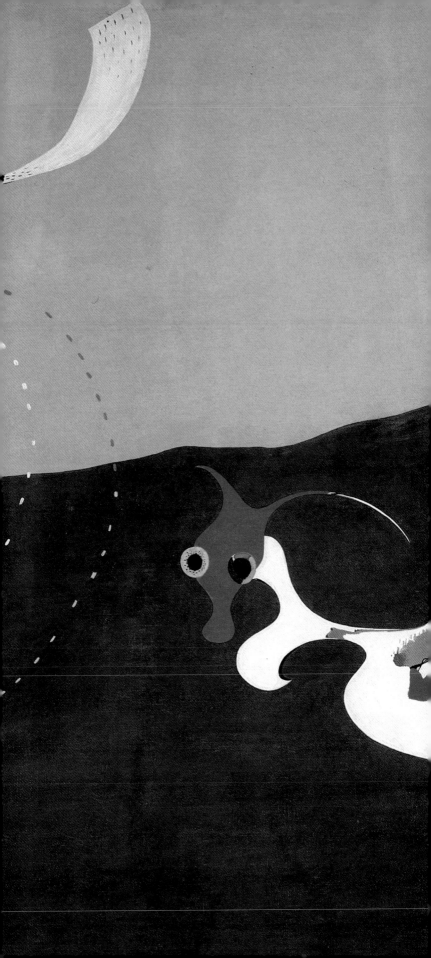

K

*"His storming
riders are his coat
of arms."
—August Macke
on Kandinsky*

Vasily Kandinsky
b. 1866, Moscow; d. 1944, Neuilly-sur-Seine, France

Vasily Kandinsky's use of the horse-and-rider motif symbolized his crusade against conventional aesthetic values and his dream of a better, more spiritual future through the transformative powers of art. The rider is featured in many woodcuts, temperas, and oils, from its first appearance in the artist's folk-inspired paintings, executed in his native Russia at the turn of the century, to his abstracted landscapes made in Munich during the early 1910s. The horseman was also incorporated into the cover designs for Kandinsky's theoretical manifesto of 1911, *On the Spiritual in Art,* and the contemporaneous *Blue Rider Almanac*, which he co-edited with Franz Marc.

In 1909, the year he completed *Blue Mountain*, Kandinsky painted no less than seven other canvases with images of riders. In that year his style became increasingly abstract and expressionistic and his thematic concerns shifted from the portrayal of natural events to apocalyptic narratives. By 1910 many of the artist's abstract canvases shared a common literary source, the Revelation of Saint John the Divine; the rider came to signify the Horsemen of the Apocalypse, who will bring epic destruction after which the world will be redeemed. In both *Sketch for Composition II* and *Improvisation 28* (second version) Kandinsky depicted—through highly schematized means—cataclysmic events on one side of the canvas and the paradise of spiritual salvation on the other. In the latter painting, for instance, images of a boat and waves (signaling the global deluge), a serpent, and, perhaps, cannons emerge on the left, while an embracing couple, shining sun, and celebratory candles appear on the right.

—N. S.

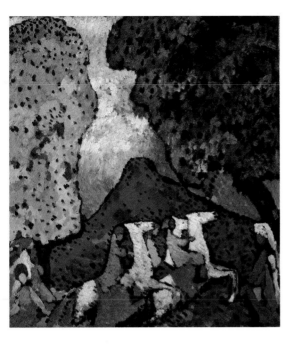

Blue Mountain,
*1908–9. Oil on
canvas, 41 ³/₄ x 38
inches. Gift,
Solomon R.
Guggenheim.*
41.505

Sketch for
Composition II,
*1909–10. Oil on
canvas, 38 ³/₈ x
51 ⁵/₈ inches.*
45.961

Improvisation 28
*(second version),
1912. Oil on
canvas, 43 ⁷/₈ x
63 ⁷/₈ inches. Gift,
Solomon R.
Guggenheim.*
37.239

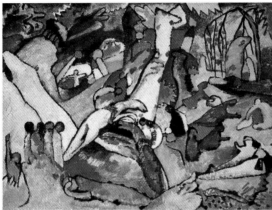

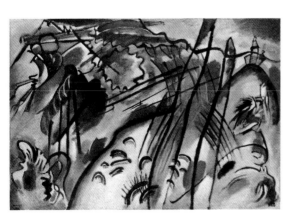

Vasily Kandinsky

With its undulating colored ovals traversed by animated brushstrokes, *Black Lines* is among the first of Kandinsky's truly non-objective paintings. The network of thin, agitated lines indicates a graphic, two-dimensional sensibility, while the floating, vibrantly hued forms suggest various spatial depths.

By 1913 Kandinsky's aesthetic theories and aspirations were well developed. He valued painterly abstraction as the most effective stylistic means through which to reveal hidden aspects of the empirical world, express subjective realities, aspire to the metaphysical, and offer a regenerative vision of the future. Kandinsky wanted the evocative power of carefully chosen and dynamically interrelated colors, shapes, and lines to elicit specific responses from viewers of his canvases. The inner vision of an artist, he believed, could thereby be translated into a universally accessible statement.

He realized, however, that it would be necessary to develop such a style slowly in order to foster public acceptance and comprehension. Therefore, in most of his work from this period he retained fragments of recognizable imagery. "We are still firmly bound to the outward appearance of nature and must draw forms from it," he wrote in his essay *Picture with the White Edge*, but suggested that there existed a hidden pictorial construction that would "emerge unnoticed from the picture and [would thus be] less suited to the eye than the soul." *Painting with White Border*, for instance, was explained by Kandinsky as a response to "those . . . extremely powerful impressions I had experienced in Moscow—or more correctly, of Moscow itself." To illustrate the spirit of the city, Kandinsky included an extremely abbreviated image of a Russian troika driven by a trio of horses (the three diagonal black lines in the upper-left portion of the canvas). The mass of swirling colors and lines in the center has been convincingly interpreted as the figure of a lance-bearing St. George on horseback, an allusion to Moscow's tsarist tradition (the state seal of Peter the Great included an emblem of the saint). *Small Pleasures* is filled with veiled imagery of the Last Judgment, as in many of his canvases, but its title suggests other readings. In an essay on the painting, Kandinsky wrote that his goal "was to let . . . [himself] go and scatter a heap of small pleasures upon the canvas."

—N. S.

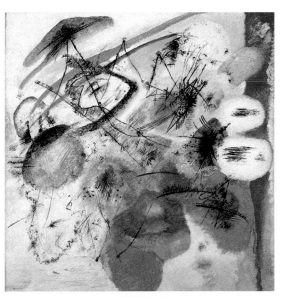

Black Lines, *Dec. 1913. Oil on canvas, 51 x 51 ⁵/₈ inches. Gift, Solomon R. Guggenheim.* 37.241

Painting with White Border, *May 1913. Oil on canvas, 55 ¹/₄ x 78 ⁷/₈ inches. Gift, Solomon R. Guggenheim.* 37.245

Small Pleasures, *June 1913. Oil on canvas, 43 ¹/₄ x 47 ¹/₈ inches.* 43.921

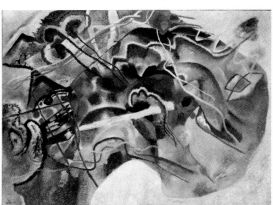

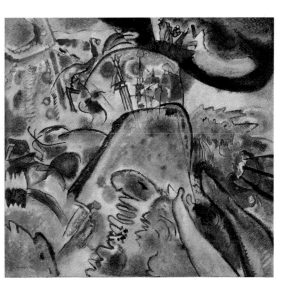

"It is said that in art it is not necessary and even dangerous to have intuition. This is the point of view of a few young {Russian} painters who push the materialistic viewpoint to absurdity."

Vasily Kandinsky

When Kandinsky returned to his native Moscow after the outbreak of World War I, his expressive abstract style underwent changes that reflected the utopian artistic experiments of the Russian avant-garde. The emphasis on geometric forms, promoted by artists such as Kazimir Malevich, Aleksandr Rodchenko, and Liubov Popova in an effort to establish a universal aesthetic language, inspired Kandinsky to expand his own pictorial vocabulary. Although he adopted some aspects of the geometrizing trends of Suprematism and Constructivism—such as overlapping flat planes and clearly delineated shapes—his belief in the expressive content of abstract forms alienated him from the majority of his Russian colleagues, who championed more rational, systematizing principles. This conflict led him to return to Germany in 1921. *In the Black Square*, executed two years later, epitomizes Kandinsky's synthesis of Russian avant-garde art and his own lyrical abstraction: the white trapezoid recalls Malevich's Suprematist paintings, but the dynamic compositional elements, resembling clouds, mountains, sun, and a rainbow, still refer to the landscape.

In 1922 Kandinsky joined the faculty of the Weimar Bauhaus, where he discovered a more sympathetic environment in which to pursue his art. Originally premised on a Germanic, expressionistic approach to art making, the Bauhaus aesthetic came to reflect Constructivist concerns and styles, which by the mid-1920s had become international in scope. While there, Kandinsky furthered his investigations into the correspondence between colors and forms and their psychological and spiritual effects. In *Composition 8*, the colorful, interactive geometric forms create a pulsating surface that is alternately dynamic and calm, aggressive and quiet. The importance of circles in this painting prefigures the dominant role they would play in many subsequent works, culminating in his cosmic and harmonious image, *Several Circles*. "The circle," claimed Kandinsky, "is the synthesis of the greatest oppositions. It combines the concentric and the eccentric in a single form and in equilibrium. Of the three primary forms, it points most clearly to the fourth dimension."

—N. S.

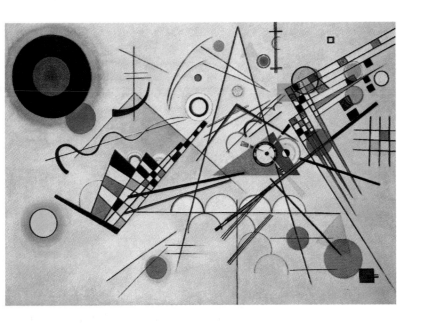

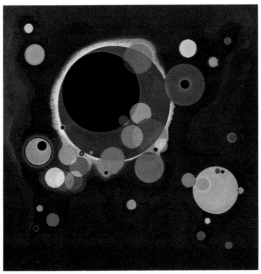

Composition 8,
*July 1923. Oil on
canvas, 55 $^{1}/_{8}$ x
79 $^{1}/_{8}$ inches. Gift,
Solomon R.
Guggenheim.
37.262*

Several Circles,
*Jan.– Feb. 1926.
Oil on canvas,
55 $^{1}/_{4}$ x 55 $^{3}/_{8}$
inches. Gift,
Solomon R.
Guggenheim.
41.283*

In the Black
Square, *June
1923. Oil on
canvas, 38 $^{3}/_{8}$ x
36 $^{5}/_{8}$ inches. Gift,
Solomon R.
Guggenheim.
37.254*

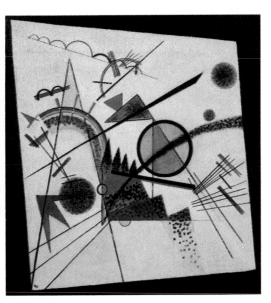

"Abstract art, despite its emancipation, is subject here also to 'natural laws,' and is obliged to proceed in the same way that nature did previously, when it started in a modest way with protoplasm and cells, progressing very gradually to increasingly complex organisms."

Vasily Kandinsky

Although Kandinsky was forced to leave Germany in 1933 due to political pressures, he did not allow the mood of desolation pervading war-torn Europe to enter the paintings and watercolors that he produced in France, where he remained until his death in 1944. His late works are marked by a general lightening of palette and the introduction of organic imagery; breaking away from the rigidity of Bauhaus geometry, he turned to the softer, more malleable shapes used by Paris-based artists associated with Surrealism, such as Jean Arp and Joan Miró. Kandinsky's late, often whimsical, paintings were also influenced by the playful, intricately detailed compositions of his longtime friend and Bauhaus colleague Paul Klee.

During his first years in France, Kandinsky experimented with pigments mixed with sand, a technical innovation practiced during the 1930s by many Parisian artists, including André Masson and Georges Braque. Although Kandinsky utilized this method only until 1936, he created several paintings with rich, textured surfaces such as *Accompanied Contrast*, in which the interconnected colored planes and smaller floating patterns project slightly from the canvas. Always attentive to and appreciative of contemporary stylistic innovations, Kandinsky inevitably brought his own interests to bear on any aspects he would borrow. As art historian Vivian Barnett has pointed out, his employment of biomorphic forms—a motif favored by Surrealist painters as well as by Klee—attests more to his fascination with the organic sciences themselves, particularly embryology, zoology, and botany. During his Bauhaus years, Kandinsky had clipped and mounted illustrations of microscopic organisms, insects, and embryos from scientific journals for pedagogical purposes and study. He also owned several important sourcebooks and encyclopedias from which depictions of minuscule creatures found abstract equivalences in his late paintings. A schematized pink-toned embryo, for instance, floats in the upper-right corner of *Dominant Curve*, while the figures contained within the green rectangle in the upper-left corner resemble microscopic marine animals. *Various Actions* is imbued with similar organic figures hovering above a celestial blue field. These buoyant, biomorphic images, often presented in pastel hues, may be read as signs of Kandinsky's optimistic vision of a peaceful future and hope for postwar rebirth and regeneration.

—N. S.

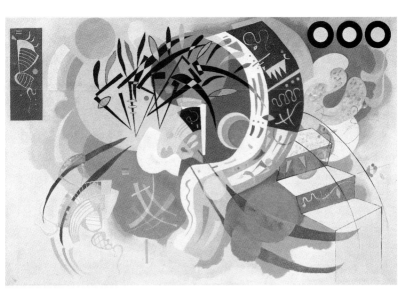

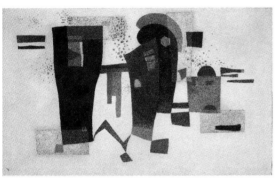

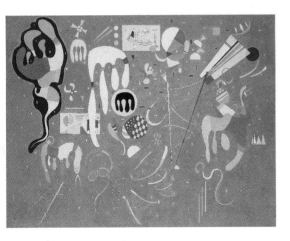

Dominant Curve, *April 1936. Oil on canvas, 50 $^7/_8$ x 76 $^1/_2$ inches.* 45.989

Accompanied Contrast, *March 1935. Oil with sand on canvas, 38 $^1/_4$ x 63 $^7/_8$ inches. Gift, Solomon R. Guggenheim.* 37.338

Various Actions, *Aug.–Sept. 1941. Oil and enamel on canvas, 35 $^1/_8$ x 45 $^3/_4$ inches.* 47.1159

"I am less interested in marks on the panels than in the presence of the panels themselves."

Ellsworth Kelly
b. 1923, Newburgh, N.Y.

When Jasper Johns and Frank Stella sought to draw attention to the flatness of the canvas, they did so with imagery and an aesthetic sensibility that are quintessentially American. Johns's flags and Stella's pinstripe patterns were perfectly suited to articulate the artists' denial of illusion and perspectival artifice. Their compatriot Ellsworth Kelly, however, spent his formative years in France, where he was exposed to work by artists of the School of Paris and developed a different, perhaps more European, sensibility.

Just as in concrete poetry, where the words of a poem are arranged on a page in a particular shape that *looks* like the poem's subject, the elements of Kelly's *Blue, Green, Yellow, Orange, Red* are arranged to conform to the order of the chromatic spectrum. The work consists of five separately constructed, monochrome panels, in the primary colors blue, yellow, and red alternating with the secondary colors green and orange. This choice of palette makes symbolic reference to the basic colors of Western European painting, thereby placing the painting in a tradition roughly dating back to Giotto and the early Renaissance. It also refers to the color choices made by László Moholy-Nagy, Josef Albers, and others in the 20th-century European tradition of geometric abstraction. At the same time, the reductive simplicity of Kelly's work links it to Jean Arp's reliefs and Henri Matisse's cutouts, wherein color and shape render surface drawing superfluous.

By the 1960s geometric abstraction had become a dominant force in American art and had contributed to the transition from Abstract Expressionism to what art critic Clement Greenberg called Post-painterly abstraction.

Kelly was grouped with Kenneth Noland, Jules Olitski, and other artists working in the U.S. who seemed to reject the tactile surfaces favored by the Abstract Expressionists. But the hard-edged matter-of-factness of Kelly's paintings is their most American quality, and may be likened to the plain manner of speech that has characterized the pragmatism of American visual culture from Shaker furniture, Grant Wood, and the films of Jimmy Stewart (the quintessential pinstripe-suited man), to the early work of Johns and Stella.

—C. L.

Blue, Green, Yellow, Orange, Red, 1966. Oil on canvas; five panels, each 60 ¹/₄ x 48 ¹/₈ inches. 67.1833

"I work with symbols which link our consciousness with the past. The symbols create a kind of simultaneous continuity and we recollect our origins."

Anselm Kiefer
b. 1945, Donaueschingen, Germany

Born in Germany just two months before the final European battle of World War II, Anselm Kiefer grew up witnessing the tragic results of modern warfare and the division of his homeland. He also experienced the rebuilding of a fragmented nation and its struggle for spiritual renewal. Kiefer has devoted himself to investigating the interwoven patterns of German mythology and history and the way they contributed to the rise of Fascism; he has also addressed the repression of its memory and the dismissal of its legacy. Kiefer confronts these issues by violating aesthetic taboos and resurrecting sublimated icons. For example, in his 1969 *Occupations* series, Kiefer photographed himself striking the "Sieg Heil" pose. Subsequent paintings—immense landscapes and architectural interiors, often encrusted with sand and straw—invoke Germany's literary, philosophical, and political heritage. References abound to the Nibelungen and Wagner, Albert Speer's Fascist structures and Adolf Hitler.

Seraphim is part of Kiefer's *Angel* series, which treats the theme of spiritual salvation through fire, an ancient belief perverted by the Nazis in their brutal quest for an exclusively Aryan nation. In this painting, a ladder connects a desolate, charred landscape to the sky. At its base, a serpent—symbolizing a fallen angel—refers to the prevalence of evil on earth; it also serves as a reminder that ladders can be used for descent as well as for ascent. According to the *Doctrine of Celestial Hierarchy*, a fifth-century text, the seraphim, who are among the heavenly beings closest to God, "purify through fire and burnt offering." Kiefer used fire to create the scorched and tortured surface of *Seraphim*, and it is evident from this and many other works that he associates fire with the critical and cathartic powers of art. This equivalence was suggested in the 1974 canvas *Painting = Burning*, in which the outline of a painter's palette is superimposed on a view of the war-torn earth. In *Resumptio*, also 1974, this palette, now winged, ascends from a tomb toward heaven. With its symbolic allusions, *Seraphim* reiterates Kiefer's belief that painting (burning) prompts remembrance and offers redemption through the destruction of illusion. The actual burning of materials used in this work enforces a more specific reading: the Latin word used to describe a sacrificial offering consumed by flames is "holocaust."

—N. S.

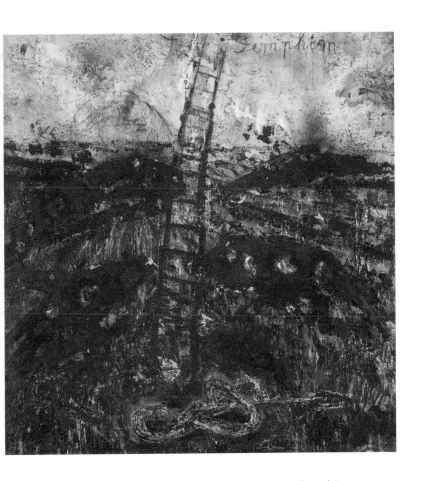

Seraphim,
1983–84. *Oil,*
straw, emulsion,
and shellac on
canvas, 126 1/4 x
130 1/4 *inches.*
Purchased with
funds contributed by
Mr. and Mrs.
Andrew M. Saul.
84.3216

"The pressure of the war and the increasingly prevailing superficiality weigh more heavily than everything else."

Ernst Ludwig Kirchner

b. 1880, Aschaffenburg, Germany; d. 1938, Davos, Switzerland

In 1905 Ernst Ludwig Kirchner joined Fritz Bleyl, Erich Heckel, and Karl Schmidt-Rottluff—all former architecture students who had turned to painting in search of greater self-expression and more immediate means of communication—to found a new art coalition: Die Brücke. The Dresden-based group, part of the larger German Expressionist movement, developed an aesthetic style defined by agitated, coarse lines and intense, blunt colors. Their intention was to wage battle against the constricting forces of bourgeois culture, which they associated with mediocrity, corruption, and weakness. Kirchner's emphasis on self-empowerment and absolute freedom from convention was manifested in his early art by the predominance of erotic subject matter. The female nude—crudely rendered as "primitive" and submissive—served him and his colleagues as a sign of male domination and virility.

Artillerymen, painted two years after Die Brücke's dissolution, marked a change in subject matter. The picture depicts an assembly of naked male soldiers, overseen by a clothed military official. Their attenuated bodies are compressed into an airless, low-ceilinged chamber. Created after Kirchner had been drafted into the German army in 1914 and subsequently released on the grounds of mental instability, this image suggests the artist's sense of overwhelming vulnerability. The naked, showering soldiers are powerless as individuals; their wills have been subjected to the rigidity and anonymity of military life. The view that *Artillerymen* represents Kirchner's horror of the war (and fear for his own life) is corroborated in a more overtly autobiographical painting from the same period, *Self-Portrait as Soldier*. In this oft-reproduced work, a gaunt uniformed Kirchner presents his own severed arm to the viewer, an allusion to the terror of artistic impotence and, ultimately, of death. The presence of a nude female model behind him extends the metaphor to include the possibility of castration, the fear of which would be particularly powerful given Kirchner's conflation of sexual prowess, cultural liberation, and aesthetic achievement.

—N. S.

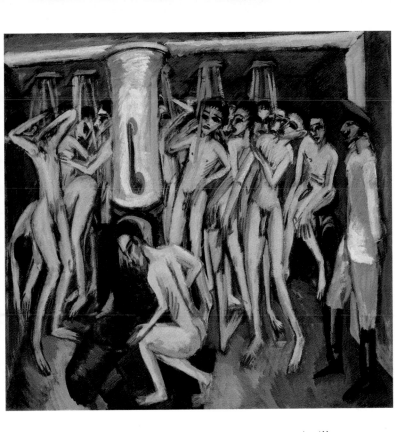

Artillerymen,
*1915. Oil on
canvas, 55 $^{1}/_{8}$ x
59 $^{1}/_{8}$ inches. By
exchange. 88.3591*

Kitsch

What is the quintessential icon of kitsch? Perhaps a plastic Venus de Milo statuette complete with working clock embedded in the stomach. An image such as this affords, among other things, a convenient reference point from which to draw a line between *us*, those who can be counted upon to know kitsch when they see it, and *them*, the untutored masses. Unfortunately for "us," whoever we might be, the reliability of such distinctions is more often than not questionable, if not illusory.

It was Clement Greenberg who, in his 1939 essay *Avant-Garde and Kitsch*, strove to define the avant-garde as a last bastion against kitsch. In treating the vagaries of mass culture as a moral contaminant, however, he seriously under-estimated its overall revolutionary potential and the extent to which traditional culture would be irrevocably transformed by the ongoing processes of industrialization. The dissolution of so-called high art was already well under way when the Dadaists incorporated imagery from popular magazines and newspapers into their photomontages. By the time *Avant-Garde and Kitsch* appeared, Surrealism, with its hybrid dream objects, had heralded an onslaught of Venus de Milo clocks to come. But beyond the progression of various art movements per se, Greenberg failed to comprehend how mass culture-as-spectacle enabled kitsch to gobble up authentic masterpieces, even the Venus de Milo herself. No less than Charles Baudelaire foresaw this involution in his 1863 essay *The Painter of Modern Life*: "The world—and even the world of artists—is full of people who can go to the Louvre, walk rapidly, without so much as a glance, past rows of very interesting, though secondary, pictures, to come to a rapturous halt in front of a Titian or Raphael—one of those that would have been most popularized by the engraver's art; then they will go home happy, not a few saying to themselves, 'I know my Museum.'" Pop artists grappled with this condition in an effort to keep their art from becoming too corny. They showed that artists must address how spectacle inexorably saturates everyday life; failure to acknowledge this truth only perpetuates kitsch. This marked a curious reversal of the accustomed battle lines. Ironically, it is purist aesthetics that then became most vulnerable to kitschification.

—John Miller

Jim Dine, Bedspring *(detail).*

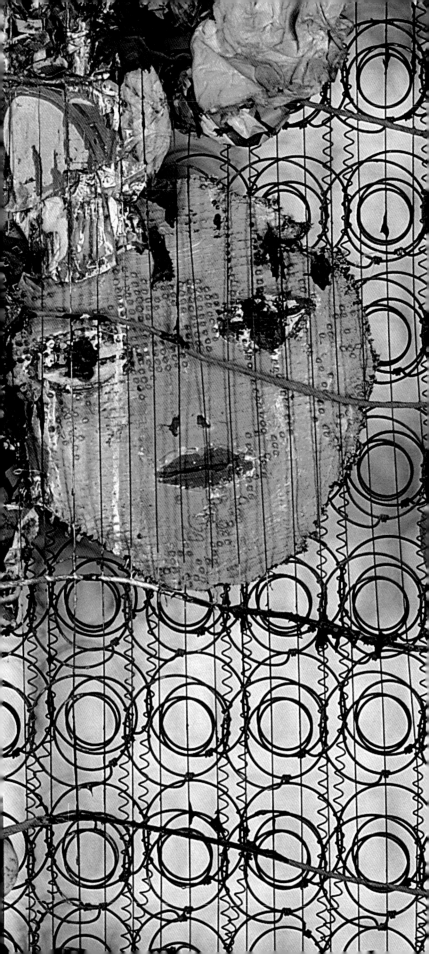

"My self . . . is a dramatic ensemble."

Paul Klee

b. 1879, Münchenbuchsee, Switzerland; d. 1940, Muralto-Locarno, Switzerland

Paul Klee's persistent shifts in style, technique, and subject matter indicate a deliberate and highly playful evasion of aesthetic categorization. Nevertheless, it is virtually impossible to confuse a work by Klee with one by any other artist, even though many have emulated his idiosyncratic, enigmatic art. So accepted was his work that Klee was embraced over the years by the Blue Rider group, the European Dada contingent, the Surrealists, and the Bauhaus faculty, with whom he taught for a decade in Weimar and Dessau.

As part of the early 20th-century avant-garde, Klee formulated a personal abstract pictorial language. His vocabulary, which oscillates freely between the figurative and the nonrepresentational, communicates through a unique symbology that is more expressive than descriptive. Klee conveyed his meanings through an often whimsical fusion of form and text, frequently writing the titles to his works on the mats upon which they are mounted and including words within the images themselves. Such is the case with *The Bavarian Don Giovanni*, in which Klee indicated his admiration for the Mozart opera as well as for certain contemporary sopranos, while hinting at his own amorous pursuits. A veiled self-portrait, the figure climbing the ladder is surrounded by five women's names, an allusion to the operatic scene in which Don Giovanni's servant Leporello recites a list of his master's 2,065 love affairs. Citing Klee's confession that his "infatuations changed with every soubrette at the opera," art historian K. Porter Aichele has identified the Emma and Thères of the watercolor as the singers Emma Carelli and Thérèse Rothauser. The others—Cenzl, Kathi, and Mari—refer to models with whom Klee had fleeting romantic interludes.

Although much of Klee's work is figurative, compositional design nearly always preceded narrative association. The artist often transformed his experiments in tonal value and line into visual anecdotes. *Red Balloon*, for example, is at once a cluster of delicately colored, floating geometric shapes and a charming cityscape. *Runner at the Goal* is an essay in simultaneity; overlapping and partially translucent bars of color illustrate the consecutive gestures of a figure in motion. The flailing arms and sprinting legs add a comic touch to this figure, on whose forehead the number "one" promises a winning finish.

—N. S.

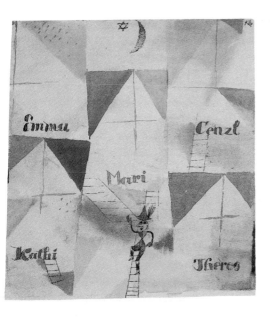

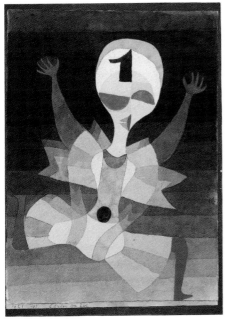

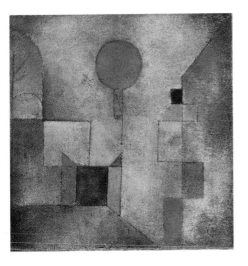

The Bavarian
Don Giovanni,
*1919. Watercolor
and ink on paper,
8 7/8 x 8 3/8 inches.
48.1172x69*

Runner at the
Goal, *1921.
Watercolor and
pencil on paper,
bordered with
watercolor on the
cardboard mount;
paper: 12 7/8 x 9 3/8
inches; paper and
border: 12 7/8 x
9 3/8 inches;
cardboard: 15 1/2 x
11 7/8 inches.
48.1172x55*

Red Balloon,
*1922. Oil (and oil
transfer drawing?)
on chalk-primed
gauze mounted on
board, 12 1/2 x
12 1/4 inches.
48.1172x524*

Paul Klee

An assiduous student of music, nature, mathematics, and science, Paul Klee applied this constellation of interests to his art at every turn. Even his purely abstract works have their own particular subject matter. *In the Current Six Thresholds*, an austere composition of horizontal chromatic stripes divided into smaller units and intersected by vertical bands, has been compared to landscape painting. A late Bauhaus work, it is part of a series of gridlike canvases that Klee painted after he returned from a trip to Egypt. His visual impressions of the Nile river valley are represented here through a highly schematized, geometric analogy composed of a square lattice motif and restrained tonal variations. Another geometric painting, *New Harmony*, demonstrates the artist's longstanding interest in color theory. Such flat configurations of painted rectangles appeared in Klee's work as early as 1915 and evolved as expressions of his equation of chromatic division with musical notation. This late canvas, painted in 1936, is the last such composition and, in typical Klee fashion, looks toward the new and innovative, rather than nostalgically backward. According to art historian Andrew Kagan, the composition is based on the principle of bilateral inverted symmetry (the right side of the canvas is an upside-down reflection of the left) and the tonal distribution of juxtaposed, noncomplementary colors evokes the nonthematic, monodic 12-tone music of Arnold Schönberg. Kagan notes, in conjunction with this reading, that Klee used 12 hues in *New Harmony*, save for the neutral gray and the black underpainting.

Klee revealed a more socially and politically relevant side in his 1937 painting *Revolution of the Viaduct*, of which the Guggenheim's *Arches of the Bridge Break Ranks* is an earlier version. Created when Fascism was on the rise in Europe, the image of rebellious arches escaping from the conformity of a viaduct invokes public dissension while promoting individuality. It is a flippant but foreboding reference to Albert Speer's monolithic Nazi architecture as well as to official Soviet imagery of workers marching forward in unison. There is a poignant postscript to Klee's social critique: after the artist fled Germany in 1937 to his native Switzerland, 17 of his works were displayed in the Nazis' *Degenerate Art* exhibition, a show of Modern painting and sculpture that they considered too free-spirited and libertarian.

—N. S.

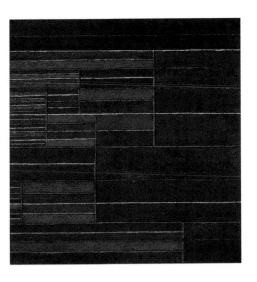

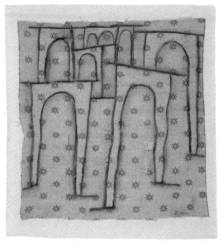

In the Current
Six Thresholds,
1929. *Oil and
tempera on canvas,
17 ¹/₈ x 17 ¹/₈
inches. 67.1842*

Arches of the
Bridge Break
Ranks, 1937.
*Charcoal on cloth
mounted on paper;
cloth: 16 ³/₄ x
16 ¹/₂ inches; paper:
19 ⁵/₈ x 18 ³/₈
inches.
48.1172x59*

New Harmony,
1936. *Oil on
canvas, 36 ⁷/₈ x
26 ¹/₈ inches.
71.1960*

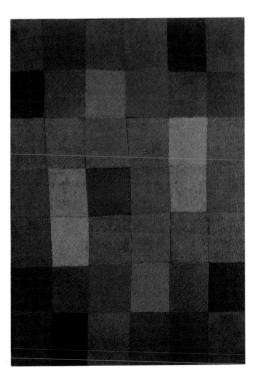

*"It is that
extraordinary
faculty of the
sponge to become
impregnated with
whatever may be
fluid that
seduced me."*

Yves Klein
b. 1928, Nice; d. 1962, Paris

Yves Klein's first passion in life was judo. In 1952 he moved to Tokyo and studied at the Kodokan Judo Institute, where he earned a black belt. When he returned to Paris in 1955 and discovered to his dismay that the Fédération Française de Judo did not extol him as a star, he shifted his attentions and pursued a secondary interest—a career in the arts. During the ensuing eight years Klein assembled a multifarious and critically complex body of work ranging from monochrome canvases and wall reliefs to paintings made with fire. He is renowned for his almost exclusive use of a strikingly resonant, powdery cobalt pigment, which he patented under the name "International Klein Blue," claiming that it represented the physical manifestation of cosmic energy that, otherwise invisible, floats freely in the air. In addition to monochrome paintings, Klein applied this pigment to sponges, which he attached to canvases as relief elements or positioned on wire stands to create biomorphic or anthropomorphic sculptures. First exhibited in Paris in 1959, the sponge sculptures—all essentially alike, yet ultimately all different—formed a forest of discrete objects surrounding the gallery visitors. About these works Klein explained, "Thanks to the sponges—raw living matter—I was going to be able to make portraits of the observers of my monochromes, who . . . after having voyaged in the blue of my pictures, return totally impregnated in sensibility, as are the sponges."

Klein's activities also included using nude female models drenched in paint as "brushes"; releasing thousands of blue balloons into the sky; and exhibiting an empty, white-walled room and then selling portions of the interior air, which he called "zones" of "immaterial pictorial sensibility." His intentions remain perplexing 30 years after his sudden death. Whether Klein truly believed in the mystical capacity of the artist to capture cosmic particles in paint and to create aesthetic experiences out of thin air and then apportion them at whim is difficult to determine. The argument has also been made that he was essentially a parodist who mocked the metaphysical inclinations of many Modern painters, while making a travesty of the art market.

—N. S.

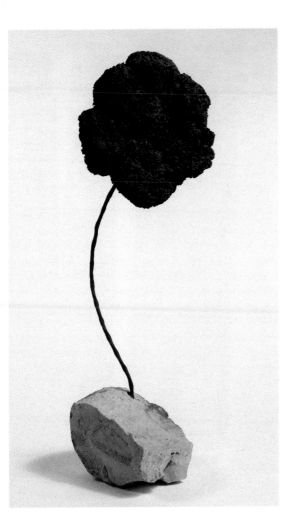

Blue Sponge,
*1959. Dry pigment
in synthetic resin on
sponge with metal
rod and stone base,
39 inches high.
Gift, Mrs. Andrew
P. Fuller. 64.1752*

> *"People sometimes think I take a white canvas and paint a black sign on it, but this is not true. I paint the white as well as the black, and the white is just as important."*

Franz Kline

b. 1910, Wilkes-Barre, Pa.; d. 1962, New York City

Throughout the 1940s, while many artists of the nascent New York School were experimenting with Surrealist-inspired biomorphic abstraction, Franz Kline was painting landscapes and portraits. Consequently in 1950, when the artist showed large, gestural abstract paintings in his first solo exhibition, it appeared that he had experienced a wholesale conversion. Much has been made of a 1949 visit he paid to his friend Willem de Kooning, who asked Kline for some of the drawings he always carried in his pockets and projected them onto the wall, monumentalizing details of the sketches. While this episode may have been a catalyst for Kline's mature style, by the end of the 1940s his work was already yielding to a looser application of paint and a more emphatic expressionistic technique.

Kline scored his success in the early 1950s with large canvases onto which he applied black and white commercial paint with housepainter's brushes. He became known as an Action painter because his work expressed movement and energy, emphasizing dynamic line. The characteristic

Painting No. 7,
*1952. Oil on
canvas*, 57 ¹/₂ x
81 ³/₄ *inches.*
54.1403

black slashes of *Painting No. 7* suggest the full
body movement of the artist as he spontaneously
applied the paint, incorporating chance splatters
and smearing. In fact, Kline's paintings were
constructed only to *look* as if they were painted in
a moment of inspiration—they usually resulted
from the transfer of a sketch to the canvas.

Unlike de Kooning and Jackson Pollock,
Kline never flirted with figuration in his abstract
paintings and avoided spatial ambiguity. *Painting
No. 7* is among the artist's most straightforward
statements; it also demonstrates his knowledge of
art history. Kline's emphasis on the square in this
and other works suggests his interest in Josef
Albers and Kazimir Malevich. Art historian
Harry Gaugh cites Piet Mondrian's
Composition 1A as an influence, and also contends
that the compositional structure of *Painting No. 7*
recalls James McNeill Whistler's *Arrangement in
Black and Gray: The Artist's Mother*. Though the
similarity between the latter two paintings might
appear incidental, Kline referred to Whistler in
other paintings, and the austere geometry of
Whistler's canvas would have appealed to him.

—J. B.

137

"This state of alertness of the soul or consciousness, expectant and receptive, is like an unborn child whose own mother might not be aware of it and to whom nothing from the outside world slips through."

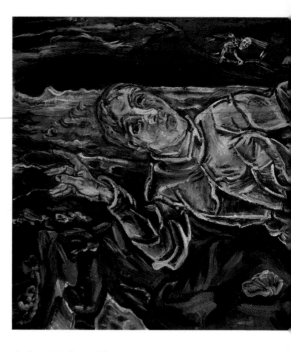

Oskar Kokoschka

b. 1886, Pöchlarn, Austria; d. 1980, Montreux, Switzerland

In the Vienna of 1914, a woman having an abortion was cause for scandal, even within the confines of the relatively open-minded art world. When such a woman was the widow of a famous composer, unwed, and carrying on two love affairs simultaneously, her decision would alarm even the most sympathetic souls. Thus it is that the agonized knight errant of Oskar Kokoschka's painting is to this day read as an expression of the artist's pain over the death of an unborn child and the crumbling of his relationship with the fascinating, and quite unrepentant, Alma Mahler.

The central figure appears to be a self-portrait of Kokoschka, clad in the armor of a medieval knight. He lies errant, or lost, in a stormy landscape, his two attributes—a winged bird-man and a sphinxlike woman—in close proximity. The bird-man has been interpreted either as the figure of death or another self-portrait, while the sphinx-woman has been seen as a stand-in for Mahler. A funereal sky bears the letters "E S," which probably refer to Christ's lament, "Eloi, Eloi, lama sabachthani" ("My God, my God, why hast Thou forsaken me?"). As if the self-equivalence with chivalry and the martyred Christ were not enough, the agitated brushwork and disturbing composition convince us of Kokoschka's spiritual discomfort.

If we look at *Knight Errant* within the context of Austrian art and compare it to the measured and ornate works of Hans Makart or even Gustav

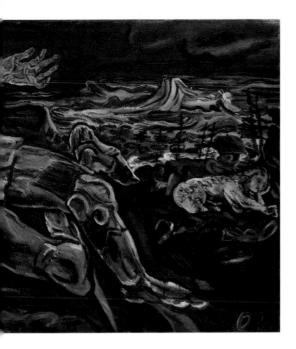

Knight Errant,
*1915. Oil on
canvas, 35 1/4 x
70 1/8 inches.*
48.1172x380

Klimt, Kokoschka's radicality emerges clearly. In
what was still fin-de-siècle Vienna, *Knight Errant*
was a notable exception for the immediacy of its
imagery, which seemed to come more from the
realm of psychoanalysis than from contemporary
artistic trends. Indeed, Alma Mahler's first
husband, Gustav, had consulted Sigmund Freud
about his marriage, and the famous couple was
apparently versed in psychoanalytic principles.
But perhaps Kokoschka was equally influenced by
his admiration for Baroque allegorical and literary
motifs. Whatever their source, his emotion-
charged images stem from a turbulently personal
interpretation of Expressionism.

—C. L.

"When you describe art, you are also describing how meaning is produced, and subjectivity is formed. In other words, you are describing reality."

Joseph Kosuth
b. 1945, Toledo, Ohio

In his 1969 essay *Art After Philosophy*, artist and theoretician Joseph Kosuth argued that traditional art-historical discourse had reached its end. In its place he proposed a radical investigation of the means through which art acquires its cultural significance and its status as art. "Being an artist now," commented Kosuth, "means to question the nature of art. If one is questioning the nature of painting, one cannot be questioning the nature of art. . . . That's because the word 'art' is general and the word 'painting' is specific. Painting is a *kind* of art. If you make paintings you are already accepting (not questioning) the nature of art."

During this formative stage in his work, Kosuth made the tautological nature of art explicit. As an analytical proposition, art presupposes the existence of an aesthetic entity that fulfills the criteria of "artness." This criteria, as Marcel Duchamp proved with his ready-mades, could consist merely of the declaration "this is a work of art." Kosuth used this linguistic approach to explore the social, political, cultural, and economic contexts through which art is presented and thus defined. To demonstrate this discursive aspect of art, Kosuth employed language itself as his medium. What resulted was a rigorously conceptual art devoid of all morphological presence; intellectual provocation replaced perception as words displaced images and objects. This shift was signaled in Kosuth's *First Investigations* (subtitled *Art As Idea As Idea*), a series that includes photostats of dictionary definitions of words such as "water," "meaning," and "idea." Accompanying these photographic images are certificates of documentation and ownership (not for display) indicating that the works can be made and remade for exhibition purposes. This strategy of presentation represents Kosuth's attempt to undermine the preciousness of the unique art object and its privileged place in the museum. He sought to demonstrate that the "art" component is not located in the object itself but rather in the *idea* or concept of the work.

Along with other Conceptual artists Kosuth waged an attack on conventional aesthetics that has informed the strategies of many recent Postmodern artists. From Kosuth's initial enterprise, a younger generation has inherited a deconstructive approach to art in which a critique of the production of meaning takes precedence over the communication of meaning.

—N. S.

wa-ter (wâ'tėr), *n.* [AS. *wæter* = D. *water* = G. *wasser*, akin to Icel. *vatn*, Goth. *wató*, water, also to Gr. ὕδωρ, Skt. *udan*, water, L. *unda*, a wave, water; all from the same root as E. *wet*: cf. *hydra, otter*[1], *undine*, and *wash*.] The liquid which in a more or less impure state constitutes rain, oceans, lakes, rivers, etc., and which in a pure state is a transparent, inodorous, tasteless liquid, a compound of hydrogen and oxygen, H_2O, freezing at 32° F. or 0° C., and boiling at 212° F. or 100° C.; a special form or variety of this liquid, as rain, or (often in *pl.*) as the liquid ('mineral water') obtained from a mineral spring (as, "the *waters* of Aix-la-Chapelle".

'Titled (Art As Idea As Idea)' *{Water}*, *1966. Photostat, 48 x 48 inches. Gift, Leo Castelli, New York. 73.2066.1-.2*

Jannis Kounellis
b. 1936, Piréa, Greece

Though born and raised in Greece, Jannis Kounellis reached artistic maturity in Italy. He immersed himself in his adopted homeland's rich aesthetic history, and came to trust that art's importance lies in its reflection of the complex web of beliefs and values at the heart of cultural development. Throughout history, Kounellis concluded, art evolved in response to and in expression of fundamental theological, intellectual, and political thought patterns. But he determined that postwar European society lacked appropriate aesthetic forms through which to reflect the fragmentary nature of contemporary civilization. Conventional painting and sculpture, as products of cultural unity, were no longer germane to the erratic situation he perceived. In 1967 he began producing sculptures, installations, and theatrical performances that intentionally embraced the fragmentary and the ephemeral. At that time, he was associated with a number of Italian artists who, for similar political and aesthetic reasons, were pursuing an analogous goal. Grouped together under the name Arte Povera, their work incorporated organic and industrial materials resulting in poetic confrontations between nature, culture, and the fabricated environment. To this end, Kounellis has blocked doorways and windows with accumulations of stones or wood fragments. He even went as far as including live animals in his work in the attempt to formulate an entirely new paradigm through which to experience art. He also utilized fire in the form of butane torches and smoke residue to evoke the alchemical, transformative potential of the flame, while simultaneously referring to its destructive force.

By the end of the 1960s Kounellis's repertoire of materials included rock, wood, burlap, wool, steel, lead, gold, fire, and fragments of classical sculpture, which he has since employed in numerous combinations to formulate a body of work that is iconographically consistent yet stylistically variable. The recent metal wall reliefs, such as this work, are morphologically reminiscent of painting but conceptually distant. The fusion of organic and inorganic substances—here, a circle of golden wax embedded into a sheet of lead—symbolizes the shifting and unpredictable nature of meaning in art. Such a juxtaposition of contradictory materials serves perhaps as an allegory for human fragility and the inevitability of historical imperatives.

—N. S.

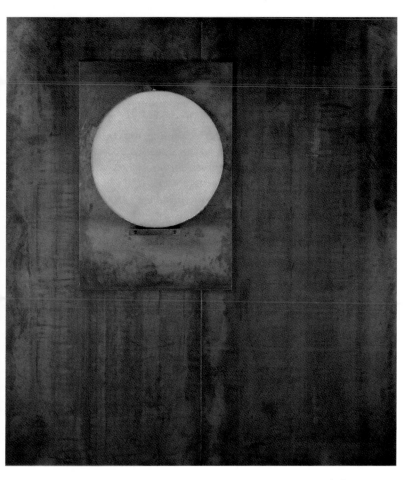

Untitled, 1987.
*Lead, wax, and
metal, 79 x
71 1/8 x 7 1/2
inches. Gift,
Annika
Barbarigos.*
87.3515

"I work with pictures and words because they have the ability to determine who we are, what we want to be, and what we become."

Barbara Kruger

b. 1945, Newark, N.J.

Barbara Kruger juxtaposes photographs culled from the mass media with pithy slogans in a vigilantly constructed attack on the ways in which self-identity, desire, and public opinion are manipulated and perpetuated. Her often caustic presentations—ranging from billboards, T-shirts, and posters to the signature red-bordered montages of words and images—play on clichés and cultural stereotypes to underscore and, eventually, undermine the persuasive power of representation. Distinctively feminist in orientation, the work also examines how gender difference is reinforced through media presentation. Traditionally, women have been displayed in film and advertising as objects of desire for the male viewer. The exception occurs when women are targeted by the media as consumers; only then do they become subjects, but merely as patrons of desirable images of themselves.

Kruger brings the issue of gender identification into question through her ambiguous use of the neutral pronouns "I," "you," and "we" in her phrases, such as the following: YOUR GAZE HITS THE SIDE OF MY FACE; YOU MAKE HISTORY WHEN YOU DO BUSINESS; YOU INVEST IN THE DIVINITY OF THE MASTERPIECE; WHEN I HEAR THE WORD CULTURE, I TAKE OUT MY CHECKBOOK. To some extent, Kruger reconfigures the conventional gendered subject/object relationship by bestowing the female voice with authority, but quickly subverts this mere reversal of power by scrambling the identities of speaker and audience.

Untitled (Not Perfect) is an early example of Kruger's mature work; it marks the transitional period between the artist's provocative, embroidered wall hangings and her photographic pieces. It is best understood when examined in concert with another work from 1980, *Untitled (Perfect)*, in which the word "perfect" is written across an image of a woman's discreetly sweatered torso; her hands are clasped as if in prayer. In contrast to this image of chaste propriety—suggestive of the socially condoned behavior often required of women—*Not Perfect* depicts a pair of soiled male hands resting in a washbasin. The word "stain," albeit crossed out, points to the questionable source of the hands' discoloration. Is it spilled coffee or dirt or blood? Although intentionally indecipherable, the image suggests the sense of recklessness, adventure, and destruction stereotypically associated with the male in our culture.

—N. S.

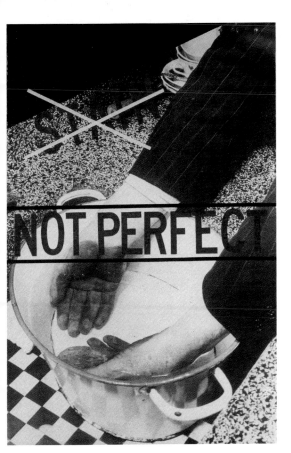

Untitled (Not Perfect), *1980. Photostat and text on paper, 60 x 40 inches. Exxon Corporation Purchase Award.* 81.2809

Wifredo Lam

b. 1902, Sagua la Grande, Cuba; d. 1982, Paris

"I wanted with all my heart to paint the drama of my country, but by thoroughly expressing the negro spirit, the beauty of the plastic art of the blacks. In this way I could act as a Trojan horse that would spew forth hallucinating figures with the power to surprise, to disturb the dreams of the exploiters."

When Wifredo Lam arrived in Paris in 1938 he carried a letter of introduction to Pablo Picasso, with whom he had an immediate rapport. Soon he met many other leading artistic figures, among them André Breton, the dominant publicist and theorist of Surrealism. The Surrealists, who attempted to unleash the power of the unconscious through explorations of dream states and automatist writing, were fascinated by the mythologies of "primitive" people. They subscribed to an anthropology that perceived modern "primitive" cultures as the heirs to an integrated understanding of myth and reality, which they hoped to achieve themselves. Lam, as a Cuban of African, Chinese, and European descent, seemed to the Surrealists to have privileged access to that undifferentiated state of mind. In 1942 the artist returned to Cuba, where he constructed a body of work in a Surrealist idiom, creating symbolic creatures engaged in ritual acts of initiation. Lam's vocabulary of vegetal-animal forms was inspired by Afro-Cuban and Haitian Santeria deities. He also associated with the nationalist poets of the Négritude movement, who relied in their work on the images and rhythms of their native culture.

Rumblings of the Earth represents a synthesis of Lam's concerns in his work of the 1940s. This painting melds his reaction to the European artistic legacy with his own goals and the indigenous traditions of his country. Here, Lam referred to Picasso's 1937 *Guernica* through direct quotations and more abstract correspondences, but he transformed Picasso's political statement by replacing the central victim of *Guernica*, the horse, with a spectral presence bearing a large knife, described by Lam as "the instrument of integrity." An aggressive painting, *Rumblings of the Earth* includes vaginal and phallic references that focus the work thematically on the cycle of birth and death while suggesting ritual initiation and violence. For Lam, revolutionary violence was a means of liberation; in his hands, the victim in Picasso's canvas has become the aggressor.

In *Zambezia, Zambezia* Lam depicted an iconic woman partly inspired by the *femme-cheval* (horse-headed woman) of the Santeria cult. He frequently used the device of transmogrification of body parts to suggest magical metamorphosis, inspired by indigenous American and African ritual objects. In this painting it is manifested in the testicle "chin" of the figure.

—J. B.

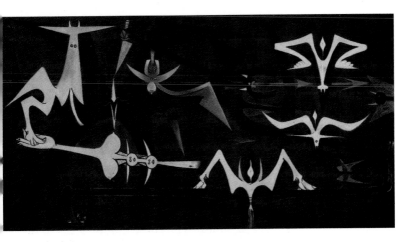

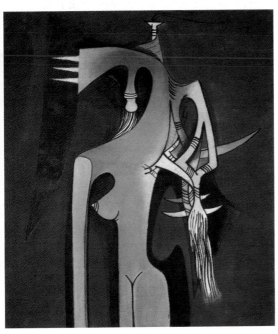

Rumblings of the Earth, *1950. Oil on canvas, 59 ³/₄ x 112 inches. Gift, Mr. and Mrs. Joseph Cantor. 58.1525*

Zambezia, Zambezia, *1950. Oil on canvas, 49 ³/₈ x 43 ⁵/₈ inches. Gift, Mr. Joseph Cantor, Carmel, Indiana. 74.2095*

Language

When language becomes plastic, it is art. When art melts it becomes language.

There are two ways to have and to hold language: either one writes it down and the sounds become words and phrases that are saved and read, or one memorizes it and repeats it aloud over and over again. Most of the time it just vanishes into thin air rather quickly.

Art, on the other hand, is destined to be conserved. Made to stand on its own, it asserts its independence as long as the materials it is composed of retain their consistency (Wright).

From the dawn of Modernism, words have been inserted into art works: a fragment of newspaper or the word itself was objectified by the Cubists; the Fascists made posters in which word and image were juxtaposed in a collage of orders; Dadaists did it to achieve disorder; and the Surrealists utilized words to get beyond representation. Recently words have returned to the canvas as propositions relating how much we are saturated by language. Consciousness and language are now more than ever hand in hand in this overdeveloped world, where communication engulfs expression. Language needs art to perform the endless task of taking out its garbage, as birth control for the overpopulation of signs.

Just as lines, planes, colors, forms, and objects cohabitate to transform worldy things, the materiality of language (sound, marks, and gestures) must be articulated to make art (Schwitters, Michaux, Chagall). In other words, the familiar and the unknown must be joined. Examples include a smooth miracle seal (Brancusi), a magic square (Morris), or a transparent cube (Bell). The art of composition (Kandinsky, Proust, Glass) *is art*.

But what does it mean to say that art too is a kind of language?

Art is a special kind of language, both private and a product of social existence. When the materiality of language is seen as a play of forces, tensions, or intensities, and a selection and composition of these ooze from some localized frame, art and language rediscover each other. The physicality of language is not only to be found in bodily movements, but also in all that bodies can feel: coarseness, rigidity, expansion (Hesse), enclosure (Cornell), balance (Mondrian), depth, dispersion (Pollock), darkness, vibration, and vertigo before the void.

Art is the language of sensations, whether it uses words, colors, sounds, or stones.

—Lysa Hochroth

Jenny Holzer, Untitled (Selections from Truisms, Inflammatory Essays, The Living Series, The Survival Series, Under a Rock, Laments, and Child Text) *(detail)*.

148

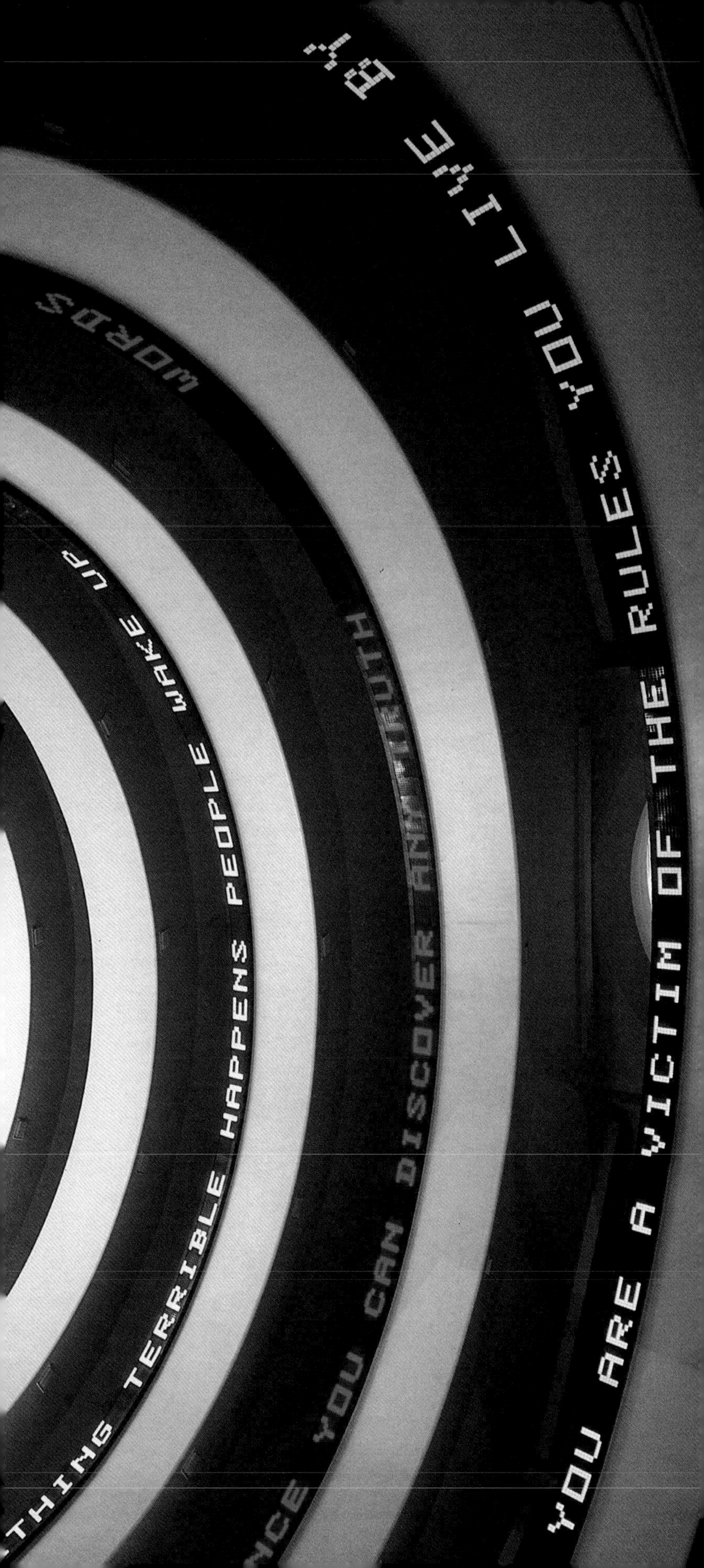

RULES YOU LIVE BY

WORDS

...THING TERRIBLE HAPPENS PEOPLE WAKE UP

...CE YOU CAN DISCOVER ANY TRUTH

YOU ARE A VICTIM OF THE RULES

"Beauty is everywhere, in the arrangement of your pots and pans, on the white wall of your kitchen, more perhaps than in your 18th-century salon or in the official museum."

Fernand Léger

b. 1881, Argentan, Normandy, France; d. 1955, Gif-sur-Yvette, France

Art historian and critic Michel Seuphor proclaimed that 1912 was "perhaps the most beautiful date in the whole history of painting in France." That year marked the culmination of Analytic Cubism in the work of Pablo Picasso and Georges Braque as well as the maturation of Fernand Léger's idiosyncratic Cubist style, as manifested in his lively painting *The Smokers*. All three artists were inspired by Paul Cézanne in their quest for a means by which to accurately describe three-dimensional objects on a two-dimensional canvas. By breaking the represented figures or items into series of splintered planes and rendering them against—or within—a similarly faceted background, they created an entirely integrated space in which field and object interpenetrate one another. Of the three painters, Léger developed a vocabulary of more precisely delineated forms—his fragmented units are larger, arcs predominate, and color prevails.

In both *The Smokers* and *Nude Model in the Studio* the curving, overlapping planes describe the corporeal forms of each painting's subject while articulating an allover, rhythmically patterned surface. The resulting oscillation between volumetric body and dynamic space owes as much to Futurist aesthetics as to Analytic Cubism. By 1913 Léger had pushed his abstracting grammar to its logical extreme in a series of non-objective paintings entitled *Contrast of Forms*. Premised on the visual disparity between discrete geometric volumes, the series presents assorted calibrations of cylindrical, cubic, and planar units. As variations on a theme, each composition of alternating solids and voids offers a different play of light and shadow. This gouache study for *Contrast of Forms* accentuates the linear armature and abbreviated modeling of the shifting geometric shapes. With these thoroughly abstract images, Léger's explorations of the Cubist idiom approached those of Robert Delaunay, whose *Simultaneous Windows* and brilliantly colored circular motifs of 1913 neared complete detachment from empirical reality. For Léger, however, this foray into total non-objectivity was only temporary, as he would soon revive his penchant for figurative subjects.

—N. S.

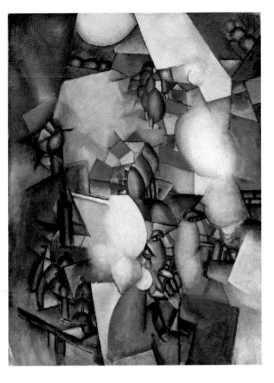

The Smokers,
Dec. 1911–
Jan. 1912. Oil on
canvas, 51 x
38 inches. Gift,
Solomon R.
Guggenheim.
38.521

Study for
Contrast of
Forms, *1913.*
Gouache on buff
wove paper mounted
on cardboard,
19 1/2 x 24 inches.
48.1172x50

Nude Model in
the Studio,
1912–13. Oil on
burlap, 50 3/8 x
37 5/8 inches.
49.1193

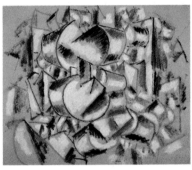

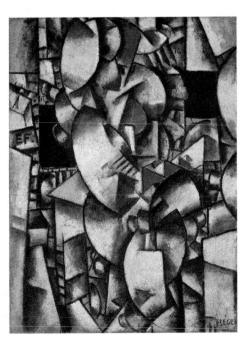

Fernand Léger

Fernand Léger's streamlined forms date from World War I, when he served in the French army. His predilection for military hardware and its gleaming surfaces coincided with his hope of creating a truly popular art form that would describe and inspire modern life. After the war, he turned away from the experiments with pure abstraction that had characterized his earlier work and infused social meaning into his art; quasi-representational motifs emerged in lively paintings depicting soldiers, factory workers, bargemen, and the pulsating urban environment. In works such as *The City* of 1919 and *The Mechanic* of 1920, Léger incorporated elements of Cubist fragmentation into his new pristine, mechanical syntax to evoke the energy of contemporary experience.

As a call to political and aesthetic order resounded throughout postwar French society in a nationalistic attempt to restore its rationalist heritage, Léger introduced the monumental, classical figure into his art. The absolute calm and stasis of *Woman Holding a Vase* demonstrates his affinities with the neo-antique depictions of women by Pablo Picasso and Gino Severini. It also shows Léger's sympathies with the Purist ideals of Amedée Ozenfant and Le Corbusier, who called for a revival of classical aesthetic consonance as a symbol of renewed social harmony. Léger's palette of blue, yellow, red, and black was indebted to Piet Mondrian's De Stijl paintings of the time, further evincing Léger's identification with utopian and reconstructivist postwar ideals.

—N. S.

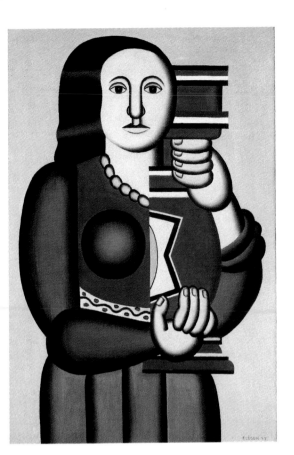

Woman Holding a Vase *(definitive state)*, 1927. *Oil on canvas, 57 5/8 x 38 3/8 inches.* 58.1508

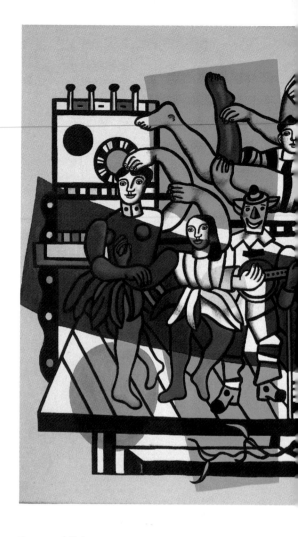

"This freedom, this new space, could help . . . in the transformation of individuals, in the modification of their way of life."

Fernand Léger

Unlike many of his School of Paris colleagues, Léger eschewed using collaged fragments to represent everyday life, instead developing proletarian themes that he executed in ever larger formats. *The Great Parade* is the summation of his lifelong attempt to devise an imagery of the everyday within the realm of painting. It was preceded by hundreds of preparatory studies in which Léger methodically resolved every detail of the complex composition. The stately procession of figures is couched in the rhetoric of monumental history painting, with only the integrity of its subject matter saving it from the pomposity of a modern allegory.

This subject matter reveals Léger's political sympathies and intentions. An ardent believer in the equality of people, and apparently of the sexes, Léger depicted men and women as indistinguishable equals on a wide swath of blue; in a related fresco for the International Women's Congress (1948), he showed women in a variety of professional guises that are a far cry from the

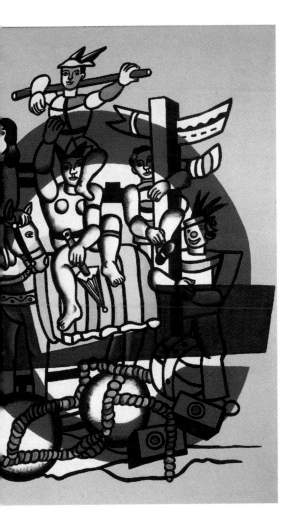

The Great Parade
(*definitive state*),
1954. *Oil on
canvas, 117³/₄ x
157¹/₂ inches.*
62.1619

roles they were usually accorded in art and society of the time. To call this procession of revelers a work about the "society of spectacle" would be an anachronism. That term postdates it by a good ten years, but as defined by the critic Guy Debord and the Situationists, the concept of leisure and its indexation to class does apply to Léger's painting. The lower classes did not know leisure time until the late 19th century, when labor-saving industrialization and transportation advances made vacations possible. The circus is a place where all people are equal, united in their enjoyment of the spectacle. Its capacity to entertain became a metaphor for Léger's vision of art as a vehicle for the transformation of society. His hope was to create a painting with universally appealing values. Seemingly timeless, Léger's work was didactically intended to remind people of their fundamental right to self-fulfillment.

—C. L.

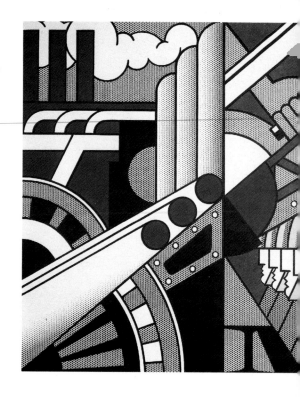

> "{Pop art} is an involvement with what I think to be the most brazen and threatening characteristics of our culture, things we hate, but which are also powerful in their impingement on us."

Roy Lichtenstein
b. 1923, New York City

In 1963 Roy Lichtenstein defended Pop art against its critics, contending that "there are certain things that are usable, forceful, and vital about commercial art." He and other Pop artists wanted to harness the power of contemporary mass communication and merchandising techniques, for better or worse. By choosing comic-book illustrations as a theme, and using simulated Benday dots to suggest cheap printing, Lichtenstein acknowledged (and perhaps questioned) the role of this popular form of entertainment in daily life. There is also an element of playfulness in creating fine art out of what has customarily been considered "low."

Lichtenstein has cultivated imagery from the history of art while continuing to use the conventions of comics. In *Preparedness* he used the Benday-dot technique to make a wall-size painting (it is 10 feet high by 18 feet wide) that suggests the work of Fernand Léger and the WPA art of the 1930s. Using means that previously had been reserved for history painting, altars, and commercial billboards, Léger and the WPA artists painted monumental murals, readable at a distance, on themes of workers and everyday life. Lichtenstein followed this practice to an ironic and somewhat subversive end. Painted during a year when public opinion on the Vietnam War shifted dramatically, Lichtenstein's massive

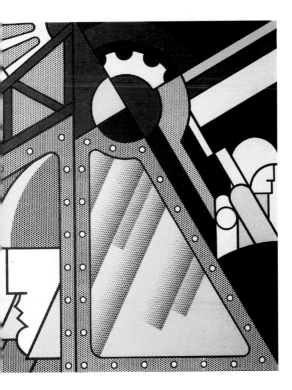

Preparedness, 1968. Oil and Magna on canvas; three panels, each 120 x 72 inches; total 120 x 216 inches. 69.1885.a-.c

depiction of machinery and soldiers probes the conventions of selling the promises of the military-industrial complex, while quietly alluding to the naive optimism underlying a call to arms.

Lichtenstein often focuses on the way his traditional and mass-media sources resolve the dilemmas of representing three dimensions on a flat picture plane, incorporating their solutions into his own work with witty exaggeration. In *Preparedness* he played the fragmented Cubist collage space of Léger against comic-strip modes of suggesting form and the surface quality of objects. There may even be a joke on Minimalism and its industrially inspired seriality: the artist's three-panel painting includes rows of machine parts and soldiers in an industrial landscape. Lichtenstein's inclusion of an airplane window in the third panel of the painting foreshadows his engagement with modes of conveying the illusion of reflective glass, which he went on to explore in a series of paintings of mirrors.

—J. B.

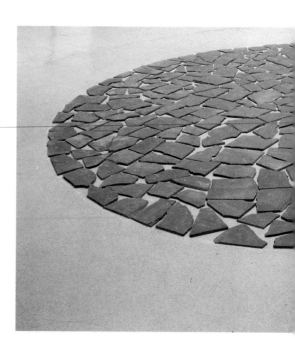

"Nature has more effect on me than I on it."

Richard Long
b. 1945, Bristol, England

To create his art, Richard Long walks hundreds of miles for days, even weeks at a time, through uncultivated areas of land: the countryside of England, Ireland, and Scotland; the mountains of Nepal and Japan; the plains of Africa, Mexico, and Bolivia. He documents these journeys with captioned large-scale photographs, maps, and lists of descriptive terms, which are exhibited as individual works. While traveling, Long sets specific tasks for himself, such as traversing an absolutely straight line for a predetermined distance, following the side of a river wherever it may lead, or picking up and then dropping stones at certain intervals along the way. While on these trips, the artist interacts with the landscape by creating modest sculptures from indigenous materials, thus attesting to his presence in the land. Circles or lines—Long's signature motifs—rubbed into the ground by repeated footprints or composed of assembled stones, driftwood, or seaweed are eventually dissolved by the wind, the rain, and rising tides, thus negating human dominance over nature. His photographs remain the only evidence of these organic sculptures after erosion has run its course. Unlike other artists who have manipulated the landscape to create Earthworks, such as Michael Heizer, Dennis Oppenheim, Robert Morris, Robert Smithson, Walter De Maria, and James Turrell, Long does not significantly alter the terrain by digging, burrowing, sculpting, or constructing. He simply adjusts nature's placement of rocks and wood to

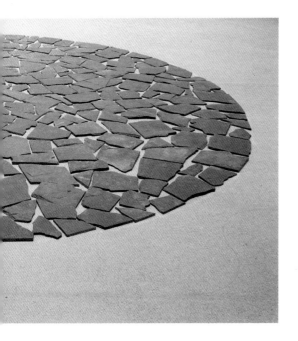

Red Slate Circle, 1980. Red slate stones, diameter 336 inches. Purchased with funds contributed by Stephen and Nan Swid. 82.2895

subtly demarcate geometric shapes.

Long translates his deeply personal experiences in the wilderness into Site-specific sculptures and mud wall-drawings that are created for exhibition spaces and private collections. Pieces composed of flint, slate, feathers, pine needles, sticks, and other rustic materials become metaphors for the paths taken on his ramblings: the spirals, circles, and lines, if extended beyond the gallery walls, would trace actual distances traveled by the artist. The sculptures are not, therefore, representations of nature per se but rather aesthetic documents of Long's engagement with the land and poetic evocations of the beauty and grandeur of the earth. Such is the case with *Red Slate Circle*, which consists of 474 stones from a New York State quarry. When it is installed in the Guggenheim's rotunda, the monumental ring echoes the building's unique spiral while conjuring images of vast canyons, still lakes, and stone pathways leading into the distance.

—N. S.

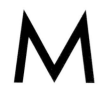

Kazimir Malevich

b. 1878, near Kiev; d. 1935, Leningrad

The paintings of the Russian avant-garde have, in general, elicited two types of interpretation: one focuses on issues of technique and style, the other concentrates on social and political issues. The former method is usually applied to Malevich's early paintings, grounded as they are in the forms of Cubism, Futurism, and other contemporaneous art movements; the latter largely avoids Malevich in favor of more politically engaged artists such as Aleksandr Rodchenko, El Lissitzky, and Vladimir Tatlin.

From the formalist's standpoint, *Morning in the Village after Snowstorm* is, in its mastery of complex colors and shapes, a perfect example of the newly created Russian style, Cubo-Futurism. The figures have been called a continuation of the genre types Malevich portrayed in his Neo-primitive paintings, their depiction seemingly reliant on the work of Fernand Léger, whose work Malevich could have known from an exhibition in Moscow in February 1912 or through reproductions. This phase in his career has been seen as Malevich's formidable stopover on his journey toward abstraction and the development of Suprematism.

But to ignore the political and social dimensions of Malevich's art is to pay it a disservice. Malevich came from humble circumstances and it is clear in autobiographical accounts that vivid memories of his country childhood compensated for his lack of a formal art education. *Morning in the Village after Snowstorm* demonstrates that Malevich's hard-won skills as a sophisticated painter were rooted in an unmistakably Russian experience. If art can be said to augur the future, then Malevich's repeated decision—on the brink of the October Revolution—to depict peasants cannot have been merely coincidental.

—C. L.

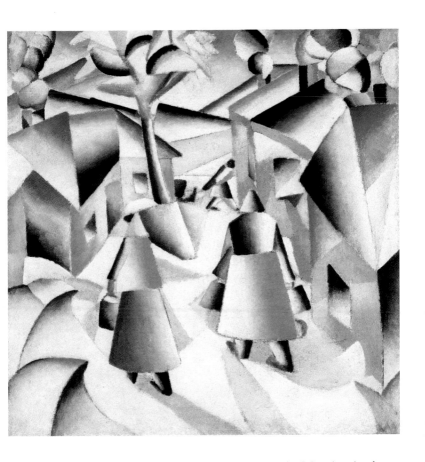

Morning in the
Village after
Snowstorm,
*1912. Oil on
canvas, 31 ³/₄ x
31 ⁷/₈ inches.
52.1327*

Edouard Manet
b. 1832, Paris; d. 1883, Paris

In 1865 Manet shocked Parisian audiences at the Salon with his painting *Olympia* (1863), an unabashed depiction of a prostitute lounging in bed, naked save for a pair of slippers and a necklace. While not an unpopular subject in 19th-century French painting, the courtesan had rarely been portrayed with such honesty. The artist provoked a similar scandal when his painting of *Nana* (1877)—a coquettish young woman in a state of partial undress powdering her nose in front of an impatient client—was exhibited in a shop window on the boulevard des Capucines. Manet's attention to a motif conventionally associated with pornography reflected his desire to render on canvas the truths of modern life. It was a theme that symbolized modernity for many late-19th-century artists and writers, including Edgar Degas and Emile Zola, who devoted their work to realistic portrayals of the shifting class structures and mores of French culture. Images of courtesans may be found throughout Manet's oeuvre; *Before the Mirror* is thought to be one such painting, related iconographically to *Nana*, but more spontaneous in execution. The artist's vigorous brushstrokes lend an air of immediacy to the picture. As in *Nana*, the corseted woman represented here admires her reflection in a mirror; but this particular scene is extremely private—the woman, in quiet contemplation of her own image, is turned with her back to the viewer.

Manet's endeavor to capture the flavor of contemporary society extended to portraits of barmaids, street musicians, ragpickers, and other standard Parisian "types" that were favorite subjects of popular illustrated literature. Since the subject of *Woman in Evening Dress* is unidentified—conjecture that she might be the French actress Suzanne Reichenberg remains purely speculative—it is tempting to view this portrait as Manet's rendering of one such type: the fashionable Parisian bourgeois woman, complete with Japanese fan.

Both paintings exemplify Manet's use of seemingly improvised, facile brushstrokes that emphasize the two-dimensionality of the canvas while simultaneously defining form and space. From our vantage point, it is less Manet's choice of subject matter than the tension between surface and subject, in which the paint itself threatens to dissolve into decorative patterns, that defines his work as quintessentially Modern.

—N. S.

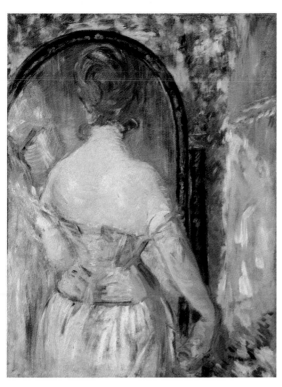

Before the Mirror, *1876. Oil on canvas, 36 1/4 x 28 1/8 inches. Thannhauser Collection, Gift, Justin K. Thannhauser. 78.2514 T27*

Woman in Evening Dress, *1877–80. Oil on canvas, 68 5/8 x 32 7/8 inches. Thannhauser Collection, Gift, Justin K. Thannhauser. 78.2514 T28*

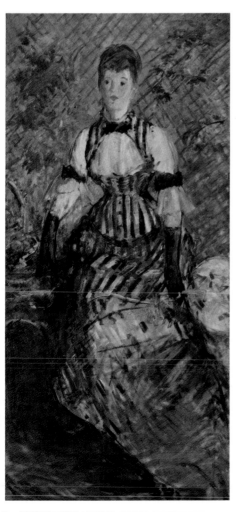

"When all is said and done, I am a maker of images—nothing more and nothing less."

Robert Mangold

b. 1937, North Tonawanda, N.Y.

Shortly after receiving an M.F.A. from Yale in 1963, Robert Mangold worked as a guard at the Museum of Modern Art in New York. Reminiscing about the months he spent there, Mangold commented that even the greatest paintings began to lose their appeal after hours of uninterrupted viewing. The Mondrians were the exception, however, and actually looked "better and better over time."

Inspired, perhaps, by Piet Mondrian's reductivist tendency, Mangold emptied his painting of all external references, focusing instead on internal formal relationships. For this reason, his work is often described as Minimalist. But whereas much Minimalist painting and sculpture is premised upon predetermined, mathematical progressions, rigid configurations, and industrial materials, Mangold's work is quite unsystematic. The difference between Mangold's art and that of many of his contemporaries lies in its idiosyncratic, intuitive nature. His geometric compositions are frequently distorted: what appears to be a perfect circle or square drawn on a two-dimensional surface is partially contorted in order to fit within the confines of the shaped canvases. While he has worked in series to explore the various permutations of such designs, Mangold has not limited himself to one specific strategy and often makes unique images. His palette, consisting of warm ochers, saturated blues, olive greens, and chocolate browns, among other hues, is more reminiscent of Italian frescoes than of the cool, detached tones or commercially mixed colors commonly used by Minimalist artists.

In 1973 Mangold created at least four versions of *Circle In and Out of a Polygon*; two were executed on canvas and two on Masonite. In all four the interior graphite line becomes interchangeable with the top, left, and bottom borders of the support. Similarly, half of the circle is outlined on the acrylic surface, while the other half continues as the curved edge on the painting's right. Mangold challenges his viewers to mentally reverse such images in order to comprehend the compositional nuances of the geometric abstraction. It is this emphasis on the conceptual basis of vision that truly links Mangold to the Minimalists, who brought their audiences to an unprecedented level of perceptual awareness.

—N. S.

Circle In and Out
of a Polygon II
(Blue), *1973.*
Acrylic and black
pencil on canvas,
72 3/16 x 72 7/16
inches. Panza
Collection.
91.3771

"Is there a more mysterious idea for an artist than to imagine how nature is reflected in the eyes of an animal? . . . We should contemplate the soul of the animal to divine its way of sight."

Franz Marc
b. 1880, Munich; d. 1916, Verdun

During the early years of this century, a back-to-nature movement swept Germany. Artists' collectives and nudist colonies sprung up in agricultural areas in the conviction that a return to the land would rejuvenate what was perceived to be an increasingly secularized, materialistic society. A seminarian and philosophy student turned artist, Marc found this nature-oriented quest for spiritual redemption inspiring. His vision of nature was pantheistic; he believed that animals possessed a certain godliness that men had long since lost. "People with their lack of piety, especially men, never touched my true feelings," he wrote in 1915. "But animals with their virginal sense of life awakened all that was good in me." By 1907 he devoted himself almost exclusively to the representation of animals in nature. To complement this imagery, through which he expressed his spiritual ideals, Marc developed a theory of color symbolism. His efforts to evoke metaphysical realms through specific color combinations and contrasts were similar to those of Vasily Kandinsky, with whom, in 1911, he founded the Blue Rider, a loose confederation of artists devoted to the expression of inner states.

For Marc, different hues evoked gender stereotypes: yellow, a "gentle, cheerful and sensual" color, symbolized femininity, while blue, representing the "spiritual and intellectual," symbolized masculinity. Marc's color theories and biography have been used by art historian Mark Rosenthal to interpret *Yellow Cow*. The frolicking yellow cow, as a symbol of the female principle, may be a veiled depiction of Maria Franck, whom Marc married in 1911. Extending this reading, Rosenthal sees the triangular blue mountains in the background as Marc's abstract self-portrait, thereby making this painting into a private wedding picture. Not all of Marc's paintings of animals are so sanguine, however. He often depicted innocent creatures in ominous scenes. Painted in 1913, *The Unfortunate Land of Tyrol* reflects the desolation caused by the Balkan War and its anticipation of pan-European battle; an Austro-Hungarian border sign included in the lower-left portion of the canvas indicates the vulnerability of this province. The cemetery and emaciated horses portend doom, but Marc's faith in the ultimate goodness of nature and the regenerative potential of war prevails: the rainbow and bird with outstretched wings reflect a promise of redemption through struggle.

—N. S.

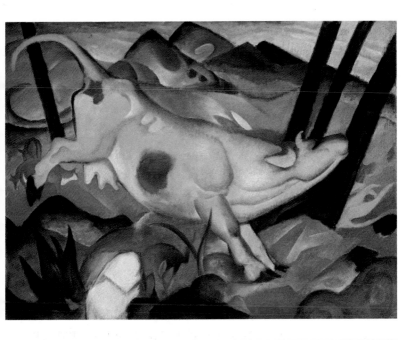

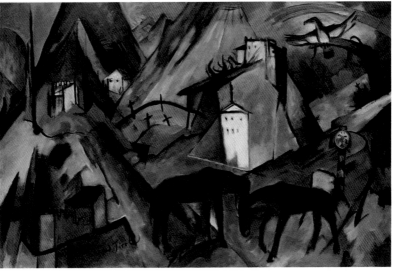

Yellow Cow,
1911. *Oil on
canvas, 55 ³/₈ x
74 ¹/₂ inches.*
49.1210

The Unfortunate
Land of Tyrol,
1913. *Oil on
canvas, 51 ⁵/₈ x
78 ³/₄ inches.*
46.1040

"I believe these are highly emotional paintings not to be admired for any technical or intellectual reason but to be felt."

Brice Marden

b. 1938, Bronxville, N.Y.

Brice Marden began to paint single monochrome canvases in 1964, after his first trip to Paris. In 1968 he broadened their scope by creating two- and three-paneled works, such as *Paris Painting*. These works reward a Zen-like contemplation of their subtle variations in color, their surface inflection, and the tension between the separate surfaces and their united silhouette.

Paris Painting is composed of two canvases joined together, each with thick skins built up from many layers of oil paint mixed with wax. The right panel is a lighter hue than the matte-gray canvas beside it. The lower edge and sides of the painting reveal the canvas support and the layering of paint, thus suggesting the laborious process of accumulation required to create a surface that recalls the cool, gessoed veneer of frescoed walls as well as the legacy of European postwar painters such as Antoni Tàpies.

Marden's work has been seen as a measured response to second-generation Abstract Expressionist gestural bravado. His relentlessly subdued monochromatic canvases of the 1960s, with their suppressed brushstrokes and serial rectangles, are considered Minimalist; yet Marden has never relinquished his commitment to a decidedly handmade production with evocative associations, as opposed to the industrial and anonymous approach favored by Minimalist artists. In his 1963 M.F.A. thesis at Yale he professed his goals: "The paintings are made in a highly subjective state within Spartan limitations. Within these strict confines, confines which I have painted myself into and intend to explore with no regrets, I try to give the viewer something to which he will react subjectively."

Marden emphasizes the metaphorical quality of his paintings by giving them allusive titles taken from places and the seasons. The works' titles and atmospheric coloration recall nature and the earth; *Paris Painting* brings to mind the kind of cold, gray day typical of the French capital. By making his canvases conform to the heights of specific people, Marden has proposed an analogy between his works and the body. Through an extension of this metaphor, the two somber panels of *Paris Painting* can be read as individuals; the unremittingly impenetrable gray surfaces become a melancholy acknowledgment of their eternal separation, despite their union.

—J. B.

Paris Painting,
1969. *Oil and wax
on canvas; two
panels; a:* 72 ¹/₈ *x
24 inches;
b:* 72 ¹/₈ *x 24 ¹/₈
inches. Panza
Collection.
91.3783.a,.b*

> *"My paintings have neither objects, nor space, nor time, not anything—no forms. They are light, lightness, about merging, about formlessness, breaking down form."*

Agnes Martin
b. 1912, Maklin, Saskatchewan, Canada

Agnes Martin's earliest experiments with an abstract idiom were based on her observations of the desert terrain of New Mexico, where she lived during the 1940s. It was there that she developed a personal vocabulary of provocative, abstract forms—similar to the formative biomorphic or pictographic works of Adolph Gottlieb, Mark Rothko, and William Baziotes—at a time when American artists were searching for the aesthetic means to convey subjective states and to intimate the existence of other, higher realities. By 1960 Martin had developed her signature grid pattern; the compositional motifs of these pristine, monochromatic paintings consist of a simple system of interlocking horizontal and vertical lines in an almost exclusively six-foot-square format. The titles of these geometrically organized pictures—*Mountains, Dark River, Starlight, Leaf in the Wind, Orange Grove, Spring*, and *White Flower*, to cite just a few—attest to Martin's persistent engagement with themes of the organic world, albeit in an abstract manner. At this time she distilled the appearance of empirical entities and expressed her own emotional response to nature through the most extreme economy of formal means. "Anything," Martin claimed in 1972, "can be painted without representation."

Unlike the more rigidly formulaic art of much Minimalist work, there is nothing systematic about Martin's use of the grid; the arrangement of coordinates shifts in scale and rhythm from work to work. The grid in *White Flower*—composed of intersecting white lines that form individual rectangles punctuated by symmetrical white dashes—resembles woven fabric. Consistent throughout Martin's mature oeuvre is an absolute equivalence of form. The compositions are emphatically nonhierarchical; no one component is privileged over another. The delicacy of Martin's style—promoted by the artist's frequent use of light graphite lines and cool tones such as pink and pale gray—masks her impulse toward stringent formal equality. Her paintings must be read as unitary entities, not as assemblies of single elements. This does not mitigate the complexity of their construction, however. The freely drawn grids, fragile, almost dissolving lines, and hushed tones of the paintings require quiet contemplation in order for the subtleties of their individual compositions to be revealed.

—N. S.

White Flower,
*1960. Oil on
canvas, 71 $^7/_8$ x 72
inches. Anonymous
gift. 63.1653*

Materials

The use of artistic materials in the 20th century can be divided into two periods: the first, through the 1940s, was one of insemination and gestation, while the second, spanning the 1950s through the present, has been one of birth and growth. For the Modernists, artistic material was viewed as a means by which art could capture life. In this sense, materials were a nutriment for feeding the embryonic eyesight in the womb of an affirmed and secure history. Thought was superimposed upon this history, shaking it up with dynamic explosions of energy, conscious and unconscious notions, rational and mystical suggestions. Although it tapped other cultures, it always stuck to its own terrain and its boundaries remained defined by the perimeters of a frame or base.

After World War II a new material body was born, revealing its obstacles and vitality. Action Painting in America and Art Informel in Europe brought the material of art into the light. Leaving its womb, material began an active, howling life. During the late 1950s, Neo-Dada and Pop artists began exalting the "lowly" materials of our world. These new materials could be a body and its organic traces, or cultural remnants that fetishize the icons of communication and consumerism. Painting and sculpture plunged into the maelstrom of things and objects, actions and bodies, possessing them and thereby transfiguring them. In the 1960s an effluvium of material passed through the wonders and witchcraft of Arte Povera and Environmental Art. Their materials fascinated and awakened the viewers by putting them in touch with the breath, the inspiration of nature. With Minimalism and Conceptualism, the eruption of material led to the point of its disappearance. Such were the ecstasies of logic and planning that art was designated a pure condition of consciousness, in which neither subject nor object exists, and the process itself comes to light. Today, after entering the world, material has returned to itself, becoming persona through a second birth, claiming the right to be disparate and multiple. From Louise Bourgeois to Robert Mapplethorpe, this process carries the energy charge of an enigma, that of the "inner view," which can be evoked by the formulations of a morbid and ironic art or a profound and transgressive art. Thus, after insemination and gestation, after birth and adolescence, artistic material, in its growth, has begun to ponder its sensual and sexual identity.

—Germano Celant

(*Translated from the Italian by Joachim Neugroschel.*)

Alberto Burri, Composition *(detail).*

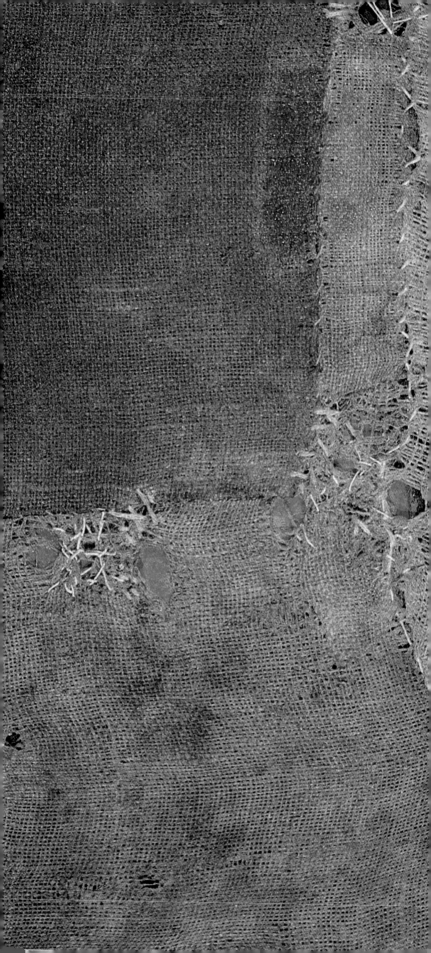

Henri Matisse

b. 1869, Le Cateau-Cambrésis, France; d. 1954, Nice

> "What interests me most is neither still life nor landscape but the human figure. It is through it that I best succeed in expressing the nearly religious feeling that I have towards life."

Henri Matisse often painted the same subject in versions that range from relatively realistic to more abstract or schematic. At times the transition from realism to abstraction could be enacted in a single canvas, as is the case with *The Italian Woman*, the first of many portraits Matisse painted of a professional Italian model named Laurette. The purposefully visible pentimenti and labored convergence of lines bear witness to his perpetual struggle "to reach that state of condensation of sensations which constitutes a picture." Matisse was not interested in capturing momentary impressions; he strove to create an enduring conception.

From the earlier state of the portrait, which depicts a heavier woman, Matisse pared down Laurette's image, in the process making her less corporeal and more ethereal. Using the conventions of religious painting—a frontal pose, introspective countenance, and flat background devoid of any indication of location—he created an icon of Woman. The emphatic eyes and brow, elongated nose, and pursed lips of her schematic face resemble an African mask, implying that Matisse, like so many Modern artists, equated the idea of Woman with the foreign, exotic, and "primitive"; he continued in this vein, posing the same model with a turban and a mantilla.

The spatial ambiguity of this portrait—the way the arms appear flat while the background overtakes a shoulder, for example—reveals Matisse's relationship to Paul Cézanne via the bolder experiments of Cubism. In a 1913 portrait of his wife, Matisse had played with the distinctions between volume and plane by including a flattened scarf that wraps around her arm. This treatment anticipates the shawl-like background of *The Italian Woman*. These paintings recall Cézanne's series of portraits of Madame Cézanne (one of which was owned by Matisse) both formally and iconographically, although Matisse's images are more radically schematized and distilled.

The austerity of color and severe reduction of *The Italian Woman* is characteristic of Matisse's work from 1914 to 1918. The art historian Pierre Schneider has suggested that these elements embody the artist's response to the devastation of World War I.

—J. B.

174

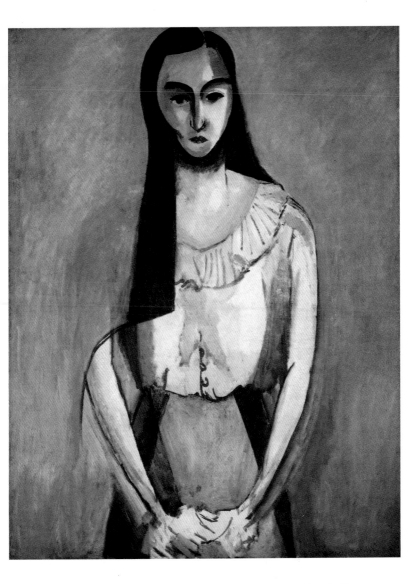

The Italian
Woman, *1916.*
Oil on canvas,
45 $^{15}/_{16}$ x 35 $^{1}/_{4}$
inches. By
exchange. 82.2946

"The igloo functions
as a moldable
hemisphere,
transparent and
luminous. . . . This
creates a highly
luminous
intermediary space,
becoming a study of
transparency and
light, like a
gorgeous ampule
from Murano or
certain ancient glass
vessels."

Mario Merz

b. 1925, Milan

Mario Merz envisions the contemporary artist as a nomad, shifting from one environment to another and resisting stylistic uniformity while mediating between nature and culture. Since 1968 Merz has used the hemispherical form of the igloo—a transitory dwelling—to express his faith in the liberating powers of restlessness with the world and its values. He assembles the rounded structures with segmented, metal armatures, usually covering them with a net and bits of clay, wax, mud, burlap, or leather, glass fragments, or bundles of twigs. Phrases with political or literary references, spelled out in neon, often span the domes. The earliest such example, *Giap Igloo* (1968), bears a slogan attributed to the North Vietnamese military strategist General Vo Nguyen Giap: "If the enemy masses his forces, he loses ground; if he scatters, he loses strength." The contradiction inherent in this phrase captures Merz's conception of the igloo as a momentary shelter that, despite its perpetual relocation, remains a constant.

Merz often uses materials indigenous to the sites of his exhibitions to reinforce the nomadic essence of the igloo and its references to a humble economic system close to nature. For a 1979 show in Australia, for instance, he used eucalyptus leaves to blanket an igloo. He also adjusts the structure's scale and intricacy of design—more recent examples have been pierced by curving tables, surrounded by stacks of newspapers, or clustered in groups—to correspond to the environment in which they are exhibited. *Unreal City*, created for the Guggenheim Museum's spiraling rotunda on the occasion of a 1989 retrospective, is a tripartite igloo: the large, glass-covered structure is transparent and reveals smaller wood and rubber versions nestled within. As in all of Merz's sculptures (and much Arte Povera work in general), this piece embodies both beauty and violence: the shards of broken glass clamped onto this fragmented edifice are at once delicate and dangerous. The neon phrase "Città irreale" (Italian for "unreal city"), suspended across a wire-mesh triangle on the dome, refers to the intensely subjective, surreal quality of Merz's art. Although the nomadic artist may shift from one location or style or medium to another, creating momentary theaters of meaning, the sites visited are, ultimately and essentially, places in the mind.

—N. S.

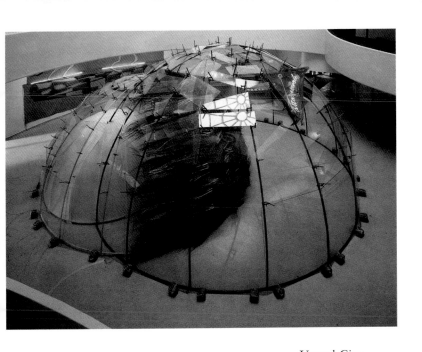

Unreal City,
Nineteen
Hundred Eighty-
Nine, *1989.*
Glass, mirror,
metal pipes, twigs,
rubber, clay, and
clamps; three igloos:
196 7/8 inches high,
392 inches in
diameter; 157 3/8
inches high, 315
inches in diameter;
98 7/16 inches high,
196 inches in
diameter. Gift of
the artist.
89.3631.a-.g

"The most
Surrealist of
us all."
—André Breton
on Miró

Joan Miró

b. 1893, Barcelona; d. 1983, Palma de Mallorca

During the summer of 1923 Joan Miró began painting *The Tilled Field*, a view of his family's farm in Montroig, Catalonia. Although thematically related to his earlier quasi-realistic, Fauvist-colored rural views such as *Prades, The Village*, this painting is the first example of Miró's Surrealist vision. Its fanciful juxtaposition of human, animal, and vegetal forms and its array of schematized creatures constitute a realm visible only to the mind's eye, and reveal the great range of Miró's imagination. While working on the painting he wrote, "I have managed to escape into the absolute of nature." *The Tilled Field* is thus a poetic metaphor that expresses Miró's idyllic conception of his homeland, where, he said, he could not "conceive of the wrongdoings of mankind."

The complex iconography of *The Tilled Field* has myriad sources, and attests to Miró's longstanding interest in his artistic heritage. The muted, contrasting tones of the painting recall the colors of Catalan Romanesque frescoes, while the overt flatness of the painting—space is suggested by three horizontal bands indicating sky, sea, and earth—and the decorative scattering of multicolored animals throughout were most likely inspired by medieval Spanish tapestries. These lively creatures are themselves derived from Catalan ceramics, which Miró collected and kept in his studio. The stylized figure with a plow has its source in the prehistoric cave paintings of Altamira, which Miró knew well. Even the enormous eye peering through the foliage of the pine tree and the eye-covered pine cone beneath it can be traced to examples of early Christian art, in which the wings of angels were bedecked with many tiny eyes. Miró found something alive and magical in all things: the gigantic ear affixed to the trunk of the tree, for example, reflects his belief that every object contains a living soul.

Miró's spirited depiction of *The Tilled Field* also has political content. The three flags—French, Catalan, and Spanish—refer to Catalonia's attempts to secede from the central Spanish government. Primo de Rivera, who assumed Spain's dictatorship in 1923, instituted strict measures, such as banning the Catalan language and flag, to repress Catalan separatism. By depicting the Catalan and French flags together, across the border post from the Spanish flag, Miró announced his allegiance to the Catalan cause.

—N. S.

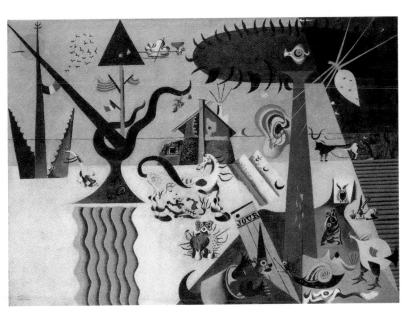

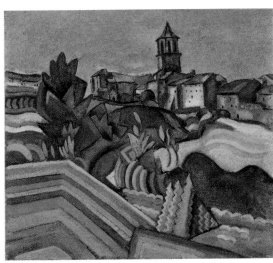

The Tilled Field,
*1923–24. Oil on
canvas, 26 x 36 ¹/₂
inches.* 72.2020

Prades, the
Village, *summer
1917. Oil on
canvas, 25 ⁵/₈ x
28 ⁵/₈ inches.*
69.1894

Joan Miró

"I went quite a bit that year with poets because I felt that it was necessary to go a step beyond the strictly plastic and bring some poetry into painting."

In 1925 Miró's work took a decisive turn, stimulated, according to the artist, by hunger-induced hallucinations involving his impressions of poetry. These resulted in the artist's "dream paintings," such as *Personage*, in which ghostly figures hover in a bluish ether. Miró explored Surrealist automatism in these canvases, attempting to freely transcribe his wandering imagination without preconceived notions. Although these images are highly schematic, they are not without references to real things, as the artist made clear. "For me a form is never something abstract," he said in 1948. "It is always a sign of something. It is always a man, a bird, or something else." In these works Miró began to develop his own language of enigmatic signs: the forms in *Personage* depict a large vestigial foot and a head with three "teeth" in its grinning mouth. The star shape often represents female genitalia in Miró's oeuvre, and the dot with four rays symbolizes the vision of a disembodied eye.

Two years later Miró reverted to imagery somewhat more grounded in reality. In *Landscape (The Hare)*, among other works, he also returned to one of his favorite subjects, the countryside around his family's home in Catalonia. Miró said that he was inspired to paint this canvas when he saw a hare dart across a field on a summer evening. In *Landscape (The Hare)* this event has been transformed to emphasize the unfolding of a heavenly event. A primeval terrain of acid oranges and red is the landscape in which a hare with bulging eyes stares transfixed by a spiraling "comet."

By the late 1940s Miró was making canvases on a much larger scale and with broader markings. *Painting* of 1953 is more than six feet high by twelve feet wide and is characterized by loose, gestural brushstrokes and stained pigments. The calligraphic drawing style and open field of works such as *Personage* has, in *Painting*, metamorphosed into bold, energetic lines in a vast, cosmic atmosphere. Yet the star and sun, the animal-like forms, and the sprays of dots are signs of the artist's symbolic language developed in the 1920s.

—J. B.

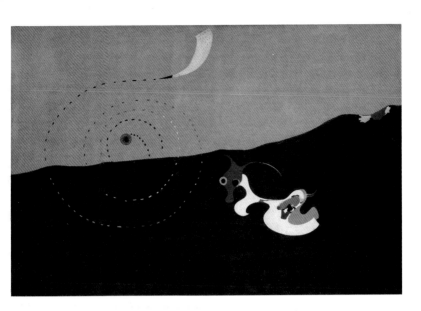

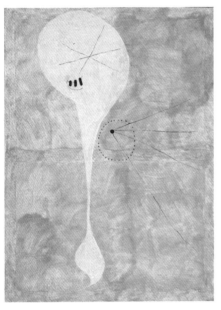

Landscape (The Hare), *autumn 1927. Oil on canvas, 51 x 76 5/8 inches. 57.1459*

Personage, *summer 1925. Oil and egg tempera (?) on canvas, 51 1/4 x 37 7/8 inches. 48.1172x504*

Painting, *1953. Oil on canvas, 76 3/4 x 148 3/4 inches. 55.1420*

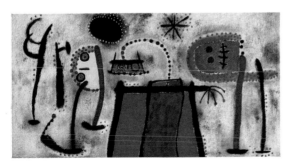

Amedeo Modigliani

b. 1884, Livorno, Italy; d. 1920, Paris

When Amedeo Modigliani moved from Italy to Paris in 1906, the leading artists of the avant-garde were exploring the forms and construction of "primitive" objects. Inspired by Paul Gauguin's directly carved sculptures, which were exhibited in a retrospective that year, Pablo Picasso, André Derain, Henri Matisse, and Constantin Brancusi began to make archaizing stone and wood sculptures. Brancusi, with whom Modigliani developed a close friendship, exerted a strong influence on the Italian; this is particularly obvious in his attempts at carving between the years 1909 and 1915, when he made idol-like heads and caryatids with monumental and simplified forms.

Modigliani's sculptural concerns were translated into paint in *Jeanne Hébuterne with Yellow Sweater*, in which he portrayed his young companion as a kind of fertility goddess. With her highly stylized narrow face and blank eyes she has the serene countenance of a deity, and the artist's emphasis on massive hips and thighs mimics the focus of ancient sculptures that fetishize reproduction. Both this work and *Nude*, with their simplified, elongated oval faces, gracefully attenuated noses, and button mouths, suggest the artist's interest in African masks.

Modigliani painted the human figure almost exclusively and created at least 26 reclining female nudes. Although the impact of Modernist practice on his art was great, he was also profoundly concerned with tradition; the poses of *Nude* and similar works echo precursors by Titian, Goya, and Velázquez. Nevertheless, Modigliani's figures differ significantly by the level of raw sensuality they transmit. His nudes have often been considered lascivious, even pornographic, in part because they are depicted with body hair, but perhaps also due to the artist's reputation for debauchery. His nickname, Modi, rhymes with the French word *maudit* (accursed), a name he very likely acquired because of his lifestyle. Modigliani died of tuberculosis and complications probably brought on by substance abuse and hard living. The tragic fact that Jeanne Hébuterne, pregnant with their second child, committed suicide the next day has only contributed to the infusion of romantic speculation concerning Modigliani's work.

—J. B.

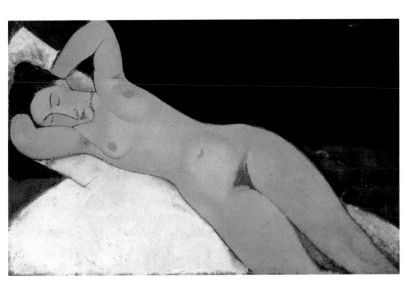

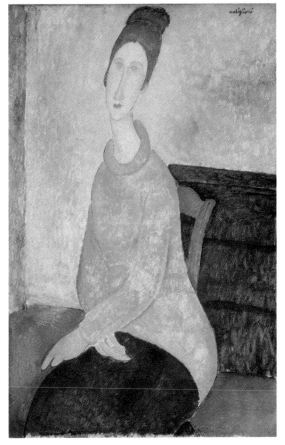

Nude, 1917. *Oil
on canvas, 28 3/4 x
45 7/8 inches. Gift,
Solomon R.
Guggenheim.
41.535*

Jeanne Hébuterne
with Yellow
Sweater,
*1918–19. Oil on
canvas, 39 3/8 x
25 1/2 inches. Gift,
Solomon R.
Guggenheim.
37.533*

*"This urge of mine
to supersede pigment
with light has its
counterpart in a
drive to dissolve
solid volume into
defined space. When
I think of sculpture,
I cannot think of
static mass.
Emotionally,
sculpture and
movement are
interdependent."*

László Moholy-Nagy

b. 1895, Bacsbarsod, Hungary; d. 1946, Chicago

László Moholy-Nagy's utopian view that the transformative powers of art could be harnessed for collective social reform—a tenet embedded in much Modernist theory—reflected his early association with the leftist Hungarian group MA (Today), a coalition of artists devoted to the fusion of art and political activism. It was also tied to his longstanding affiliation with the Bauhaus, the German artistic and educational community founded by Walter Gropius and dedicated to the development of a universally accessible design vocabulary. With his Bauhaus colleagues, who included Josef Albers, Vasily Kandinsky, Paul Klee, and Oskar Schlemmer, he strove to define an objective science of essential forms, colors, and materials, the use of which would promote a more unified social environment.

Moholy-Nagy firmly believed that the art of the present must parallel contemporary reality in order to successfully communicate meaning to a public surrounded by new technological advancements. Hence, he considered traditional, mimetic painting and sculpture obsolete and turned to pure geometric abstraction filtered through the stylistic influence of Russian Constructivism. Inspired by the structural and formal capacities of modern, synthetic materials, Moholy-Nagy experimented with transparent and opaque plastics, particularly Celluloid, Bakelite, Trolitan, and Plexiglas. In 1923 he created his first painting on clear plastic, giving physical form to his profound interest in the effects of light, which would later be manifest in film and photography as well as in transparent sculptures, such as the kinetic *Dual Form with Chromium Rods*.

A II and *AXL II* illustrate how Moholy-Nagy translated his efforts to manipulate light "as a new plastic medium" onto the painted canvas. In the first painting, the colored parallelograms and circles appear to be almost translucent as one plane overlaps the next and their hues shift accordingly. In the second, the intersecting transparent forms read as converging beams of light. A sense of layered space, echoing the artist's three-dimensional plastic "paintings" constructed with clear, projecting planes, was thus achieved. The contrived play of shadow and illumination on these canvases underscores the artist's conviction that light could be harnessed as an effective aesthetic medium, "just as color in painting and tone in music."

—N. S.

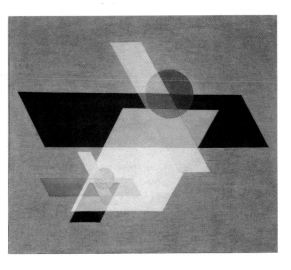

A II, *1924.*
Oil on canvas,
45 ⁵/₈ x 53 ⁵/₈
inches. 43.900

AXL II, *1927. Oil*
on canvas, 37 x
29 ¹/₈ inches. Gift,
Mrs. Andrew P.
Fuller. 64.1754

Dual Form with
Chromium Rods,
1946. Plexiglas
and chrome-plated
steel rods, 36 ¹/₂ x
47 ⁷/₈ x 22 inches.
48.1149

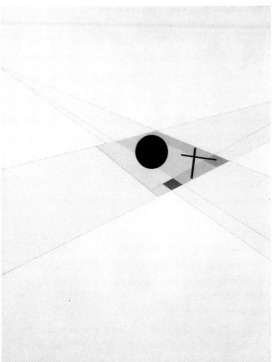

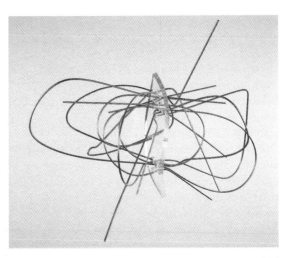

*"We must see deeper,
see abstractly and
above all
universally."*

Piet Mondrian

*b. 1872, Amersfoort, The Netherlands; d. 1944,
New York City*

When Piet Mondrian saw Cubist paintings by
Pablo Picasso and Georges Braque at a 1911
exhibition in Amsterdam, he was inspired to go
to Paris. *Composition VII*, painted a year after his
arrival in 1912, exemplifies Mondrian's regard for
the new technique. With a procedure indebted to
high Analytic Cubism, Mondrian broke down his
motif—in this case a tree—into a scaffolding of
interlocking black lines and planes of color;
furthermore, his palette of close-valued ocher and
gray tones resembles Cubist canvases. Yet
Mondrian went beyond the Parisian Cubists'
degree of abstraction: his subjects are less
recognizable, in part because he eschewed any
suggestion of volume, and, unlike the Cubists,
who rooted their compositions at the bottom of
the canvas in order to depict a figure subject to
gravity, Mondrian's scaffolding fades at the
painting's edges. In works such as *Composition
No. 8*, based on studies of Parisian building
façades, Mondrian went even further in his refusal
of illusionism and the representation of volume.

During the war years, Mondrian continued to
move toward greater abstraction, rejecting
diagonal lines and decreasing his reliance on his
favored subjects—trees, seascapes, and
architecture. *Composition 1916*, which developed
from studies of a church, is among the last of his
works that can be traced to an observable source.
Canvases like this make it clear that Mondrian's
interest lay foremost in coming to terms with the
two-dimensionality of the painted surface. For
this work, the artist designed a strip frame (now
lost), which he said prevented the sensation of
depth created by traditional carved frames.

The inexorable consistency and internal logic
of his solutions hint at a larger conceptual
principle, which is outlined in great depth in the
artist's extensive theoretical writings. Like many
pioneers of abstraction, Mondrian's impetus was
largely spiritual. He aimed to distill the real
world to its pure essence, to represent the
dichotomies of the universe in eternal tension. To
achieve this, he privileged certain principles—
stability, universality, and spirituality—through
the yin/yang balancing of horizontal and vertical
strokes. His philosophical framework was
grounded in the Neoplatonic and Tantric-inspired
texts of authors connected to the Theosophical
Society, the Dutch branch of which had counted
Mondrian as a member since 1909.

—J. B.

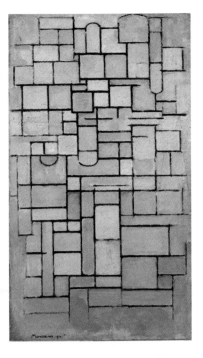

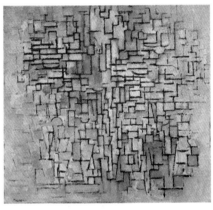

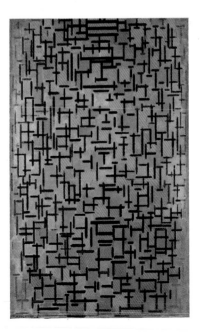

Composition
No. 8, *1914. Oil
on canvas, 37 ¹/₈ x
21 ⁷/₈ inches.
49.1227*

Composition VII,
*1913. Oil on
canvas, 41 ¹/₈ x
44 ³/₄ inches.
49.1228*

Composition
*1916, 1916. Oil
on canvas with
wood strip at
bottom edge,
46 ⁷/₈ x 29 ⁵/₈
inches. 49.1229*

"In painting the straight line is certainly the most precise and appropriate means to express free rhythm."

Piet Mondrian

Mondrian was a member of the Dutch De Stijl movement from its inception in 1917. By the early 1920s, in line with De Stijl practice, he restricted his compositions to predominantly off-white grounds divided by black horizontal and vertical lines that often framed subsidiary blocks of individual primary colors. *Composition 2*, a representative example of this period, demonstrates the artist's rejection of mimesis, which he considered a reprehensibly deceptive imitation of reality.

In 1918 Mondrian created his first "losangique" paintings, such as the later *Composition IA*, by tilting a square canvas 45 degrees. Most of these diamond-shaped works were created in 1925 and 1926 following his break with the De Stijl group over Theo van Doesburg's introduction of the diagonal. Mondrian felt that in so doing van Doesburg had betrayed the movement's fundamental principles, thus forfeiting the static immutability achieved through stable verticals and horizontals. Mondrian asserted, however, that his own rotated canvases maintained the desired equilibrium of the grid, while the 45-degree turn allowed for longer lines.

Art historian Rosalind Krauss identifies the grid as "a structure that has remained emblematic of modernist ambition." She notes in these paintings by Mondrian, whose work has become synonymous with the grid, two signal opposing generative tendencies. *Composition IA*, in which the lines intersect just beyond the picture plane (suggesting that the work is taken from a larger whole), exemplifies a centrifugal disposition of the grid; *Composition 2*, whose lines stop short of the picture's edges (implying that it is a self-contained unit), evinces a centripetal tendency. Krauss argues that these dual and conflicting readings of the grid embody the central conflict of Mondrian's—and indeed of Modernism's—ambition: to represent properties of materials or perception while also responding to a higher, spiritual call. "The grid's mythic power," Krauss asserts, "is that it makes us able to think we are dealing with materialism (or sometimes science, or logic) while at the same time it provides us with a release into belief (or illusion, or fiction)."

—J. B.

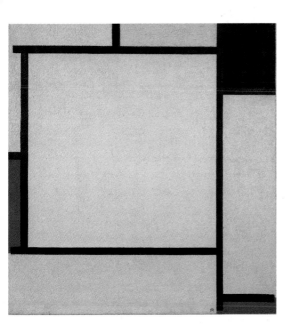

Tableau 2;
Composition 2,
1922. *Oil on
canvas, 21 7/8 x
21 1/8 inches.*
51.1309

Composition No. I;
Composition 1A,
1930. *Oil on
canvas, 29 5/8 x
29 5/8 inches
(lozenge). Hilla
Rebay Collection.*
71.1936 R96

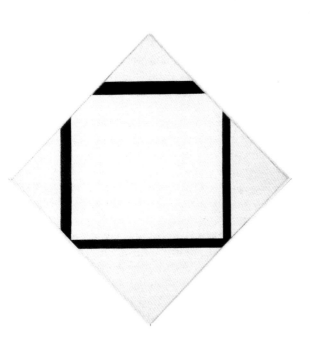

"Simplicity of shape does not necessarily equate with simplicity of experience."

Robert Morris
b. 1931, Kansas City, Mo.

In 1964, at New York's Green Gallery, Robert Morris exhibited a suite of large-scale polyhedron forms constructed from two-by-fours and gray-painted plywood. This kind of simple geometric sculpture came to be called Minimalist because it seemed to be stripped of extraneous distractions such as figural or metaphorical reference, detail or ornament, and even surface inflection. Sculptures like the Corner Piece, one component of the 1964 suite, boldly delineate the space in which they are located, thus defining the physical and temporal relationship of the viewer to the sculptural object.

Morris's sculptures often consist of industrial or building materials such as steel, fiberglass, and plywood, and were commercially fabricated according to the artist's specifications. The value of the "artist's hand"—the unique gesture that defines an individual's skill and style—was inimical to Morris, and the work of art became, in theory, not an "original" object but a representation of the idea from which it was conceived. This notion allowed for the creation and destruction of a piece when necessary; Corner Piece, for example, is refabricated each time it is to be exhibited.

In 1968 Morris introduced an entirely different aesthetic approach, which he articulated in an essay entitled *Anti-Form*. In this and later writings he reassessed his assumptions underlying Minimalist art and concluded that, contrary to earlier assertions, the construction of such objects *had* relied on subjective decisions and therefore resulted in icons—making them essentially no different than traditional sculpture. The art that he, Eva Hesse, Richard Serra, and others began to explore at the end of the 1960s stressed the unusual materials they employed—industrial components such as wire, rubber, and felt—and their response to simple actions such as cutting and dropping. Pink Felt, for example, is composed of dozens of sliced pink industrial felt pieces that have been dropped unceremoniously on the floor. Morris's scattered felt strips obliquely allude to the human body through their response to gravity and epidermal quality. The ragged irregular contours of the jumbled heap refuse to conform to the strict unitary profile that is characteristic of Minimalist sculpture. This, along with its growing referentiality, led Morris's work of the late-1960s and early 1970s to be referred to by such terms as Anti-Form, Process Art, or Post-Minimalism.

—J. B.

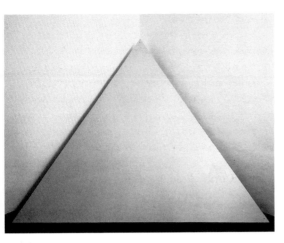

Untitled *{Corner Piece}*, 1964. *Gray-painted plywood and pine; height and width of individual sides: side A: 71 ³/₄ x 71 ³/₄ inches; side B: 71 ¹³/₁₆ x 71 ¹/₂ inches; unlabeled side: 88 x 101 ⁷/₁₆ inches. Panza Collection.* 91.3791

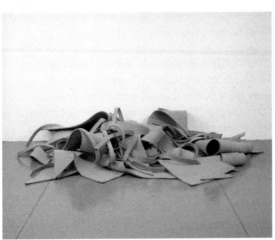

Untitled *{Pink Felt}*, 1970. *Pink felt pieces of various sizes, installation variable. Panza Collection.* 91.3804

"The 'Spanish
Elegies' are not
'political,' but my
private insistence
that a terrible
death happened that
should not be
forgot{ten}. They
are as eloquent as I
could make them.
But the pictures are
also general
metaphors of the
contrast between life
and death
and their
interrelations."

Robert Motherwell

b. 1915, Aberdeen, Wash.; d. 1991, Provincetown

Robert Motherwell was only 21 years old when the Spanish Civil War broke out in 1936, but its atrocities made an indelible impression on the artist, who later devoted a series of more than 200 paintings to the theme. The tragic proportions of the three-year battle—more than 700,000 people were killed in combat and it occasioned the first air-raid bombings of civilians in history—roused many artists to respond. Most famously, Pablo Picasso created his monumental 1937 painting *Guernica* as an expression of outrage over the events. From Motherwell's retrospective view, the war became a metaphor for all injustice. He conceived of his *Elegies to the Spanish Republic* as majestic commemorations of human suffering and as abstract, poetic symbols for the inexorable cycle of life and death.

Motherwell's allusion to human mortality through a nonreferential visual language demonstrates his admiration for French Symbolism, an appreciation he shared with his fellow Abstract Expressionist painters. Motherwell was particularly inspired by Symbolist poet Stéphane Mallarmé's belief that a poem should not represent some specific entity, idea, or event, but rather the emotive effect that it produces. The abstract motif common to most of the *Elegies*—an alternating pattern of bulbous shapes compressed between columnar forms— may be read as an indirect, open-ended reference to the experience of loss and the heroics of stoic resistance. The dialectical nature of life itself is expressed through the stark juxtaposition of black against white, which reverberates in the contrasting ovoid and rectilinear slab forms. About the *Elegies*, Motherwell said, "After a period of painting them, I discovered Black as one of my subjects—and with black, the contrasting white, a sense of life and death which to me is quite Spanish. They are essentially the Spanish black of death contrasted with the dazzle of a Matisse-like sunlight." This and other remarks Motherwell made regarding the evolution of the *Elegies* indicate that form preceded iconography. Given that the *Elegies* date from an ink sketch made in 1948 to accompany a poem by Harold Rosenberg that was unrelated to the Spanish Civil War, and that their compositional syntax became increasingly intense, it seems all the more apparent that the "meaning" of each work in the series is subjective and evolves over time.

—N. S.

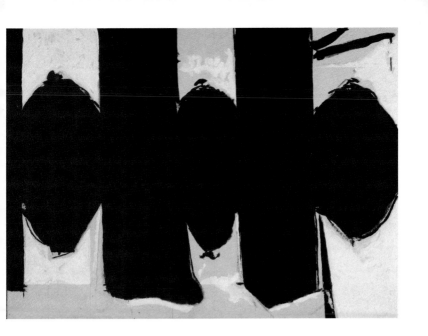

Elegy to the
Spanish Republic
No. 110, *Easter
Day, 1971.
Acrylic with pencil
and charcoal on
canvas, 82 x 114
inches. Gift, Agnes
Gund. 84.3223*

N

Bruce Nauman
b. 1941, Fort Wayne, Ind.

Bruce Nauman defies the traditional notion that an artist should have one signature style and a visually unified oeuvre. Since the mid-1960s the artist has created an open-ended body work that includes fiberglass sculptures, abstract body casts, performances, films, neon wall reliefs, interactive environments, videos, and, recently, motorized carousels displaying cast-aluminum animal carcasses. If anything links such diverse endeavors, it is Nauman's insistence that aesthetic experience supersedes the actual object in importance. Perception itself—the viewer's encounter with his or her body and mind in relation to the art object—can be interpreted as the subject matter of Nauman's work. Using puns, claustrophobic passageways with surveillance cameras, and videotaped recitations of bad jokes, he has created situations that are physically or intellectually disorienting, forcing viewers to confront their own experiential thresholds.

Nauman adopted neon signage during the 1960s (perhaps in response to Pop art) to illustrate his word plays. *None Sing/Neon Sign* is an anagram that, like Nauman's other semiotically playful neon pieces—*Raw War* and *Run from Fear/Fun From Rear*, for example—underscores the arbitrary relationship between a word's definition, what it sounds like, and what it looks like. A circular sign from 1967 of the spiraling neon phrase THE TRUE ARTIST HELPS THE WORLD BY REVEALING MYSTIC TRUTHS suggests, in retrospect and with irony, that these truths may be nothing more than the subtle distinctions between aesthetic illusion, artistic hype, and meaning.

Nauman enforces the contrast between the perceptual and physical experience of space in his sculptures and installations. Looking at the brilliant color emanating from *Green Light Corridor* prompts quite a different phenomenological experience than does maneuvering through its narrow confines. *Lighted Performance Box* provokes another experiential situation. As a rectangular column, it resembles the quintessential unitary Minimalist sculpture, yet the square of light cast on the ceiling from the lamp encased inside alters one's reading of the piece: the sense of a hidden, unattainable space, one that can only be experienced vicariously, is evoked. Thus, the performance alluded to in the title is only a private, conceptual act, initiated when viewers attempt to mentally project their own bodies into this secret, enclosed place.

—N. S.

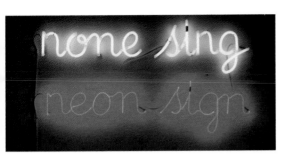

None Sing/
Neon Sign, *1970.*
Ruby-red and cool-
white neon tubing;
none sing: 7 ¹/₂ x
22 ¹³/₁₆ inches;
neon: 5 ¹/₂ x 11 ¹³/₁₆
inches; sign:
6 ¹¹/₁₆ x 11 ⁷/₁₆
inches. (Edition
of 6.) Panza
Collection.
91.3825.a-.c

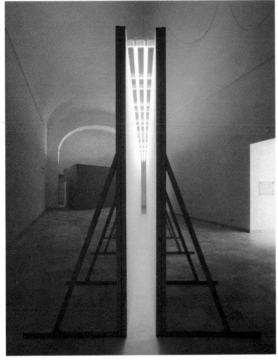

Green Light
Corridor,
1970–71. Wall-
board and green
fluorescent lights,
120 x 12 x 480
inches. Promised
gift, Count
Giuseppe Panza di
Biumo.

Lighted
Performance Box,
1969. Aluminum
box with spotlight,
78 x 20 x 20
inches. Panza
Collection.
91.3820

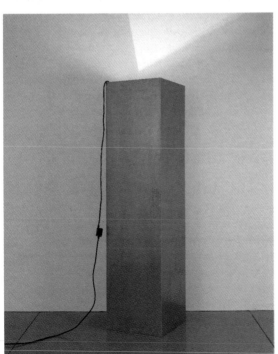

"No matter how individual we humans are, we are a composite of everything we are aware of. We are the mirror of our times."

Louise Nevelson
b. 1899, Kiev; d. 1988, New York City

Louise Nevelson's mature work emerged in the mid-1950s, when she began to assemble found wooden objects into constructions, most of which she painted uniformly black. In so doing she aligned herself with many contemporary artists who embraced found objects to create what has become known as Junk Art, an aesthetic that stems from Pablo Picasso's invention, early in this century, of a sculpture of accumulation. Nevelson's large-scale wall constructions reflect her interest in pre-Columbian stelae as well. The scale and formal purity of the all-black and all-white sculptures, in which the frontal relief surface and uniform coloration focus the viewer on the play of light and shadow, also suggest the solemnity and grandeur of altar paintings.

In *Luminous Zag: Night,* 105 boxes are filled with rows of saw-toothed wooden beams or, in approximately a dozen cases, with column fragments or jumbles of finials. A complicated rhythmic pattern, suggesting a fuguelike musical composition, is created by the play of vertical and horizontal zigzags. Like Piet Mondrian's *Broadway Boogie Woogie* (1942–43), Nevelson's *Luminous Zag: Night* appears to be inspired by jazz music and its emphasis on improvisation within an established structure. The emphatic chiaroscuro of the zigzag blocks suggests the dynamism of Broadway at night. In an interview, Nevelson addressed the prominent use of the color black in her work, saying that "it's only an assumption of the Western world that it means death, for me it may mean finish, completeness, maybe eternity."

White Vertical Water is the opposite of *Luminous Zag: Night* in terms of tension and color. While the geometric regularity of the latter recalls urban architecture, the spontaneous irregularity of *White Vertical Water* evokes images of nature. The long undulating curves of the forms in the work's narrow vertical boxes mimic the cascading streams of a waterfall or the froth of white water, while the biomorphic cutout layers in the upper-right squares, which recall the work of Jean Arp, suggest squirming fish. The materials and wall-like structure of Nevelson's monumental sculptures are akin to the fundamental elements of architecture, through which she created metaphorical analogies to urban and natural environments.

—J. B.

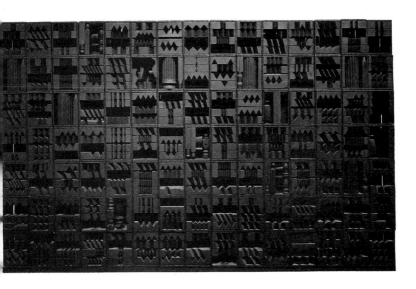

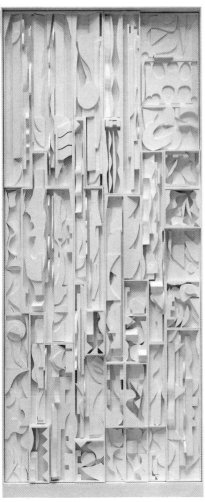

Luminous Zag: Night, *1971.* *Painted wood, 105 boxes, 120 x 193 x 10 ³/₄ inches overall. Gift, Mr. and Mrs. Sidney Singer.* *77.2325.a-.bbbb*

White Vertical Water, *1972.* *Painted wood, 26 sections, 216 x 108 inches overall. Gift, Mr. and Mrs. James J. Shapiro.* *85.3266.a-.z*

The Cry, *1959.*
Balsa wood on steel
base, 86 ¹/₄ x
29 ¹/₂ x 19 ¹/₄
inches overall.
66.1812

Isamu Noguchi
b. 1904, Los Angeles; d. 1988, New York City
Isamu Noguchi was an American artist whose
artistic education took place in the requisite arena
for the avant-garde of the first half of the century:
Paris. Yet he was of Japanese origin, and as he
slowly came in touch with his own cultural roots
he increasingly shifted his emphasis away from a
formal aesthetic vocabulary founded on the works
of sculptors such as Constantin Brancusi in favor
of a uniquely Japanese appreciation for the innate
beauty of even the simplest materials. His art
reveals both a debt to 20th-century sculptural
canons and a rare understanding of the means by
which geological and organic materials can be
transformed. He once remarked, "Abandoned
stones which I become interested in invite me to
enter into their life's purpose. It is my task to
define and make visible the intent of their being."

Carl Andre made a similar transition to a Zen-
like minimalism. Yet the works of the two artists
are entirely different, perhaps because Noguchi
belonged to the previous generation, for which, as
he said, "sculpture comes from time-consuming
difficulty, not industrial reproduction." This
existentialist emphasis on the mastery of life's

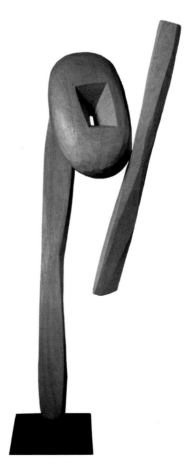

circumstances characterizes his early sets for the dances of Martha Graham and such sculptures as *The Cry* and *Lunar*.

The *Lunar* series came about in the 1940s, when Noguchi became fascinated by the reflection of light on form. *Lunar* is cut out of anodized aluminum and mounted, in contrast, on a wooden base. The aluminum is a softly reflective surface, sensitive to variations in light. *The Cry*, on the other hand, is malleable as a result of another natural force—wind. It was made in 1959 out of balsa wood, although it was cast in bronze a few years later. The Guggenheim Museum owns the balsa original, in which Noguchi attempted to create the lightest possible form of solid sculpture. Its elements are loosely connected so that they vibrate in response to air currents. Many of the qualities explored in *The Cry* and *Lunar* are also found in Noguchi's *akari*, the ethereal lamps for which he has become best known. Patterned on the paper lanterns hanging outside of traditional homes in Japan, the *akari* continued Noguchi's earlier interest in the potential luminosity and weightlessness of sculpture.

—C. L.

Lunar, 1959–60. Anodized aluminum with wood, 74 1/2 x 24 x 11 5/8 inches. 61.1596

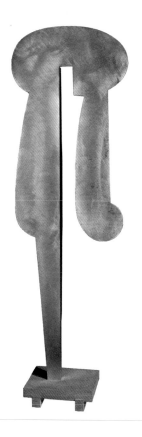

Non-Objective

The term "non-objective" is a very free (and misleading) translation of the German word *gegenstandslos*. Although "without objects" or "objectless" is a more accurate translation, "non-objective" has been used in the U.S. as a synonym for abstract art since its introduction and popularization by the German artist and curator Hilla Rebay. Rebay, who had come to the States in 1927, helped the industrialist Solomon R. Guggenheim assemble a group of primarily abstract works, including paintings by Vasily Kandinsky, Robert Delaunay, and László Moholy-Nagy, and became the first director of the Museum of Non-Objective Painting, as the Guggenheim was called from 1939 to 1952. She used the term "non-objective" in the first catalogue of the collection, which she prepared for a traveling exhibition in 1936. In this catalogue and in others that followed, Rebay attempted to divide abstract painting in general and Kandinsky's paintings in particular into evolutionary stages of partly abstract ("objective abstraction") and abstract ("non-objective"). Kandinsky and other pioneering abstract painters such as Piet Mondrian did not like this translation of *gegenstandslos*. They felt it evoked the negative connotation of philosophical subjectivity, whereas they wanted to emphasize the universal and international aspects of their work. In Kandinsky's correspondence with Rebay from the 1930s, he agreed that for some paintings, such as his *Black Lines* of 1913, he had not utilized concrete objects to arrive at his imagery, but he indicated his dislike for her schematic quantifications. He had used the term *gegenstandslos* in earlier essays—in his 1913 autobiography, for example—to describe his goal of obscuring specific, material objects in his paintings, but Kandinsky more often relied on the word *abstrakt* to indicate the direction of his work. In an essay of 1935 he critiqued the tone of both *gegenstandslos* and "non-objective," explaining that the "non" and the "los" were devoid of positive meaning.

By the time the Frank Lloyd Wright building that now houses the Guggenheim collection opened in 1959, the Museum of Non-Objective Painting had changed its name to the Solomon R. Guggenheim Museum. In the ensuing years, usage of "non-objective," with its convoluted hierarchical classification of different types of abstraction and its suggestion of philosophical subjectivity, has steadily fallen out of favor.

—Rose-Carol Washton Long

Vasily Kandinsky, Black Lines *(detail).*

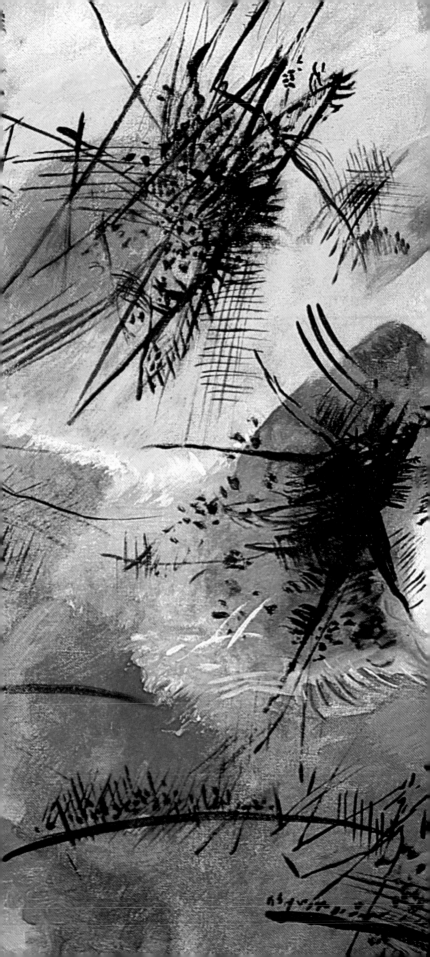

*"I never make
representations of
bodies but of things
that relate to bodies
so that the body
sensation is passed
along to the
spectator either
literally or by
suggestion."*

Claes Oldenburg
b. 1929, Stockholm, Sweden

Claes Oldenburg's absorption with the common-place was first manifested in his personal collection of toys, plastic food, and kitschy knick-knacks. These objects served as prototypes for the pieces the artist included in his early Happenings and installations. The burlesque *Freighter and Sailboat*—one of the first soft pieces—originated as a playfully sagging prop in his 1962 performances *Store Days I & II* and *Injun I*. Such sculptural articles played a more central role in Oldenburg's fabricated environment *The Store* (1961–62), in one version of which he filled a Manhattan storefront with colorfully painted plaster simulations of ordinary items—including articles of clothing (lingerie, in particular) and sundry food products—which he sold as merchandise. Because of its conflation of creativity with commerce, *The Store* is often cited as a quint-essential moment in the emergence of Pop art.

Oldenburg's enterprise, however, suggests many interpretations. The lumpy wares sold at *The Store* and their later incarnations as large-scale, stuffed vinyl sculptures—including a light switch, a toaster, and the pay telephone shown here—may be seen as substitutions for and references to the human body. Through their malleable forms and susceptibility to the effects of gravity, these supple sculptures often suggest specific anatomical parts: hamburgers are breasts, a tube of toothpaste is a phallus. Passive and limp, but potentially arousable, the pieces allude to the sexual, a realm that has been repressed in much Modern, abstract art. By asserting the sensual through the mundane, Oldenburg explores the ways in which everyday objects are so much an extension of ourselves. Anyone familiar with Freud's interpretation of dreams, in which domestic items are surrogates for human anatomy, will find a similar equation in Oldenburg's art.

After 1964 the artist expanded the range of his work to include monumental public projects while continuing to maintain his engagement with the ordinary and to demonstrate his remarkable sense of humor. The proposed projects (which generally exist only as drawings, prints, and maquettes) include an enormous, buttered baked potato for Brooklyn's Grand Army Plaza. When actually constructed—such as the 24-foot-high lipstick set on an army tank at Yale University—the monuments activate their surrounding environments through a subversive mix of political provocation and entertainment.

—N. S.

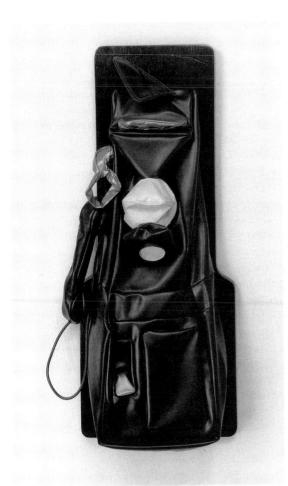

Soft Pay-Telephone, 1963. *Vinyl filled with kapok, mounted on painted wood panel, 46 1/2 x 19 x 9 inches. Gift, Ruth and Philip Zierler in memory of their dear departed son, William S. Zierler.* 80.2747

Freighter and Sailboat, 1962. *Muslin filled with shredded foam rubber, painted with spray enamel; freighter: 19 11/16 x 70 11/16 x 5 15/16 inches; sailboat: 45 1/16 x 28 15/16 x 5 5/16 inches. Gift, Claes Oldenburg and Coosje van Bruggen.* 91.3904.a,.b

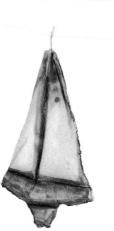

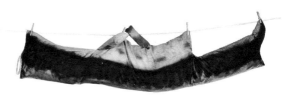

P

"The machine has become more than a mere appendix to life. It has come to form an authentic part of human existence . . . perhaps its soul."

Francis Picabia
b. 1879, Paris; d. 1953, Paris

Francis Picabia abandoned his successful career as a painter of coloristic, amorphous abstraction to devote himself, for a time, to the international Dada movement. A self-styled "congenial anarchist," Picabia, along with his colleague Marcel Duchamp, brought Dada to the New York art world in 1915, the same year he began making his enigmatic machinist portraits, such as *The Child Carburetor*, which had an immediate and lasting effect on American art. *The Child Carburetor* is based on an engineer's diagram of a "Racing Claudel" carburetor, but the descriptive labels that identify its various mechanical elements establish a correspondence between machines and human bodies; the composition suggests two sets of male and female genitals. Considered within the context created by Duchamp's contemporaneous work *The Bride Stripped Bare by Her Bachelors, Even*, as art historian William Camfield has observed, *The Child Carburetor*, with its "bride" that is a kind of "motor" operated by "love gasoline," also becomes a love machine. Its forms and inscriptions abound in sexual analogies, but because the mechanical elements are nonoperative or "impotent," the sexual act is not consummated. Whether the implication can be drawn that procreation is an incidental consequence of sexual pleasure, or simply that this "child" machine has not yet sufficiently matured to its full potential, remains unclear. Picabia stressed the psychological possibilities of machines as metaphors for human sexuality, but he refused to explicate them. Beneath the humor of his witty pictograms and comic references to copulating anthropomorphic machines lies the suggestion of a critique— always formulated in a punning fashion— directed against the infallibility of science and the certainty of technological progress. *The Child Carburetor* and his other quirky, though beautifully painted, little machines (which he continued to make until 1922) are indeed fallible. If they are amusingly naive as science fictions or erotic machines, they are also entirely earnest in placing man at the center of Picabia's universe, albeit a mechanical one.

—J. A.

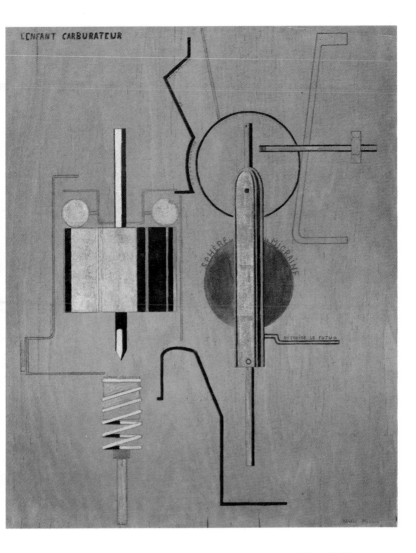

The Child
Carburetor, *1919.*
*Oil, enamel,
metallic paint, gold
leaf, pencil, and
crayon on stained
plywood, 49 ³/₄ x
39 ⁷/₈ inches.*
55.1426

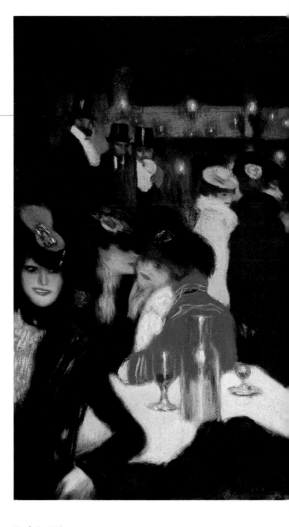

Pablo Picasso

b. 1881, Málaga, Spain; d. 1973, Mougins, France
Pablo Picasso was still living in Barcelona when the 1900 World's Fair drew him to Paris for the first time. During the course of his two-month stay he immersed himself in art galleries as well as the bohemian cafés, nightclubs, and dance halls of Montmartre. *Le Moulin de la Galette*, his first Parisian painting, reflects his fascination with the lusty decadence and gaudy glamour of the famous dance hall, where bourgeois patrons and prostitutes rubbed shoulders. Picasso had yet to develop a unique style, but *Le Moulin de la Galette* is nonetheless a startling production for an artist who had just turned 19.

Parisian night life, teeming with uninhibited hedonism and vulgarity, was a popular theme in late-19th- and early 20th-century painting; artists such as Edouard Manet and Edgar Degas documented this enticing, ribald nocturnal realm. None was a more skilled chronicler or sympathetic observer of the demimonde than Henri de Toulouse-Lautrec, whose numerous

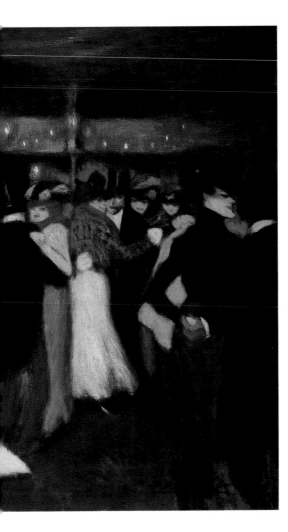

Le Moulin de la Galette, autumn 1900. Oil on canvas, 34 3/4 x 45 1/2 inches. Thannhauser Collection, Gift, Justin K. Thannhauser. 78.2514 T34

paintings and graphics from the late 1880s and early 1890s of pleasure palaces and their roguish patrons were an early and important influence on Picasso. Reproductions of his expressive paintings appeared in French newspapers that circulated in Barcelona and were well known to Picasso before he came to Paris, but the firsthand experience of these canvases and the decadent culture they portrayed increased his admiration for Toulouse-Lautrec and the tradition in which they were painted. In *Le Moulin de la Galette*, Picasso adopted the position of a sympathetic and intrigued observer of the spectacle of entertainment, suggesting its provocative appeal and artificiality. In richly vibrant colors, much brighter than any he had previously used, he captured the intoxicating scene as a dizzying blur of fashionable figures with expressionless faces.

—J. A.

Pablo Picasso

Images of labor abound in late-19th- and early 20th-century French art. From Jean-François Millet's sowers and Gustave Courbet's stone breakers to Berthe Morisot's wet nurses and Edgar Degas's dancers and milliners, workers were often idealized and portrayed as simple, robust souls who, because of their identification with the earth, with sustenance, and with survival, symbolized a state of blessed innocence. Perhaps no artist depicted the plight of the underclasses with greater poignancy than Picasso, who focused almost exclusively on the disenfranchised during his Blue Period (1901–4), known for its melancholy palette of predominantly blue tones and its gloomy themes. Living in relative poverty as a young, unknown artist during his early years in Paris, Picasso no doubt empathized with the laborers and beggars around him and often portrayed them with great sensitivity and pathos. *Woman Ironing*, painted at the end of the Blue Period in a lighter but still bleak color scheme of whites and grays, is Picasso's quintessential image of travail and fatigue. Although rooted in the social and economic reality of turn-of-the-century Paris, the artist's expressionistic treatment of his subject—he endowed her with attenuated proportions and angular contours—reveals a distinct stylistic debt to the delicate, elongated forms of El Greco. Never simply a chronicler of empirical facts, Picasso here imbued his subject with a poetic, almost spiritual presence, making her a metaphor for the misfortunes of the working poor.

Picasso's attention soon shifted from the creation of social and quasi-religious allegories to an investigation of space, volume, and perception, culminating in the invention of Cubism. His portrait *Fernande with a Black Mantilla* is a transitional work. Still somewhat expressionistic and romantic, with its bluish tonality and lively brushstrokes, the picture depicts his mistress Fernande Olivier wearing a mantilla, which perhaps symbolizes the artist's Spanish origins. The iconic stylization of her face and its abbreviated features, however, foretell Picasso's increasing interest in the abstract qualities and solidity of Iberian sculpture, which would profoundly influence his subsequent works. Though naturalistically delineated, the painting presages Picasso's imminent experiments with abstraction.

—N. S.

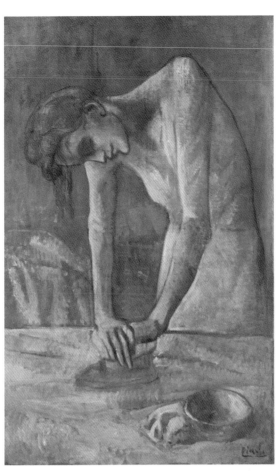

Woman Ironing,
1904. *Oil on
canvas, 45 ³/₄ x
28 ³/₄ inches.
Thannhauser
Collection, Gift,
Justin K.
Thannhauser.
78.2514 T41*

Fernande with a
Black Mantilla,
*1905/6? Oil on
canvas, 39 ³/₈ x
31 ⁷/₈ inches.
Thannhauser
Collection, Bequest
of Hilde
Thannhauser.
91.3914*

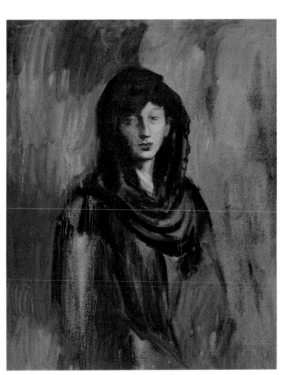

"The goal I proposed myself in making cubism? To paint and nothing more. And to paint seeking a new expression, divested of useless realism, with a method linked only to my thought—without enslaving myself or associating myself with objective reality."

Pablo Picasso

Cubism, which developed in the crucial years from 1907 to 1914, is widely regarded as the most innovative and influential art style of the 20th century. A decisive moment in its development occurred during the summer of 1911, when Georges Braque and Pablo Picasso painted side by side in Céret, in the French Pyrenees, each artist producing paintings that are difficult—sometimes virtually impossible—to distinguish from those of the other.

Picasso's still life *Carafe, Jug, and Fruit Bowl*, painted two summers before, shows an earlier stage of this style. Surfaces are broken into sharply defined planes but are not yet complexly fragmented; forms still retain an illusion of volume; and perspective, though dramatically shortened, is not obliterated. At its climax, Braque and Picasso brought Analytic Cubism to the point of almost complete abstraction. Among such works is Picasso's *Accordionist*, a baffling composition that one of its former owners mistook for a landscape because of the inscription "Céret" on the reverse. With diligence, one can distinguish the general outlines of the seated accordionist, denoted by a series of shifting vertically aligned triangular planes, semicircular shapes, and right angles; the centrally located folds of the accordion and its keys; and, in the lower portion of the canvas, the volutes of an armchair. But Picasso's elusive references to recognizable forms and objects cannot always be precisely identified and, as the Museum of Modern Art's founding director Alfred H. Barr, Jr. observed, "the mysterious tension between painted image and 'reality' remains."

In *Landscape at Céret*, another canvas painted that summer, patches of muted earthy color, schematized stairways, and arched window configurations exist as visual clues that must be pieced together. For this painting, as with all Cubist works, the total image must be "thought" as much as "seen."

—J. A.

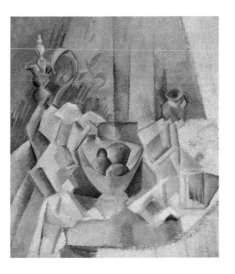

Carafe, Jug, and
Fruit Bowl,
summer 1909. *Oil
on canvas, 28 ¹/₄ x
25 ³/₈ inches. Gift,
Solomon R.
Guggenheim.*
37.536

Accordionist,
summer 1911. *Oil
on canvas, 51 ¹/₄ x
35 ¹/₄ inches. Gift,
Solomon R.
Guggenheim.*
37.537

Landscape at
Céret, *summer*
1911. *Oil on
canvas, 25 ⁵/₈ x
19 ³/₄ inches. Gift,
Solomon R.
Guggenheim.*
37.538

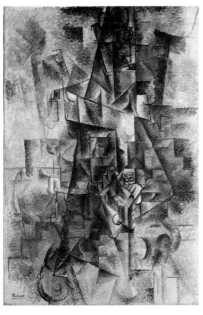

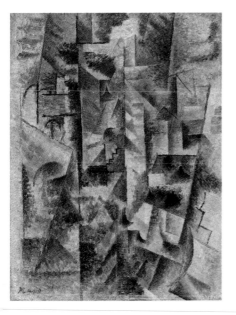

"We all know that Art is not truth. Art is a lie that makes us realize truth, at least the truth that is given us to understand."

Pablo Picasso

One year before Picasso painted the monumental still life *Mandolin and Guitar*, Cubism's demise was announced during a Dada soiree in Paris by an audience member who shouted that "Picasso [was] dead on the field of battle"; the evening ended in a riot, which could be quelled only by the arrival of the police. Picasso's subsequent series of nine vibrantly colored still lifes (1924–25), executed in a bold Synthetic Cubist style of overlapping and contiguous forms, discredited such a judgment and asserted the enduring value of the technique. But the artist was not simply resuscitating his previous discoveries in creating this new work; the rounded, organic shapes and saturated hues attest to his appreciation of contemporary developments in Surrealist painting, particularly as evinced in the work of Joan Miró and André Masson. The undulating lines, ornamental patterns, and broad chromatic elements of *Mandolin and Guitar* foretell the emergence of a fully evolved sensual, biomorphic style in Picasso's art, which would soon celebrate the presence of his new mistress, Marie-Thérèse Walter.

When Picasso met Marie-Thérèse on January 11, 1927 in front of Galeries Lafayette in Paris, she was 17 years old. As he was married at the time and she only a teenager, they were compelled to conceal their intense love affair. While their illicit liaison was hidden from public view, its earliest years are documented, albeit covertly, in Picasso's work. Five still lifes painted during 1927—incorporating the monograms "MT" and "MTP" as part of their compositions—cryptically announce the entry of Marie-Thérèse into the artist's life. By 1931 explicit references to her fecund, supple body and blond tresses appear in harmonious, voluptuous images such as *Woman with Yellow Hair*. Marie-Thérèse became a constant theme; she was portrayed reading, gazing into a mirror, and, most often, sleeping, which for Picasso was the most intimate of depictions.

The abbreviated delineation of her profile—a continuous, arched line from forehead to nose—became Picasso's emblem for his subject, and appears in numerous sculptures, prints, and paintings of his mistress. Rendered in a sweeping, curvilinear style, this painting of graceful repose is not so much a portrait of Marie-Thérèse the person as it is Picasso's abstract, poetic homage to his young muse.

—N. S.

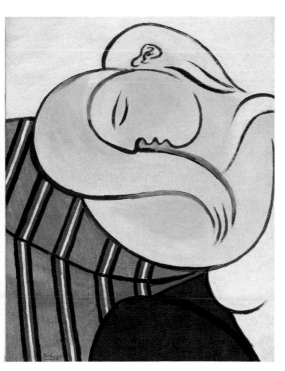

Woman with
Yellow Hair,
*Dec. 1931. Oil on
canvas, 39 ³/₈ x
31 ⁷/₈ inches.
Thannhauser
Collection, Gift,
Justin K.
Thannhauser.
78.2514 T59*

Mandolin and
Guitar, *1924. Oil
with sand on
canvas, 55 ³/₈ x
78 ⁷/₈ inches.
53.1358*

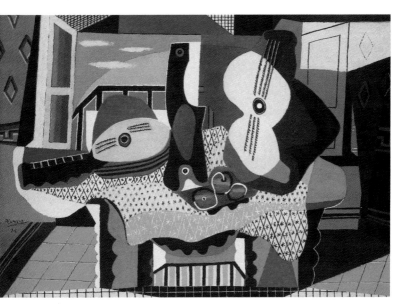

"(Pissarro) is neither a poet nor a philosopher but simply a naturalist. He paints the earth and the sky—that is what he has seen, and you may dream dreams about it if you like."
—Emile Zola

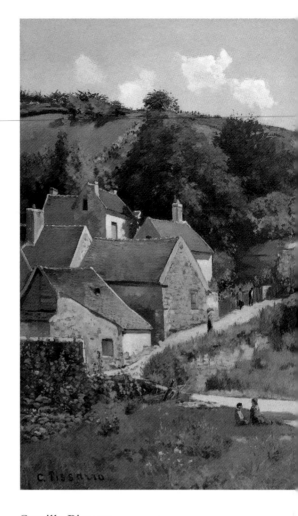

Camille Pissarro

b. 1830, Saint Thomas, West Indies; d. 1903, Paris

The view represented here is a winding village path at the base of a cluster of houses in Pontoise, France, known as the Hermitage. Camille Pissarro lived there on and off between 1866 and 1883, choosing the rural environs of the provincial capital for a series of large-scale landscapes that have been called his early masterpieces. Pissarro's idyll, replete with villagers and neatly tended gardens, is more than just the naturalist painter's attention to perceived reality. It is a continuation of the French academic landscape tradition, which stretched from the allegories of Poussin to the proto-Cubist landscapes of Paul Cézanne, who studied and worked with Pissarro.

Pissarro stripped his painting of the historical or sentimental overtones that characterized the landscapes of his immediate predecessors. And he made magisterial use of light and dark, demonstrating more than a mere interest in the effects of sun and shade. As art theorist Charles Blanc wrote at the time, this type of articulation was meant "not simply to give relief to the forms,

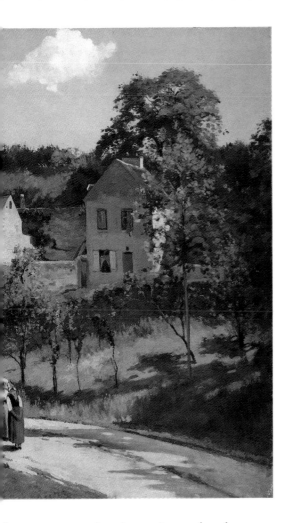

The Hermitage at Pontoise, *ca. 1867. Oil on canvas, 59 ⁵/₈ x 79 inches. Thannhauser Collection, Gift, Justin K. Thannhauser. 78.2514 T67*

but to correspond to the sentiment that the painter wishes to express, conforming to the conventions of a moral beauty as much as to the laws of natural truth."

The painterly conventions that Pissarro utilized in *The Hermitage* were established by Gustave Courbet, Edouard Manet, and the Barbizon school, but the painting is also a product of its era. In the same year that Marx published *Das Kapital*, Pissarro elected to depict a class of people that many critics considered a vulgar choice for the subject of a painting. Pissarro's later socialist sympathies aside, his work avoided the confines of traditional academic painting, which was centered on scenes far removed from the real world he hoped to describe. *The Hermitage*, however realistic an arcadian scene it appears to be, belongs to Pissarro's seemingly unfulfilled quest for a truthful manner of depiction. Shortly afterward he abandoned this Realist style for a looser brush and the atmospheric effects for which he is popularly known, the trademarks of Impressionism.

—C. L.

"A mirror is a way between visible and un-visible, as it extends sight beyond its seemingly normal faculties."

Michelangelo Pistoletto

b. 1933, Biella, Piedmont, Italy

Before 1962, when the mirror replaced the canvas in Michelangelo Pistoletto's work, he painted searching self-portraits to express a sense of cultural desolation and personal isolation. Concurrently, Pistoletto attempted to tackle what was perceived in some postwar art circles as the bankruptcy of traditional pictorial form. "It was a moment of great tension and no solution," he explained. "I had to find a way out of this dramatic situation of an art that reflected the need to recapture some indication of how to continue." Increasingly, the artist varnished the backgrounds of these portraits, thus creating reflective surfaces, and the decision to employ actual mirrors followed. For the initial incarnation of the mirror pieces, he silkscreened photographic images of men and women on highly polished steel plates. The life-size and lifelike figures seem to be observing a phantasmic world beyond the looking glass. As viewers, we encroach upon what seems to be their private space as our own reflections peer back from the picture. In actuality, it is the very space we occupy. The uneasy shift between reality and representation is startling. For Pistoletto, the introduction of the mirror provided a liberating aesthetic strategy that ventured far beyond the play between art and life, pursued to varying degrees by other members of the Arte Povera group. While the depicted figures are frozen in time, the reflective surfaces are infused with potentiality and indeterminacy. This temporal element, captured in the concept of the fourth dimension, is fundamental to Pistoletto's art. So is an appreciation of the semantic distinction between the definitions of "reflection": the word denotes both the occurrence of a visual likeness and the act of mental contemplation. Within this term is located the congruity between seeing and thinking, a phenomenon at the core of Pistoletto's conceptual project.

By the mid-1970s the artist had extended his experiments to create split reflective surfaces that, in essence, mirror themselves in an endless repetition of their own forms. Pistoletto also fragmented the mirror, breaking the reflected image into pieces and thereby exposing the deceptive nature of mimetic representation. *Broken Mirror*, as part of the larger *Division and Multiplication of the Mirror* series, is an elegant and challenging example of the artist's meditation on the nature of reflection and representation.

—N. S.

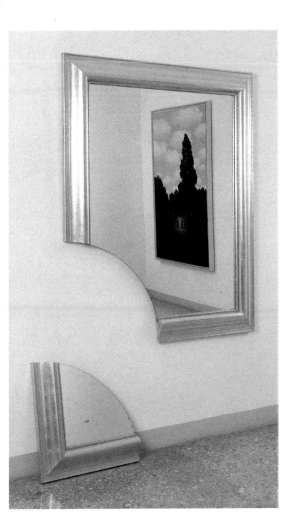

Broken Mirror, 1978. Mirror with gilded frame; frame: 64 ³/₈ x 53 ¹/₈ x 3 ¹/₈ inches; mirror: 23 ⁵/₈ x 23 ⁵/₈ inches. Gift of the artist. 90.3652.a,.b

> *"When I am in my painting, I'm not aware of what I'm doing. It is only after a sort of 'getting acquainted' period that I see what I have been about. I have no fears about making changes, destroying the image, because the painting has a life of its own."*

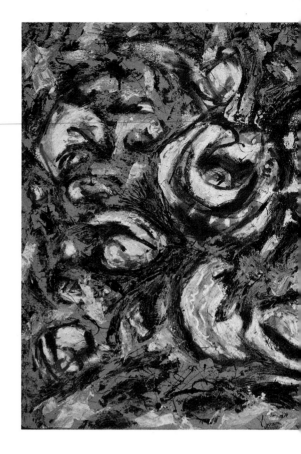

Jackson Pollock

b. 1912, Cody, Wyo.; d. 1956, The Springs, N.Y.
The critical debate that surrounded Abstract Expressionism during the late 1940s was embodied in the work of Jackson Pollock. Clement Greenberg, a leading critic and Pollock's champion, professed that each discrete art form should, above all else, aspire to a demonstration of its own intrinsic properties and not encroach on the domains of other art forms. A successful painting, he believed, affirmed its inherent two-dimensionality and aimed toward complete abstraction. At the same time, however, the critic Harold Rosenberg was extolling the subjective quality of art; fervent brushstrokes were construed as expressions of an artist's inner self, and the abstract canvas became a gestural theater of private passions. Pollock's art—from the early, Surrealist-inspired figurative canvases and those invoking "primitive" archetypes to the later labyrinthine webs of poured paint—elicited both readings. Pollock's reluctance to discuss his subject matter and his emphasis on the imme-diacy of the visual image contributed to shifting and, ultimately, dialectic views of his work.

In 1951, at the height of the artist's career, *Vogue* magazine published fashion photographs by Cecil Beaton of models posing in front of

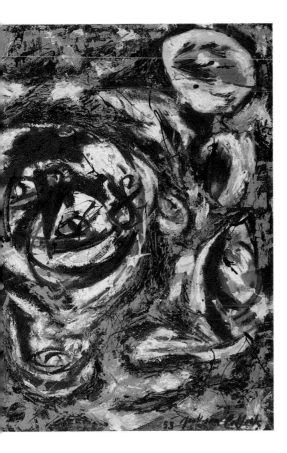

Ocean Greyness, 1953. *Oil on canvas, 57 3/4 x 90 1/8 inches. 54.1408*

Pollock's drip paintings. Although this commercial recognition signaled public acceptance—and was symptomatic of mass culture's inevitable expropriation of the avant-garde—Pollock continuously questioned the direction and reception of his art. His ambivalence about abstract painting, marked by a fear of being considered merely a "decorative" artist, was exacerbated, and it was around this time that he reintroduced to his paintings the quasi-figurative elements that he had abandoned when concentrating on the poured canvases. *Ocean Greyness*, one of Pollock's last great works, depicts several disembodied eyes hidden within the swirling colored fragments that materialize from the dense, scumbled gray ground. "When you are painting out of your unconscious," he claimed, "figures are bound to emerge." Manifest in this painting is a dynamic tension between representation and non-objectivity that, finally, constitutes the core of Pollock's multileveled oeuvre.

—N. S.

Liubov Popova

b. 1889, near Moscow; d. 1924, Moscow

Women formed an essential part of the Russian avant-garde, changing the face—and gender—of art in the process. Chief among them was Liubov Popova, the well-heeled daughter of a textile merchant. Popova's skill lay in her mastery of Parisian Cubism and Milanese Futurism, all the while maintaining her roots in a Russian artistic idiom. This is especially apparent in the commanding view of Birsk painted in 1916.

Popova began this painting on the occasion of a summer visit to her former governess, who lived in Birsk, a small town near the Urals. Popova turned to a style that was already anachronistic in 1916; the houses are fragmented and depicted in sliding planes of color that seem a cross between those favored by Georges Braque, Juan Gris, and Umberto Boccioni. These shades, however, are too intense to be characteristic of her Western mentors. They evoke paintings on glass, or the brilliance of Russian folk costumes. At this time Popova was still undecided as to her theoretical position. *Birsk* satisfied both the fragmentation of space so dear to the Cubists and the problem of luminous and shifting forms taken up by the Futurists. Like some of the works that Kazimir Malevich painted a few years earlier, it is an example of Russian Cubo-Futurism. *Birsk* was one of the last Western-oriented works that Popova painted before turning her attention to the artistic needs dictated by the October Revolution. By 1917 she adopted the theoretical implications of non-objective painting fully and began making Productivist art—art with a practical social function. In part this involved designing bold textile patterns that are anticipated in the cascading cliffs of *Birsk*.

It is ironic that Popova chose a frankly Western style to paint this work. Birsk is a city in Bashkir; its historical culture is Islamic and, until 1929, its writing system was Arabic. There, Popova may have gathered information for her later embarkation into textile design. Birsk has a strong local tradition of weaving and counted-thread embroidery, with geometric designs, diamonds, and cross-shaped figures providing an interesting parallel to the geometric solids of Popova's designs of the early 1920s.

—C. L.

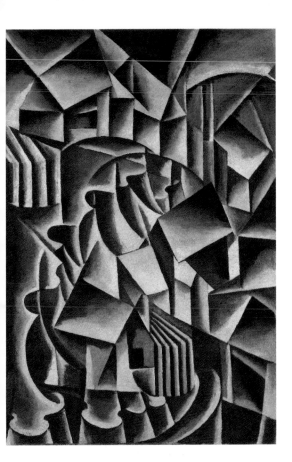

Birsk, *1916. Oil on canvas, 41 3/4 x 27 3/8 inches. Gift, George Costakis. 81.2822*

"The strongest work for me embodies contradiction, which allows for emotional tension and the ability to contain opposed ideas."

Martin Puryear
b. 1941, Washington, D.C.

Martin Puryear raises, then resolves, contrary formal issues in the making of his abstract wooden sculptures, creating a dynamic equilibrium of antithetical forces. In works such as *Seer* he strives to balance the opposition of a volumetric, closed form with one that is open yet inaccessible. There is also a linear element to this sculpture: the wire is a kind of drawing in space, reminiscent of a Renaissance exercise in perspective, while the wooden circle on the floor outlines a base from which the wire chassis appears to have been extruded. Puryear's virtuoso ability to control wood stems from his knowledge of craft traditions. Though originally trained as a painter, in the mid-1960s the artist learned about indigenous carpentry in Africa and began to make wooden sculptures while in Sweden, where he observed Scandinavian woodworking techniques.

The clarity of Puryear's forms, along with his interest in the physical response of the viewer to his objects, allies the artist to the Minimalist sculptors of the late 1960s. But the Minimalists' espousal of industrial materials and fabrication and their denial of metaphor were anathema to Puryear, who is committed to organic materials, handcraftsmanship, and poetic evocation through form. His work is more akin to that of the Post-Minimalists, such as Eva Hesse, whose constructions have organic connotations, even though they are often assembled from man-made elements.

The variety of sculptural methods and materials Puryear employs—he opposes bent wood with woven wire, for example, and integrates found objects into handmade structures—leads to myriad metaphorical interpretations. *Seer* evokes associations with man-made architecture; the wire base of the object suggests both a yurt (the temporary home of nomadic Mongols) and the hull of a boat. It also incorporates the idea of a cage. Critics have noted intimations of violence and sexuality and a sense of frustrated energy in Puryear's work. Applying such a reading to *Seer*, one could interpret the lower section of the sculpture as a trap for invisible gases that are metaphorically funneled into the cone in a Duchampian play on sexual energy. The horn atop the cage might be seen as a portent of divinity, adding another layer of meaning. Looked at straight on, it reads as a spire, becoming a divining rod directed toward a celestial mark.

—J. B.

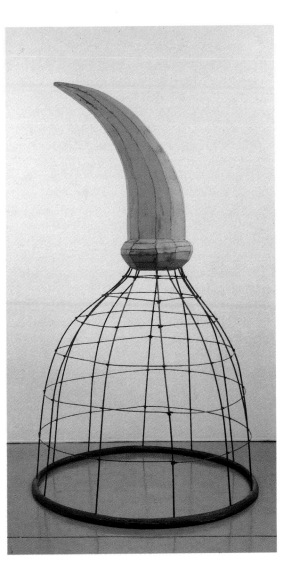

Seer, 1984.
*Water-based paint
on wood and wire,
78 x 52 1/4 x 45
inches. Purchased
with funds
contributed by the
Louis and Bessie
Adler Foundation,
Inc., Seymour M.
Klein, President.*
85.3276

R

"Painting relates to both art and life. Neither can be made. (I try to act in that gap between the two.)"

Robert Rauschenberg
b. 1925, Port Arthur, Tex.

In 1951 and 1952 Robert Rauschenberg created two series of paintings, one monochrome white and pristine, the other all black with clotted, collaged-newspaper surfaces. In 1953 he shifted to the color red. In an interview many years later he told art historian Barbara Rose, "I was trying to move away from black and white. Black *or* white, not black-and-white. So I picked the most difficult color for me to work in." *Red Painting*, like the *Black Paintings*, has a richly textured, mottled skin. The bloodlike hue and the layered, collaged paper suggesting bandages evoke the contemporaneous work of Italian artist Alberto Burri, whose studio the Texas-born artist visited in 1953.

During the remainder of the 1950s Rauschenberg developed his "combines," heterogeneous works that join aspects of both painting and sculpture through the artist's attachment of objects to two-dimensional supports. *Untitled*, with its metal engine cover and plastic dish attached to the canvas, bears witness to the artist's multimedia experiments of the 1950s; this work is also among his first investigations of the silkscreen process. From 1962 to 1964 Rauschenberg clipped images from the popular media and had silkscreens made of them. In a frenzy of activity, he would "collage" reproductions of his preferred themes onto various supports, integrating them through patches of color and smeared ink. *Untitled* includes references to technological progress in locomotion (the two rockets and the engine cover), the history of art (a classical sculpture at lower right), and signature American products (the Coca-Cola billboard). The banality of these images was considered at the time to be part of a bad-boy response to the high seriousness of Abstract Expressionism. The art of Jasper Johns met with a similar critical reaction. But the comparative coolness of the next decade's Pop art—its denial of painterly gesture, for example, and its more deadpan choice of subject matter—highlighted Rauschenberg's and Johns's expressionistic use of paint and made it clear that both artists chose imagery for its autobiographical references. Rauschenberg's combines and silkscreen paintings have been called a virtual diary of his interests. In *Untitled*, for example, Rauschenberg included an image of his friend Merce Cunningham, who dances in a white rectangle at center.

—J. B.

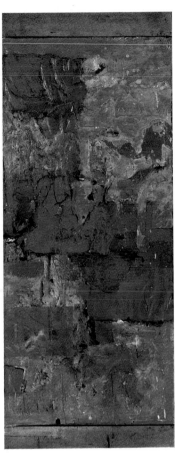

Red Painting,
1953. *Oil, cloth,
and newsprint on
canvas with wood,
79 x 33 ⅛ inches.
Gift, Walter K.
Gutman. 63.1688*

Untitled, 1963.
*Oil, silkscreen, ink,
metal, and plastic
on canvas, 82 x 48
inches. Purchased
with funds
contributed by
Elaine and Werner
Dannheisser and
The Dannheisser
Foundation.*
82.2912

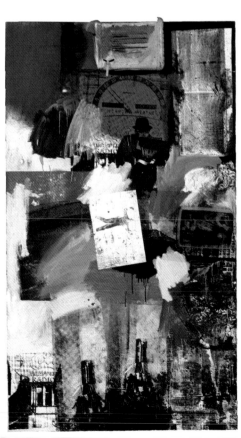

"After I decided to be an artist, the first thing that I had to believe was that I, a black woman, could penetrate the art scene and that I could do so without sacrificing one iota of my blackness, or my femaleness, or my humanity."

Faith Ringgold

b. 1930, New York City

During the late 1960s and the 1970s Faith Ringgold played an instrumental role in the organization of protests and actions against museums that had neglected the work of women and people of color. Her paintings from this period are overtly political, and present an angry, critical reappraisal of the American dream glimpsed through the filter of race and gender relations. Ringgold's most recent aesthetic strategy, however, is not one of political agitation or blatant visual provocation. Instead, she has come to embrace the potential for social change by undermining racial and gender stereotypes through impassioned and optimistic presentations of black female heroines.

Ringgold's vehicle is the story quilt—a traditional American craft associated with women's communal work that also has roots in African culture. She originally collaborated on the quilt motif with her mother, a dressmaker and fashion designer in Harlem. That Ringgold's great-great-great-grandmother was a Southern slave who made quilts for plantation owners suggests a further, perhaps deeper, connection between her art and her family history. One of Ringgold's early efforts, dating from 1982, tells the tale of the stereotyped Aunt Jemima through painted images, sewn fabric, and handwritten texts. The naive, folk-art quality of the quilts is part of Ringgold's scheme to emphasize narrative over style, to convey information rather than to dazzle with technique.

Tar Beach, the first quilt in Ringgold's colorful and lighthearted series entitled *Women on a Bridge*, depicts the fantasies of its spirited heroine and narrator Cassie Louise Lightfoot, who, on a summer night in Harlem, flies over the George Washington Bridge. "Sleeping on Tar Beach was magical . . ." explains Cassie in the text on the quilt, "only eight years old and in the third grade and I can fly. That means I am free to go wherever I want to for the rest of my life." For Ringgold, this phantasmic flight through the urban night sky symbolizes the potential for freedom and self-possession. "My women," proclaimed Ringgold about the *Women on a Bridge* series, "are actually flying; they are just free, totally. They take their liberation by confronting this huge masculine icon—the bridge."

—N. S.

226

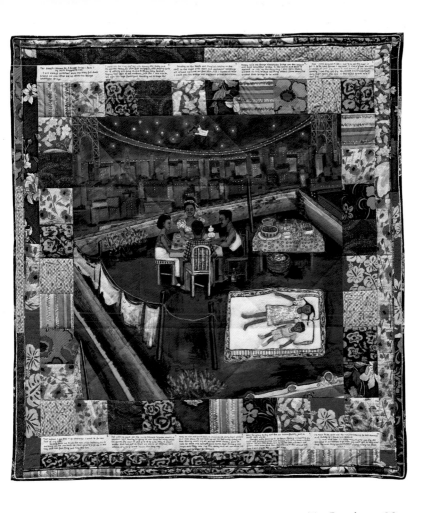

Tar Beach, 1988. Acrylic on canvas bordered with printed, painted, quilted, and pieced cloth, 74 ⁵/₈ x 68 ¹/₂ inches. Gift, Mr. and Mrs. Gus and Judith Lieber. 88.3620

*"The fact that lots
of people break
down and cry
when confronted
with my pictures
shows that I
communicate
with those basic
human emotions.
The people who
weep before my
pictures are having
the same religious
experience I had
when I painted
them."*

Mark Rothko

b. 1903, Dvinsk, Russia; d. 1970, New York City

With paintings such as *Untitled (Violet, Black, Orange, Yellow on White and Red)*, Mark Rothko arrived at his mature idiom. For the next 20 years he would explore the expressive potential of stacked rectangular fields of luminous colors. Like other New York School artists, Rothko used abstract means to express universal human emotions, earnestly striving to create an art of awe-inspiring intensity for a secular world.

In order to explain the power of his canvases, some art historians have cited their compositional similarity to Romantic landscape painting and Christian altar decoration. Anna Chave suggests that Rothko's early interest in religious iconography underlies his later work. She sees a reference to a Madonna and Child in *Number 17*, an apparently abstract work that developed out of the Surrealistic biological fantasies that he had been painting in the early 1940s. For Chave, mature paintings such as *Untitled (Violet, Black, Orange, Yellow on White and Red)* metaphorically encompass the cycle of life from cradle to grave, in part by harboring an oblique reference to both adorations and entombments. The stacked rectangles may be read vertically as an abstracted Virgin bisected by horizontal divisions that indicate the supine Christ. Even without Chave's argument, it is clear that Rothko hoped to harness the grandeur of religious painting. The principles of frontality and iconic imagery in his mature works are common to traditional altarpieces, and both formats have similar dimensions and proportions. Often larger than a human being, Rothko's canvases inspire the kind of wonder and reverence traditionally associated with monumental religious or landscape painting.

It was Rothko's euphoric veils of diaphanous pure color that led critics to praise him as a sensualist and a colorist, praise that pained him because he believed that his champions had lost sight of his serious intentions. For him the canvases enacted a violent battle of opposites—vertical versus horizontal, hot color versus cold—invoking the existential conflicts of modernity. The *Black Paintings*, begun in the year before the artist's suicide, confirm Rothko's belief that his work encompassed tragedy. The desolation of canvases such as *Untitled (Black on Grey)*, drained of color and choked by a rigid white border—rather than suggesting the free-floating forms or veiled layers of his earlier work—indicate that, as Rothko asserted, his paintings are about death.

—J. B.

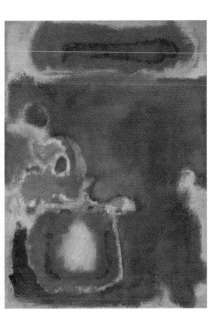

Number 17, 1947. *Oil on canvas, 47³/₄ x 35¹/₂ inches. Gift of The Mark Rothko Foundation, Inc. 86.3420*

Untitled (Violet, Black, Orange, Yellow on White and Red), *1949. Oil on canvas, 81¹/₂ x 66 inches. Gift, Elaine and Werner Dannheisser and The Dannheisser Foundation. 78.2461*

Untitled (Black on Grey), *1970. Acrylic on canvas, 80¹/₈ x 69¹/₈ inches. Gift of The Mark Rothko Foundation, Inc. 86.3422*

"We are the two
greatest painters
of the epoch."
—Henri
Rousseau to
Pablo Picasso

Henri Rousseau

b. 1844, Laval, France; d. 1910, Paris

Henri Rousseau endured the art-historical misfortune of being a working-class late bloomer—he was a Sunday painter who only began to paint seriously in his 40s—with what seemed to his critics little natural talent. His unsentimental, haunting images nonetheless drew the attention of a literary and artistic coterie hungry for fresh recruits. How did Rousseau, whose style still commands belittling adjectives such as "naive" and "simple," escape relegation to the margins of art history? It was, as the writer André Malraux has pointed out, the former toll clerk's friendship with a legion of well-established masters that has by and large guaranteed his place in the history of Modern art. During his lifetime Rousseau became something of a sensation within the relatively small Parisian art scene. His astonishing works were celebrated by Alfred Jarry, Pablo Picasso, and Guillaume Apollinaire, and he came to be considered a major force by artists such as Fernand Léger, Vasily Kandinsky, and Max Beckmann only a few years after his pauper's death.

To the extent that he had limited official success while he lived, Rousseau can be said to have invented himself—he barged uninvited into exhibitions and dinner parties alike, assuming the posture of an honored guest—just as he invented images unlike anything around him. Canvases such as *Artillerymen* and *The Football Players* have been interpreted as Rousseau's quirky attempts to depict modern times, whether with a dapper military company as in the former example, or with the four natty enthusiasts of a new sport, rugby, in the latter. It is to his credit that we still have no adequate words to describe a painting in which rugby players look like pajama-clad twins, or one in which 14 identical handlebar mustaches succeed in delivering a spirited image of an artillery battery.

—C. L.

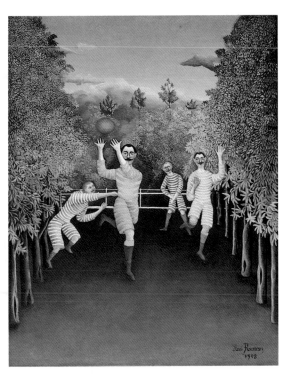

The Football
Players, *1908. Oil
on canvas, 39 ¹/₂ x
31 ⁵/₈ inches.
60.1583*

Artillerymen,
*ca. 1893–95. Oil
on canvas, 31 ¹/₈ x
39 inches. Gift,
Solomon R.
Guggenheim.
38.711*

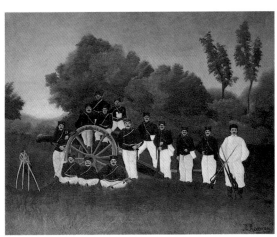

"White enables other things to become visible."

Robert Ryman
b. 1930, Nashville, Tenn.

Throughout his career, Robert Ryman has attempted to eliminate illusionism and outside references from his work, focusing instead on the fundamental properties of the materials he employs. He has confined himself to the color white, yet disclaims its importance. "It was never my intention to make white paintings," he insisted in a 1986 interview with critic Nancy Grimes. "And it still isn't. . . . The white is just a means of exposing other elements of the painting." These "other elements" include varieties of paint (oil and acrylic) and supports (canvas, paper, and metals), as well as the process of binding them. He investigates the properties of these elements methodically, yet responds spontaneously to the unpredictable exigencies caused by their interaction.

Ryman's *Classico 4* is one of a series of compositions consisting of multipanel paintings on a specific type of paper called Classico. For each work in the series, Ryman attached a configuration of heavy, creamy white sheets of the paper to a wall with masking tape, painted the sheets with a shiny white acrylic paint, removed the tape when the sheets were dry, mounted them on foamcore, and reattached them to the wall. The built-up paint edge tracing the outline of masking tape and the ripped paper left behind give witness to the process of creation. The various works in the *Classico* series differ in the organization of paper sheets, the configuration of tape traces, and the painted shape, yet they share an emphasis on the thinness of the support surface in its alignment with the wall and the monumentality conceived as an accumulation of parts.

Ryman's work achieved fame in the context of Minimal painting; his compositions were seen as essays in the reduction of his medium to essences, while his multiple-unit works were related to Minimalist seriality. Although some of the artist's goals were consistent with Minimalism, his investigations predated the movement and remained largely outside it. As Piet Mondrian had done, Ryman improvises arbitrary solutions to the problems he sets himself; unless he is surprised in the process, he feels he has failed. Ryman's preference for the perfect square, symmetry, and whiteness implies his faith in transcendental absolute qualities, a trait he shares with Mondrian as well as with Kazimir Malevich.

—J. B.

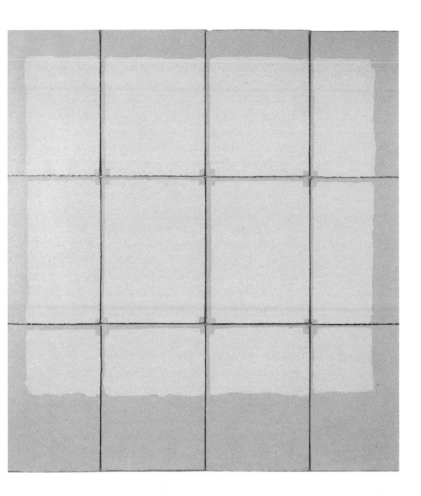

Classico 4, 1968.
Acrylic on paper,
mounted on
foamcore; 12
sections of paper,
each 30 x 22 $\frac{1}{4}$
inches. Panza
Collection.
91.3845.a-.l

S

Scale

Just as the scale of a road map reduces vast stretches of highway to scant cartographic lines, the perceptual scale established within a conventional easel painting can create hugely populated landscapes that disappear into the infinite reaches of the mind's eye. The beguiling effects of a finely painted miniature rely on the ability to maximize the scalar differential, etching great spaces and extraordinary physical presences on jewel-like surfaces no larger than the palm of one's hand.

If scale is the proportional arbiter of worlds of differing measure, it is also a sign of difference itself, calibrating the degree of dimensional discontinuity between those worlds. Many artists of the past century have focused their attention on just such discontinuities, striving to eliminate, or bring into question, the perceptual veil that allows us to speak of a separate "world" of art. The highly polished use of paint associated with the great 19th-century fine-arts academies, in which the physical presence of pigment all but vanishes under a seamless film of representational illusion, gave way to rougher brushwork that proclaimed and celebrated the literal depths of paint on canvas. Likewise, art that directly examined the idea of scale as a proportional intermediary began to appear early in this century. The scale of Marcel Duchamp's ready-made snow shovel is 1:1 by definition, an incursion into the dimensional space of the viewer, emphasized by the deliberate lack of a pedestal.

With the mural-size paintings of the Abstract Expressionists and the rigorous geometries of Minimalist sculpture, the viewer is subsumed into the spatial coordinates of the art work itself. Scale becomes less a matter of proportional relationship than of sheer size and physical concordance with one's own bodily presence. Indeed, in the past three decades, scale—as a critical element in the confrontation of art with the viewer's body, the earth, and beyond—has become subject matter itself. As artists such as Joseph Beuys, Christo, Walter De Maria, Robert Morris, and James Turrell have extended the scope of art to encompass entire streets, cities, deserts, and distant stars, the proportional, ecological, and perceptual relationship of the viewer to the work of art—and through art to the world—rises to the most challenging scale imaginable.

—Joseph Thompson

Richard Serra,
Strike *(detail).*

Egon Schiele

b. 1890, Tulln, Austria; d. 1918, Vienna

The subject of Egon Schiele's portrait is Johann Harms, his father-in-law. The painting demonstrates Schiele's sympathy for the 73-year-old man, a retired machinist with the Austrian railway. Although a family portrait, it conveys a somber monumentality. With a stateliness that transcends its subject, the painting is reminiscent of papal portraits by Raphael or Titian. The work is known as the first in a series of "painterly portraits," as opposed to earlier canvases that Schiele executed in a more graphic style.

Schiele designed the chair in the painting for his studio and used it several times for portraits. As a prop, it allowed the artist to push his subjects toward the picture plane, flattening and enlarging the contours of their bodies. The chair also recalls the furniture in Vincent van Gogh's paintings of his own bedroom; its handcrafted style reminds us of the importance of the decorative arts in Vienna at this time.

Schiele painted the portrait two years before his death from influenza. It is an example of his mature style and goes far in abolishing fixed notions of Austrian Expressionism as only an art of angst. It also demonstrates that Schiele could successfully depart from his well-known fascination with the physical and psychic dimensions of sexuality. In 1916, after initial difficulties in his marriage to Edith Harms, Schiele was beginning to enjoy a sense of domestic happiness that would lead to other intimate family portraits. Schiele's fondness for Johann Harms carried beyond this portrait—after the old man's death in 1917, Schiele made a death mask of his father-in-law.

—C. L.

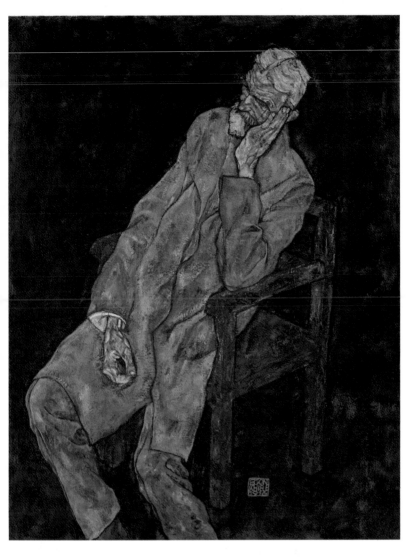

Portrait of Johann
Harms, *1916. Oil
with wax on
canvas, 54 ¹/₂ x
42 ¹/₂ inches.
Partial gift, Dr.
and Mrs. Otto
Kallir. 69.1884*

"In The Recognitions *by William Gaddis, there's a list of all the Christian saints. It was a sort of imaginary library of the names of all these characters that transgressed time. Also, there was the way these words sat on the pages. It was funny for me to see words like 'The Teddy Bears' Picnic' as the same thing as 'Pope Clement of Rome' or 'Spinoza.'"*

Julian Schnabel

b. 1951, Brooklyn, N.Y.

Julian Schnabel's swift and youthful rise to fame during the early 1980s seemed paradigmatic of the emergence of Neo-Expressionist, heroic-scale painting after two decades dominated by Minimalist and Conceptual aesthetics. Schnabel's larger-than-life presence, his beguiling rhetoric about "love," "sadness," "mortality," and "destruction," and his heavily impastoed, tortured paintings made him an art celebrity. He came to prominence with his broken-plate paintings, canvases strewn with shards of smashed crockery upon which thick, swirling layers of pigment depict legendary figures such as John the Baptist and the mythical King of the Wood. In addition to these works, inspired by Catalan architect Antonio Gaudí's bulky, mosaic benches, Schnabel brazenly executed paintings on black velvet, the quintessential kitsch medium. He followed these pictures with immense quasi-figurative images painted on recycled Kabuki theater backdrops.

In 1987 Schnabel began making paintings such as *Henner*, in which written words and proper names serve as subject matter, thus marking, for him, a radical shift from an imagery of excess to one of deliberate austerity and from pictorial narrative to oblique, linguistic reference. The series, named after William Gaddis's rambling 1952 novel *The Recognitions*, was first exhibited in 1988 in an abandoned Carmelite monastery in Seville. In place of canvases, Schnabel used tarpaulin taken from the tops and sides of army jeeps, metaphorically recalling the military occupation from 1810 to 1978 of the now-crumbling 14th-century cloister. The cruciform-shaped text paintings—with names such as *Henner*, *Ignatius of Loyola*, *Blessed Clara*, *Pope Clement of Rome*, *Diaspora*, *Spinoza*, and *Night Hunting*—collectively represent Schnabel's version of the Stations of the Cross, yet they also refer to Gaddis's story of a forger of Flemish religious masterpieces, who, as the son of a minister, equates originality with God. Schnabel's series invokes the novel's intermingled and overlapping realms of truth and deception, faith and suspicion, and fear and desire through his painted corpus of evocative linguistic fragments, pious names, and unholy events.

—N. S.

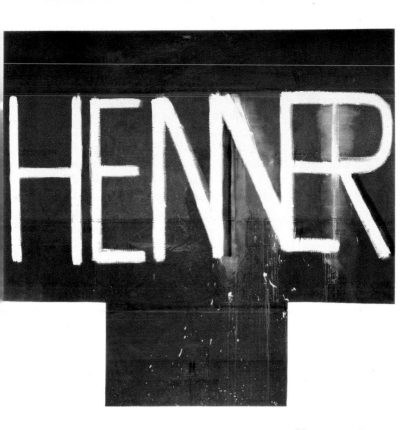

Henner, *1987.*
Gesso and oil on
tarpaulin, 132 x
144 inches.
Fractional interest
gift, Peter M.
Brant. 92.3985

"Every artist must be allowed to mold a picture out of nothing but blotting paper, for example, provided he is capable of molding a picture."

Kurt Schwitters

b. 1887, Hannover, Prussia; d. 1948, Kendal, England

An artist, poet, and typographer, Kurt Schwitters invented his own unique aesthetic style, which he dubbed Merz in 1919. Premised on the practice of assemblage—the union of sundry quotidian items with formal artistic elements—Merz exemplified Schwitters's quest for "freedom from all fetters," cultural, political, or social. The artist's collages, of which he produced more than 2,000, and his large-scale reliefs known as *Merzbilder* are kaleidoscopic, sometimes whimsical accretions of humble found material— tram tickets, ration coupons, postage stamps, beer labels, candy wrappers, newspaper clippings, fabric swatches, rusty nails, and the like—that bespeak the flux of contemporary society. In his early collages, such as *Merz 163, with Woman Sweating* and *Merz 199*, Schwitters subjected his bits of flotsam to an organizing principle resembling the vertical scaffolding of Analytic Cubism, thus transforming the diverse components into formal elements. Embedded in each collage, however, are hints of narrative.

Merzbild 5B (Picture-Red-Heart-Church) contains many such abbreviated clues, which suggest that Schwitters was not the neutral, disengaged artist described by some historians. The graphic motifs—a red heart, a simple church, and the number "69"—can all be found in Schwitters's Dadaesque line drawings dating from the same year, which contain elements that are possibly autobiographical. Their reappearance in this collaged construction suggests the artist's dedication to his subject matter. The work also harbors specifically political intimations: it includes the partially concealed front page of the German newspaper *Hannoverischer Kurier* dated February 4, 1919 and describing the overthrow of the short-lived socialist republic of Bremen in a bloody insurrection led by conservative forces. Although Schwitters was not directly involved in this conflict, his acquaintance Ludwig Bäumer, about whom he created a Merz portrait in 1920, was a leading advocate of proletarian liberation. Bäumer's politicized, utopian aspirations were analogous, in a sense, to Schwitters's optimistic embrace of Merz as an aesthetic metaphor for free will. The artist even applied his strategy of accumulation to his own home, creating the fantastic, multicomponent, fully sculptural *Merzbau* in the interior of his house.

—N. S.

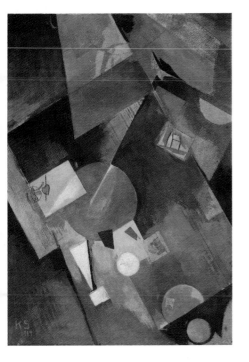

Merzbild 5B
(Picture-Red-
Heart-Church),
*April 26, 1919.
Collage, tempera,
and crayon on
cardboard, 32 ⁷/₈ x
23 ³/₄ inches.*
52.1325

Merz 163,
with Woman
Sweating, *1920.
Tempera, pencil,
paper, and fabric
collage, mounted on
paper, 6 ¹/₈ x 4 ⁷/₈
inches. Gift,
Katherine S. Dreier
Estate.* 53.1348

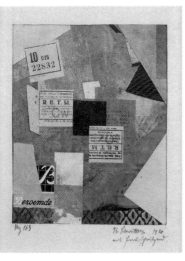

Merz 199, *1921.
Papers, fabrics, and
paint, on
newspaper, 7 ¹/₁₆ x
5 ¹¹/₁₆ inches. Gift,
Katherine S. Dreier
Estate.* 53.1350

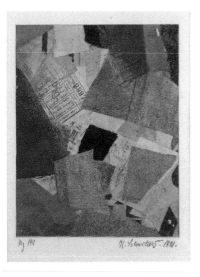

*"In all my work the
construction process
is revealed.
Material, formal,
contextual decisions
are self-evident."*

Richard Serra

b. 1939, San Francisco

Richard Serra created *Belts*—tangled clusters of
vulcanized rubber strips illuminated by an erratic
curl of neon tubing—shortly after returning from
a year of study in Italy, where he undoubtedly
witnessed the very beginnings of Arte Povera.
Like the artists who would come to be associated
with that movement, Serra employed nontraditional materials in his sculpture, in this case
belts suspended from hooks on the wall. The
piece's anthropomorphic quality—the belts
suggest limp figures or twisted harnesses—
indicates that Serra was also familiar with
contemporaneous sculptural reflections on the
human body made by Eva Hesse and Bruce
Nauman. Serra's style would change radically in
the ensuing years, but his sensitivity to the body,
its capacity for action, and its crucial role in
perception has remained a constant in the work.

Serra envisions sculpture as the physical
manifestation of transitive verbs. In 1967 and
1968 he compiled a list of infinitives that served
as catalysts for subsequent work: "to hurl"
suggested the hurling of molten lead into crevices
between wall and floor; "to roll" led to the rolling
of the material into dense, metal logs. While the
process of fabricating these pieces was, in essence,
their very subject, Serra eventually deemed them
too picturesque and he shifted strategies once
again. Continuing his employment of lead, Serra
utilized another transitive verb: "to prop." *Right
Angle Prop* is one of numerous lead constructions,
the assemblage of which is dependent on leaning
elements. Dispensing with carving and
welding—conventional methods of delineating
volume and securing mass—Serra created
precarious sculptures that stand by virtue of
equilibrium and gravity. Such pieces exist in a
constant state of tension, ever revealing the
process of their making, ever threatening to tilt
off balance. Following the perilous choreography
of propping, Serra engaged the verb "to cut" in a
series of large-scale steel sculptures, variations of
which he is still producing. *Strike* is essentially
one tall, thin steel slice that, wedged into a
corner, bisects the room and demands viewing
from both sides. As one walks around the front of
the piece, perception continually shifts: plane
gives way to edge to plane again. This cut-steel
sculpture is itself an implement for cutting space
and, in this way, serves as an analogue for the
sculptor himself, who stimulates vision by giving
material form to the transitive verb.

—N. S.

242

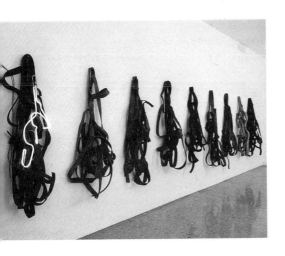

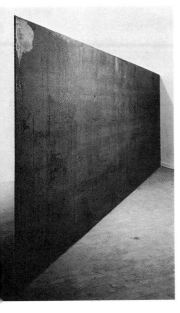

Belts, 1966–67. *Nine groups of vulcanized rubber units, two blue neon tubes, and a neon transformer, 84 x 288 x 20 inches. Panza Collection.* 91.3863

Strike (to Roberta and Rudy), *1969–71. Hot-rolled steel plate, on edge; 96 x 288 x 1 inches. Panza Collection.* 91.3871

Right Angle Prop, *1969. Lead antimony, 72 x 72 x 34 inches. Purchased with funds contributed by The Theodoron Foundation.* 69.1906

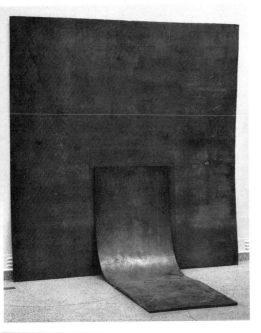

Georges Seurat

b. 1859, Paris; d. 1891, Paris

No understanding of Georges Seurat's development would be complete without consideration of the 85 oil studies he produced in the formative years prior to his first large painting, *Bathers* (1883–84). Agrarian workers and peasants are among the most consistent subjects of these early works, which reflect the important influence of Jean-François Millet, the Barbizon school painter of rural life. *Farm Women at Work* and *Peasant with Hoe* recall Millet's familiar iconographical theme of gleaners in the fields, while *Seated Woman* echoes on a small scale Millet's sense of monumentality.

Unlike Millet, who ventured deep into the countryside, Seurat found his subjects in the suburbs of Paris, which in the 1880s were zones marked by the clash of industrialization and displaced rural life. We may speculate that there is a subtle meaning in these depictions of suburban peasants who have lost their identity to modernization; yet there is also an undeniable reverie in *Farm Women at Work* and *Peasant with Hoe*. Both studies are characterized by the penetrating quality of a moment frozen in time in which the bounty of the harvest, the dignity of labor, and close communion with nature are unified. Seurat achieved his synthesis through innovative coloristic and painterly techniques. Working directly in the field, he followed the Impressionists' practice of painting outdoors to capture the fugitive effects of light; he also studied contemporaneous developments in physics, optics, and color theory assiduously. In accordance with scientific thinking, he applied pure hues rather than premixed pigments to the canvas and employed the technique of "optical mixing," in which complementary colors "vibrate" when placed in correspondence with one another. At this time, Seurat made his painting surface highly active through the use of short, crosshatched brushstrokes; he subsequently distilled these brushstrokes into tiny dots, a method now known as Pointillism.

—J. A.

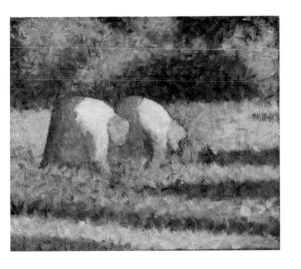

Farm Women at
Work, *ca. 1882.*
Oil on canvas,
15 ¹/₈ x 18 ¹/₄
inches. Gift,
Solomon R.
Guggenheim.
41.713

Peasant with
Hoe, *1882. Oil on*
canvas, 18 ¹/₄ x
22 ¹/₈ inches. Gift,
Solomon R.
Guggenheim.
41.716

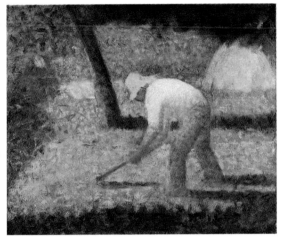

Seated Woman,
1883. Oil on
canvas, 15 x 18
inches. Gift,
Solomon R.
Guggenheim.
37.714

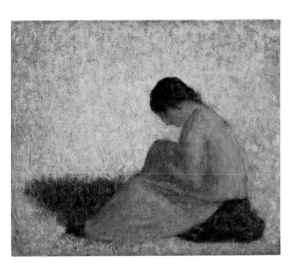

"All subjects previously used must be swept aside in order to express our whirling life of steel, of pride, of fever and of speed."

Gino Severini

b. 1883, Cortona, Italy; d. 1966, Paris

After moving from Rome to Paris in 1906, Gino Severini came into close contact with Georges Braque, Pablo Picasso, and the other leading artists of the avant-garde capital, while staying in touch with his compatriots who remained in Italy. In 1910 he signed the *Futurist Painting: Technical Manifesto* with four other Italian artists, Giacomo Balla, Umberto Boccioni, Carlo Carrà, and Luigi Russolo, who wanted their paintings to express the energy and speed of modern life.

In this painting of a train moving through the countryside, Severini split the landscape in order to impart a sense of the momentary fractured images that characterize our perception of a speeding object. The clash of intense contrasting colors suggests the noise and power of the train, which the Futurists admired as an emblem of vitality and potency.

Severini's paintings—like Futurist work in general—are informed by the legacy of Cubism, building on the Cubists' deconstruction of the motif, their collage technique, and their incorporation of graphic signs. But the Futurists' interest in depicting motion, use of bright expressive color, and politically inspired dedication to bridging the gap between art and life departed decisively from Cubist aesthetic practice, which focused on the rarefied world of the studio, investigating formal issues through often-somber portraits and still lifes.

Severini painted this canvas in the midst of World War I while living in Igny, outside Paris. Years later he recalled the circumstances: "Next to our hovel, trains were passing day and night, full of war matériel, or soldiers, and wounded." During 1915 he created many canvases in which he attempted to evoke war in paint, culminating in his January 1916 *First Futurist Exhibition of Plastic Art of the War*. This exhibition, held in Paris, included *Red Cross Train Passing a Village*.

—J. B.

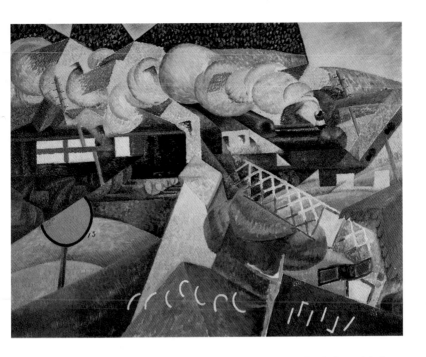

Red Cross Train
Passing a Village,
*summer 1915. Oil
on canvas, 35 x
45 3/4 inches.*
44.944

"My sculpture is part of my world. It's part of my everyday living; it reflects my studio, my house, my trees, the nature of the world I live in."

David Smith

b. 1906, Decatur, Ind.; d. 1965, near Bennington, Vt.

David Smith was foremost among the welder-sculptors who came to prominence in the U.S. after World War II. Following the example set by Pablo Picasso and Julio González, who created welded-steel sculptures as early as 1928, the Americans constructed their work directly out of iron and steel sheets and wires rather than employing the traditional method of casting. In the 1930s and 1940s, influenced by Surrealism and Constructivism, Smith created hybrid figural sculptures and dramatic mise-en-scènes. During the 1950s he began to work in stylistic series ranging from the complicated abstract drawings-in-space of the *Agricolas* to the anthropomorphic and totemic sculptures incorporating machine parts such as the *Sentinels* and *Tank Totems*. In the later part of the decade and into the 1960s his work became more volumetric and monolithic.

Smith completed 28 works in his last series of monumental abstract structures, the *Cubis*, before his death in May 1965. These celebrated sculptures were composed from a repertoire of geometric cubes and cylinders of varying proportions. All of the *Cubis* are made of stainless steel, which Smith burnished to a highly reflective surface. He told critic Thomas Hess, "I made them and I polished them in such a way that on a dull day they take on a dull blue, or the color of the sky in the late afternoon sun, the glow, golden like the rays, the colors of nature."

Some of the *Cubis* are vaguely figural, while others, such as *Cubi XXVII*, suggest architecture. This example is one of three *Cubis* usually referred to as "Gates" (although Smith called them "arches"), which rise like giant rudimentary doorways framing a central void. By counterbalancing a cylinder that appears to rest precariously on edge with two small tilted blocks that look equally unstable, Smith emphasized the potential energy captured through the welding technique. The artist activated the surface of the structure through the curling traces left by the polishing process, creating, in his words, "a structure that can face the sun and hold its own against the blaze and the power."

—J. B.

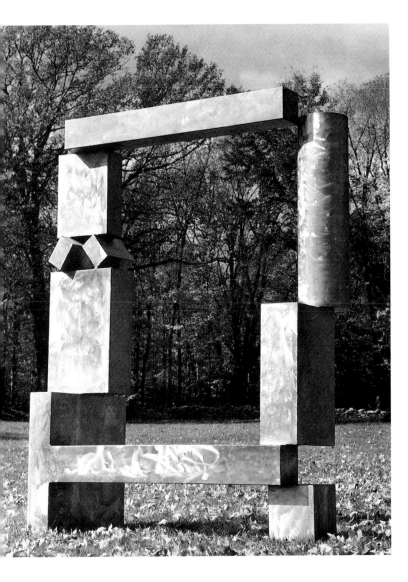

Cubi XXVII,
March 1965.
Stainless steel,
111 3/8 x 87 3/4 x
34 inches. By
exchange. 67.1862

Spiritual

Much abstract art created in the opening decades of the 20th century emanated from artists' personal, passionate belief in the expression of spiritual issues via a non-objective language. In Germany, beginning around 1910–11, Vasily Kandinsky gradually abandoned recognizable forms, replacing them with obscured motifs dictated by what he called "inner aspiration." The writings of Helena P. Blavatsky and others in the Theosophical movement, which encouraged a deeper understanding of the relationship between nature and the spirit, profoundly influenced Kandinsky, as did the teachings of Anthroposophy's founder, Rudolf Steiner, who identified specific paths by which people could perceive spiritual worlds. Kandinsky in turn was inspired to write his 1911 treatise *On the Spiritual in Art*.

The Dutch artist Piet Mondrian's association with Theosophy encouraged him to develop non-objective imagery. His early works of 1908 to 1911 incorporate references to Theosophical notions about man's place in a spiritual hierarchy and progression toward higher insight. His grid paintings reduce this spiritual hierarchy to horizontal and vertical elements, primary colors, and black and white. In Russia Kazimir Malevich and his followers sought in their Suprematist paintings to capture visual equivalents for his notion of *zaum*, a state "beyond reason."

Dada and Surrealist artists were attracted to spiritual, occult, and mystical issues as well, although such elements make intermittent, rather than programmatic, appearances in their work. Many of these artists were profoundly affected by Freudian and/or Jungian analysis and alchemical and biomorphic studies, interests that were shared by postwar artists. Jackson Pollock's involvement with psychoanalysis and his fascination with Native American rituals were both manifested in his mythic paintings of the 1940s. Mark Rothko and Barnett Newman shared Pollock's fascination with "primitive" cultures, and their most abstract paintings may be linked, via their symbol-laden early works, to their psychoanalytical and tribal studies.

The contemporary painter Frank Stella prefers an abstraction characterized by what the audience perceives. Indeed the viewer's personal response becomes the spiritual arena addressed by much recent art, including Robert Ryman's gridded voids, the glowing environments generated by Dan Flavin's works, or Walter De Maria's symbolic configurations.

—Judi Freeman

Mark Rothko, Untitled (Violet, Black, Orange, Yellow on White and Red) *(detail).*

Haim Steinbach

b. 1944, Rechovot, Israel

Haim Steinbach's shelf sculptures are devices of endless variety, but their parameters are fixed. Typically, Steinbach chooses banal objects from everyday life and arranges them on plastic-laminated triangular-wedge shelving units. The interior angles of the triangular units are constant—90, 50, and 40 degrees—and they always relate to the objects on top through volume and color. Steinbach has proposed parallels between the structure of his works and game boards, the sequence of pitches in musical scales, and the arrangement of goods on department-store shelves.

Ultra red #2, a typical Steinbach shelf sculpture, features four ruby-golden lava lamps, nine russet cooking pots, and six digital alarm clocks with blinking scarlet readouts. Just as the lava lamps and clocks continuously mutate, so too *ultra red #2* resists any fixed meaning. A fundamental issue it raises is one of language. The title, perhaps citing the names given to paint colors, focuses attention on an element that is common to the objects and the shelves—they are all some shade of red. Steinbach's approach to "red" is similar to that of the linguist remarking on the many words for "snow" used by the Eskimos. It is an anthropological perspective. Steinbach is fascinated by the way physical reality invariably shapes local linguistic or cultural customs. Because "red" exists as an idea above and beyond its infinite physical variations, we can refer to the cooking pots and lava lamps as red, and thereby find a link between them.

Steinbach's work has often been understood in terms of its implied commentary on consumer culture and on the hidden aesthetic in consumer products. *Ultra red #2* bears this out with its reference to design from the 1960s through the 1980s. But this accounts for only one aspect of the work. Steinbach highlights the contiguous illogic of the placement of objects in the world, arranging the elements of his sculptures to reflect their original accidental juxtapositions. He has also explored other kinds of juxtapositions, using objects as metaphors for race, age, and culture.

By using items that are readily available and easily replaceable, Steinbach tries to undermine the fetishizing of the art object. This monumental triptych made of household wares suggests that the artistic stacking of forms is as relative a construction as the development of different dialects.

—C. L.

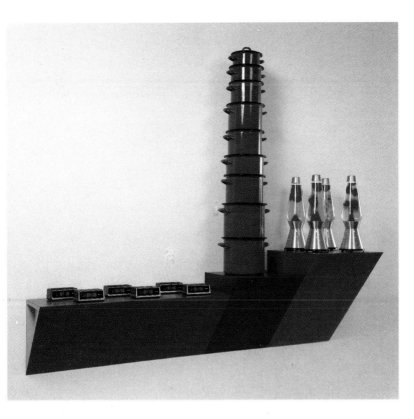

ultra red #2,
1986. Wood,
plastic laminates,
four lava lamps,
nine enamel pots,
and six digital
clocks, 67 x 76 x
19 inches. Gift,
Barbara and
Eugene Schwartz.
88.3619

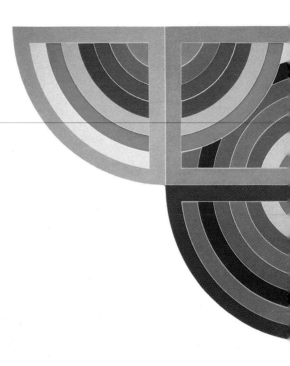

"My main interest
{in these pictures}
has been to make
what is popularly
called decorative
painting truly
viable in
unequivocal
abstract terms.
Decorative, that is,
in the good sense,
in the sense that it
is applied to
Matisse."

Frank Stella

b. 1936, Malden, Mass.

In the late 1950s and early 1960s, Frank Stella
broke the stronghold of Abstract Expressionism
with his deceptively simple paintings of black
stripes separated by narrow lines of unpainted
canvas. With their emphasis on control and
rationalism, the *Black Paintings* opened genuinely
new paths for abstraction and exerted a profound
influence on the art of the 1960s. A major shift
from this work began to develop in 1966 with his
Irregular Polygons, canvases in the shapes of
irregular geometric forms and characterized by
large unbroken areas of color. As this new
vocabulary developed into a more open and color-
oriented pictorial language, the works underwent
a metamorphosis in size, expressing an affinity
with architecture in their monumentality. Stella
also introduced curves into his works, marking
the beginning of the *Protractor* series. *Harran II*
evinces the great vaulting compositions and
lyrically decorative patterns that are the leitmotif
of the series, which is based on the semicircular
drafting instrument used for measuring and
constructing angles.

Most of the paintings' titles are taken from
the names of ancient cities in Asia Minor. A
Roman numeral following the title indicates
which of three design groups—"interlaces,"
"rainbows," and "fans"—encompasses its surface
patterning. *Harran II* is composed of a full circle
formed of two vertical protractors, each of which
interlocks with a horizontal protractor shape. In

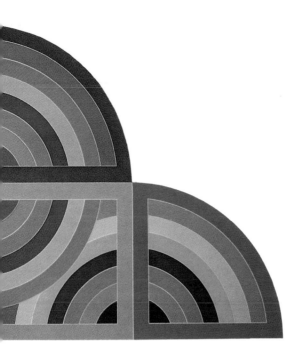

Harran II, 1967.
Polymer and fluorescent polymer paint on canvas, 120 x 240 inches. Gift, Mr. Irving Blum. 82.2976

turn, each protractor-shaped area contains eight concentric circular bands—the "rainbows"—that articulate the surface of the canvas.

Although the dominant motifs of the *Protractor* series are circular or curvilinear, every shape is actually defined by pairs of horizontal and vertical lines that intersect at right angles; the gridded rectilinear pattern that is formed is superimposed over the decorative arcs. Through the device of the protractor and the use of almost psychedelic color—a combination of acrylic and fluorescent pigments—Stella brought abstraction and decorative pattern painting into congruence in a manner that challenged the conventions of both traditions.

—J. A.

Antoni Tàpies

b. 1923, Barcelona

In the years after World War II, both Europe and America saw the rise of predominantly abstract painting concerned with materials and the expression of gesture and marking. New Yorkers dubbed the development in the U.S. Abstract Expressionism, while the French named the pan-European phenomenon of gestural painting Art Informel (literally "unformed art"). A variety of the latter was Tachisme, from the French word "tache," meaning a stain or blot. Antoni Tàpies was among the artists to receive the label Tachiste because of the rich texture and pooled color that seemed to occur accidentally on his canvases.

"And the most sensational surprise came when I suddenly discovered one day that my pictures, for the first time, had turned into walls."

Tàpies reevaluates humble materials, things of the earth such as sand—which he used in *Great Painting*—and the refuse of humanity: string, bits of fabric, and straw. By calling attention to this seemingly inconsequential matter, he suggests that beauty can be found in unlikely places. Tàpies sees his works as objects of meditation that every viewer will interpret according to personal experience. "What I do attempt," he maintains, "is to create images that will cause the observer to look upon reality in a more contemplative way."

These images often resemble walls that have been scuffed and marred by human intervention and the passage of time. In *Great Painting*, an ocher skin appears to hang off the surface of the canvas; violence is suggested by the gouge and puncture marks in the dense stratum. These markings recall the scribbling of graffiti, perhaps referring to the public walls covered with slogans and images of protest that the artist saw as a youth in Catalonia—a region in Spain that knew the harshest repression of the dictator Francisco Franco. Tàpies has called walls the "witnesses of the martyrdoms and inhuman sufferings inflicted on our people." *Great Painting* suggests the artist's poetic memorial to those who have perished and those who have endured.

—J. B.

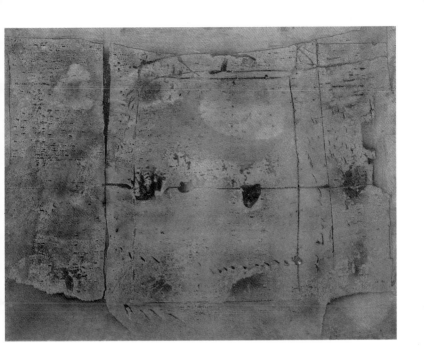

Great Painting,
1958. *Mixed
media on canvas,
78 ½ x 103
inches. 59.1551*

Theme and Variation

Until the Modern period, artists usually sought to underplay the mechanisms of composition and craft in order to emphasize the subject. By contrast, little 20th-century art is so understated or deadpan, and smoothly wrought renderings of a theme are rare. Instead, it is the variation, the reinterpretation with its rough edges and uneven surfaces, that prevails. Jasper Johns's statement—"Take an object. Do something to it. Do something else to it."—could be the anthem of much 20th-century art.

Whether one is contemplating a work of art classified as Impressionist, Cubist, Expressionist, Surrealist, or even Pop, one is almost always viewing a theme stated in such a way that its very making is as important and as obvious as the subject. Thus, a patch of sky becomes a triangle of red in a view of Paris by Marc Chagall, or a mouth is shown as a distended oval in a triptych by Francis Bacon. The work of art is a record of an artist's hand as it simplifies, fragments, abstracts, distorts, or even dissects a subject. Artists revel in their craft, overtly emphasizing lines, colors, brushstrokes, forms, and materials.

This activity may represent either a playful or serious investigation of a theme. We observe an accordion transformed into a collection of rectangular folds in Pablo Picasso's *Accordionist*, while a breast becomes a perfectly formed circle in Fernand Léger's *Woman Holding a Vase*. Paul Klee penetrates an operatic scene for its underlying dramatic rhythm and Max Beckmann examines the insidious air of Paris society. Qualities that cannot be observed in a perceptual recording are elaborated in the variation, as unseen "inner" aspects of a theme may lie side by side with the "outer" ones on the same picture plane.

With these freely inspired variations, artists invite participation in a way virtually unknown in the history of art. The viewer is persuaded, if not cajoled, into unraveling the work of art, reconvening in the mind's eye the constituent parts of the initial theme, recognizing the representational sources of purely pictorial elements, and vice versa. The aesthetic experience is made into a mental exercise, replete with clues, conundrums, and witty repartee. Relishing the rich interplay between life and art, the artist makes a fusion of the two the true subject of the work. A new kind of virtuosity is evident, in which the rendering of a theme may be less significant than the brilliance of its variation.

—Mark Rosenthal

Hans Hofmann, The Gate *(detail).*

"Every line is thus the actual experience with its unique story. It does not illustrate; it is the perception of its own realization."

Cy Twombly

b. 1929, Lexington, Va.

Cy Twombly's paintings of the early 1960s consist of white canvases upon which he has applied scribblings and scratches in a furious flurry of crayon, pencil, and paint. The pigments are squeezed from the tube, remaining as globules that appear to hang tenuously from the surface or, as in *Untitled*, ejaculations of paint that drip off the canvas and are invaded by crayon and pencil smears. Like Robert Rauschenberg and Jasper Johns, Twombly employed the Abstract Expressionists' liberating aleatory use of paint, but without their heroic pretensions or universalist goals. Twombly and his colleagues utilized an iconography of everyday life (such as representations of numbers and letters) and incorporated found objects into their work, embracing banal methods such as stenciling. The suggestion of carelessness and defilement inherent in Twombly's paintings (they elicit comparisons with the sexual graffiti in a public latrine) is also present in the work of Rauschenberg, with whom Twombly traveled to Italy in 1953.

In 1957 Twombly settled in Rome, where he inspired a small school of calligraphic painters. Some of the main elements of his mature works—the graffitilike writing on a surface that suggests a wall, and an emphasis on the material properties of his mediums—dovetail with the leading concerns of continental painters, particularly of those associated with Informale (the Italian equivalent of Art Informel). Twombly's work is filled with references to his adopted home as well as to a broader neoclassical tradition; he often alludes to mythological subjects, Old Master painters, and local places or events through his titles and scrawled words or phrases on the surfaces of the works. Idyllic landscapes and their connotation of bacchanalian pleasures have consistently provided Twombly with inspiration. The palette of his *Untitled*, for example, bears the faint echo of an 18th-century painting of a fête champêtre by Boucher or Fragonard in which sensual youths with powdered hair and strawberry-and-cream complexions gambol in sylvan glades, the breezy subject loaded with erotic innuendo. In Twombly's painting the explosive sexual charge of splatters and scribbles is complicated by a hermetic language of modern charts and graphs as if, according to art critic Roberta Smith, "an overeducated bibliophiliac suddenly—graphically, nearly obscenely—[speaks] in tongues."

—J. B.

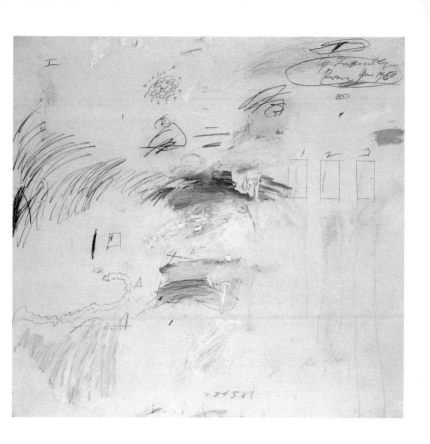

Untitled, *June 1960. Oil, pencil, and oil stick on canvas, 37 ¹/₂ x 40 ¹/₁₆ inches. Gift, Michael and Elizabeth Rea.* 91.3975

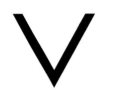

Vincent van Gogh

b. 1853, Groot-Zundert, The Netherlands; d. 1890, Auvers, France

During the years preceding his suicide in 1890, Vincent van Gogh suffered increasingly frequent attacks of mental distress, the cause of which remains unclear. *Mountains at Saint-Rémy* was painted in July 1889, when van Gogh was recovering from just such an episode at the hospital of Saint-Paul-de-Mausole in the southern French town of Saint-Rémy. The painting represents the Alpilles, a low range of mountains visible from the hospital grounds. In it, van Gogh activated the terrain and sky with the heavy impasto and bold, broad brushstrokes characteristic of his late work.

Van Gogh advocated painting from nature rather than inventing a motif from the imagination. On a personal level, he felt that painting outdoors would help to restore his health, a sentiment he often voiced when writing to his brother, Theo. He mentioned this painting several times in his letters, relating it to a passage from Edouard Rod's *Le Sens de la vie*. In one note he wrote, "I rather like the 'Entrance to a Quarry'—I was doing it when I felt this attack coming on—because to my mind the somber greens go well with the ocher tones; there is something sad in it which is healthy, and that is why it does not bore me. Perhaps that is true of the 'Mountain' too. They will tell me that mountains are not like that and that there are black outlines of a finger's width. But after all it seemed to me it expressed the passage in Rod's book . . . about a desolate country of somber mountains, among which are some dark goatherds' huts where sunflowers are blooming."

Nature had a quasi-religious or transcendental significance for van Gogh. Unlike the earlier Impressionists, who often painted urban life, van Gogh felt that the city, in particular Paris, was a place of iniquity, inherently unhealthful. In the face of industrialization and modernization (the Eiffel Tower was built the same year that this canvas was painted) van Gogh longed nostalgically for a rural environment peopled with good-natured, God-fearing peasants such as those painted by Jean-François Millet, one of his heroes. This utopian ideal, based on a belief in the regenerative capacity of a "primitive" culture, was shared by van Gogh's friend Paul Gauguin, who sought redemption farther from home, among the people of Tahiti.

—J. B.

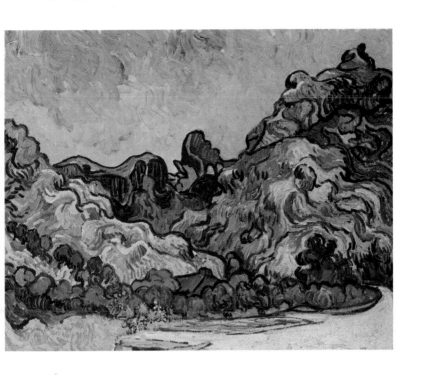

Mountains at
Saint-Rémy, *July
1889. Oil on
canvas, 28 ¹/₄ x
35 ³/₄ inches.
Thannhauser
Collection, Gift,
Justin K.
Thannhauser.
78.2514 T24*

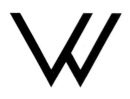

Andy Warhol
b. 1928, Pittsburgh; d. 1987, New York City

Andy Warhol announced his disengagement from the process of aesthetic creation in 1963: "I think somebody should be able to do all my paintings for me," he told art critic G. R. Swenson. The Abstract Expressionists had seen the artist as a heroic figure, alone capable of imparting his poetic vision of the world through gestural abstraction. Warhol, like other Pop artists, used found printed images from newspapers, publicity stills, and advertisements as his subject matter; he adopted silkscreening, a technique of mass reproduction, as his medium. And unlike the Abstract Expressionists, who searched for a spiritual pinnacle in their art, Warhol aligned himself with the signs of contemporary mass culture. His embrace of subjects traditionally considered debased—from celebrity worship to food labels—has been interpreted as both an exuberant affirmation of American culture and a thoughtless espousal of the "low." The artist's perpetual examination of themes of death and disaster suggest yet another dimension to his art.

Warhol was preoccupied with news reports of violent death—suicides, car crashes, assassinations, and executions. In the early 1960s he began to make paintings, such as *Orange Disaster*, with the serial application of images revolving around the theme of death. "When you see a gruesome picture over and over again," he commented, "it doesn't really have any effect." Yet *Orange Disaster*, with its electric chair repeated 15 times, belies this statement. Warhol's painting speaks to the constant reiteration of tragedy in the media, and becomes, perhaps, an attempt to exorcise this image of death through repetition. However, it also emphasizes the pathos of the empty chair waiting for its next victim, the jarring orange only accentuating the horror of the isolated seat in a room with a sign blaring SILENCE.

Warhol's death and disaster pictures underscore the importance of the vanitas theme—that death will take us all—in his oeuvre. Even his images of movie idols carry this connotation; many of the stars were dead (literally or at the box office) at the time the artist made his paintings. Warhol's vanitas imagery has a particularly American cast: he recorded American disasters, the consumption of American products (including movie stars), and, as art historian Sidra Stich has pointed out, uniquely American modes of death, such as execution by electrocution.

—J. B.

"I realized that everything I was doing must have been Death."

264

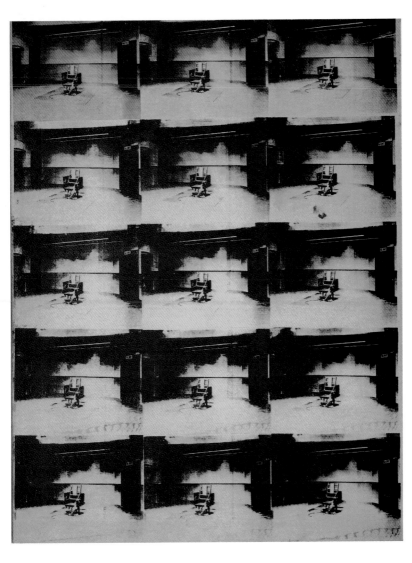

Orange Disaster,
1963. *Acrylic and*
silkscreen enamel on
canvas, 106 x
81 ¹/₂ inches. Gift,
Harry N. Abrams
Family Collection.
74.2118

Z

Gilberto Zorio

b. 1944, Andorno Micca, Italy

Gilberto Zorio exhibited his seminal work *Pink-Blue-Pink* in a Turin art gallery in 1967, just prior to his association with the Arte Povera group. Consisting of a concrete basin filled with cobalt chloride (which perpetually changes color in response to shifting levels of humidity in the room), the work reveals much about Zorio's concerns as an artist as well as his place within the development of contemporary Italian art. In art-historical terms, *Pink-Blue-Pink* refers to the works of the Italian enfant terrible Piero Manzoni, who used cobalt chloride in some of his radical wall pieces (known as *Achromes*) in order to redefine painting and its traditional role as a conveyor of predetermined meanings. *Pink-Blue-Pink* marks a continuation of the attempt to reconfigure art's role in society by demonstrating its essential malleability. The emphasis on instability and metamorphoses apparent in *Pink-Blue-Pink* would become the leitmotif of Zorio's subsequent artistic undertakings. Drawing upon the ancient science of alchemy for both form and content, he has created an oeuvre in which materials associated with chemical conversions—vessels containing water, alcohol, acids, and copper sulfate connected by suspended copper conduits—have become symbols for psychic and social transmutation. Zorio's belief in the potential for cultural change through art is apparent in the title *Per purificare le parole (To Purify Words)*, which he has applied to numerous sculptures and performances since 1968.

Zorio's notion that language can be emptied of all extraneous or corrupt facets finds a visual analogue in his work, which can be reduced to an essential symbolic typology that he combines and recombines. His fundamental aesthetic vocabulary consists of the star, which alludes to the metaphysical; the javelin, which represents mortal power; and the canoe, which suggests passage between the two realms. However utopian this project may seem, one remains aware that danger and violence constitute the underside of beauty and of harmony. Perhaps this is why Zorio pierced the broken terra-cotta star with a javelin in *Star (To Purify Words)*.

—N. S.

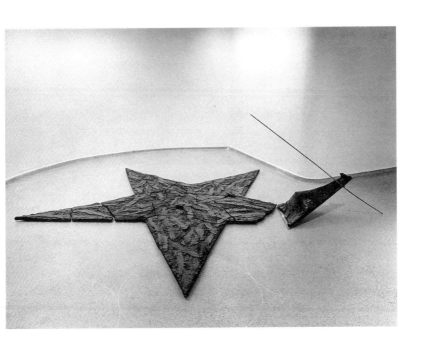

Star (To Purify
Words), *1980.*
Terra-cotta and
metal, 26 pieces,
diameter 195
inches. Exxon
Corporation
Purchase Award
with additional
funds contributed by
Sonnabend Gallery,
New York.
82.2921.a-.z

Suggested Readings

Many of the art works reproduced in this book have been fully documented in the following Guggenheim Museum publications. In some cases, the authors used these books as primary sources. They will also be of interest to the reader seeking additional information on the collection.

Barnett, Vivian Endicott. *The Guggenheim Museum: Justin K. Thannhauser Collection*. New York, 1978.

———. *Handbook: The Guggenheim Museum Collection 1900–1980*. New York, 1984.

Rudenstine, Angelica Zander. *The Guggenheim Museum Collection: Paintings 1880–1945*. 2 vols. New York, 1976.

The following books and articles are suggested for those readers seeking additional information or viewpoints on the artists whose works are discussed in this guidebook. In many cases they were used by the authors as they wrote their entries.

Josef Albers
Albers, Josef. *Interaction of Color*. New Haven, 1971.

Bucher, François. *Josef Albers: Despite Straight Lines: An Analysis of His Graphic Constructions*. New Haven, 1961.

Solomon R. Guggenheim Museum. *Josef Albers: A Retrospective*. New York, 1988.

Hamilton, George Heard. *Josef Albers: Paintings, Prints, Projects*. New Haven, 1956.

Spies, Werner. *Albers*. New York, 1970.

Carl Andre
Fuchs, Rudi H. *Carl Andre: Wood*. Eindhoven, 1978.

Solomon R. Guggenheim Museum. *Carl Andre*. New York, 1970.

Laguna Gloria Art Museum. *Carl Andre: Sculpture 1959–1977*. Austin, 1978.

Ida Applebroog
Contemporary Arts Museum, Houston. *Ida Applebroog: Happy Families*. Houston, 1990.

Ronald Feldman Fine Arts. *Ida Applebroog*. New York, 1987.

Schor, Mira. "Medusa Redux: Ida Applebroog and the Spaces of Post-Modernity." *Artforum* 28, no. 7 (March 1990), pp. 116–22.

Alexander Archipenko
National Gallery of Art and The Tel Aviv Museum. *Alexander Archipenko, A Centennial Tribute*. Washington, D.C. and Tel Aviv, 1986.

Reff, Theodore. "Harlequins, Saltimbanques, Clowns and Fools." *Artforum* 10, no. 2 (Oct. 1971), pp. 30–43.

Jean Arp

Arp, Jean. *Arp on Arp: Poems, Essays, Memories*. Ed. Marcel Jean. Trans. Joachim Neugroschel. New York, 1972.

The Minneapolis Institute of Arts. *Arp, 1886–1966*. Minneapolis, 1987.

Francis Bacon

Ades, Dawn, and Andrew Forge. *Francis Bacon*. New York, 1985.

Moorhouse, Paul. "The Crucifixion in Bacon's Art, 'A Magnificent Armature.'" *Art International*, no. 8 (autumn 1989), pp. 23–27.

Sylvester, David. *The Brutality of Fact: Interviews with Francis Bacon*. London, 1987.

Georg Baselitz

Collaboration Georg Baselitz. *Parkett*, no. 11 (Dec. 1986), pp. 28–97.

Franzke, Andreas. *Georg Baselitz*. Trans. David Britt. Munich, 1989.

Fundación Caja de Pensiones. *Georg Baselitz*. Barcelona, 1990.

Whitechapel Art Gallery. *Georg Baselitz: Paintings 1960–83*. London, 1983.

William Baziotes

Hadler, Mona. "William Baziotes: A Contemporary Poet-Painter." *Arts Magazine* 51, no. 10 (June 1977), pp. 102–10.

Weiss, Jeffrey. "Science and Primitivism: A Fearful Symmetry in the Early New York School." *Arts Magazine* 57, no. 7 (March 1983), pp. 81–87.

Bernd and Hilla Becher

Andre, Carl. "A Note on Bernhard and Hilla Becher." *Artforum* 11, no. 4 (Dec. 1972), pp. 59–61.

Arts Council of Great Britain. *Bernd and Hilla Becher*. London, 1974.

Becher, Bernd, and Hilla Becher. *Water Towers*. Cambridge, Mass., 1988.

Stedelijk van Abbemuseum. *Bernd and Hilla Becher*. Eindhoven, 1981.

Max Beckmann

Buenger, Barbara C. "Max Beckmann's Ideologues: Some Forgotten Faces." *The Art Bulletin* 71, no. 3 (Sept. 1989), pp. 453–79.

Phelan, Anthony, ed. *The Weimar Dilemma: Intellectuals in the Weimar Republic*. Manchester and Dover, N. H., 1985.

Joseph Beuys

Adriani, Götz, Winfried Konnertz, and Karin Thomas. *Joseph Beuys: Life and Works*. Trans. Patricia Lech. Woodbury, N. Y., 1979.

Stachelhaus, Heiner. *Joseph Beuys*. New York, 1991.

Tisdall, Caroline. *Joseph Beuys*. New York, 1979.

Pierre Bonnard
Newman, Sasha M., ed. *Bonnard, The Late Paintings*. New York and London, 1984.

Louise Bourgeois
Collaboration Louise Bourgeois and Robert Gober. *Parkett*, no. 27 (March 1991), pp. 26–76.

Meyer-Thoss, Christiane. *Louise Bourgeois: Designing for the Free Fall*. Zurich, 1991.

The Museum of Modern Art. *Louise Bourgeois*. New York, 1982.

Constantin Brancusi
Balas, Edith. *Brancusi and Rumanian Folk Traditions*. Boulder, 1987.

Geist, Sidney. *Brancusi: The Sculpture and Drawings*. New York, 1975.

Hulten, Pontus, Natalia Dumitresco, and Alexandre Istrati. *Brancusi*. New York, 1987.

Georges Braque
Cooper, Douglas. *The Cubist Epoch*. London, 1970.

Golding, John. *Cubism: A History and an Analysis, 1907–1914*. New York, 1959.

Solomon R. Guggenheim Museum. *Georges Braque*. New York, 1988.

Rubin, William. *Picasso and Braque: Pioneering Cubism*. New York, 1989.

Alberto Burri
Brandi, Cesare. *Burri*. Trans. Martha Leeb Hadzi. Rome, 1963.

Calvesi, Maurizio. *Alberto Burri*. Trans. Robert E. Wolf. New York, 1975.

Nordland, Gerald. *Alberto Burri: A Retrospective View 1948–77*. Los Angeles, 1977.

Alexander Calder
Calder, Alexander, and Jean Davidson. *Calder: An Autobiography with Pictures*. New York, 1966.

Lipman, Jean. *Calder's Universe*. New York, 1976.

Paul Cézanne
Loran, Erle. *Cézanne's Composition*. Berkeley and Los Angeles, 1943.

Rewald, John. *Cézanne*. New York, 1986.

Rubin, William, ed. *Cézanne: The Late Work*. New York, 1977.

Marc Chagall
Chagall, Marc. *Marc Chagall: My Life*. Trans. Elisabeth Abbott. New York, 1960.

Compton, Susan. *Chagall*. London, 1985.

Rosensaft, Jean Bloch. *Chagall and the Bible*. New York, 1987.

John Chamberlain

John and Mable Ringling Museum of Art. *John Chamberlain: Reliefs 1960–1982.* Sarasota, 1983.

Sylvester, Julie. *John Chamberlain: A Catalogue Raisonné of the Sculpture, 1954–1985.* New York and Los Angeles, 1986.

Tuchman, Phyllis. "An Interview with John Chamberlain." *Artforum* 10, no. 6 (Feb. 1972), pp. 38–43.

Joseph Cornell

Ashton, Dore. *A Joseph Cornell Album.* New York, 1974.

McShine, Kynaston, ed. *Joseph Cornell.* New York, 1980.

Starr, Sandra Leonard. *Joseph Cornell: Art and Metaphysics.* New York, 1982.

Waldman, Diane. *Joseph Cornell.* New York, 1977.

Willem de Kooning

Gaugh, Harry F. *Willem de Kooning.* New York, 1983.

Rosenberg, Harold. *Willem de Kooning.* New York, 1974.

Shapiro, David, and Cecile Shapiro, eds. *Abstract Expressionism: A Critical Record.* Cambridge, England, 1990.

Whitney Museum of American Art. *Willem de Kooning.* New York, 1983.

Robert Delaunay

Buckberrough, Sherry A. *Robert Delaunay: The Discovery of Simultaneity.* Ann Arbor, 1978.

Delaunay, Robert, and Sonia Delaunay. *The New Art of Color: The Writings of Robert and Sonia Delaunay.* Ed. Arthur A. Cohen. Trans. David Shapiro and Arthur A. Cohen. New York, 1978.

Hoog, Michel. *R. Delaunay.* Trans. Alice Sachs. New York, 1976.

Vriesen, Gustav, and Max Imdahl. *Robert Delaunay: Light and Color.* Trans. Maria Pelikan. New York, 1967.

Walter De Maria

De Maria, Walter. "The Lightning Field." *Artforum* 18, no. 8 (April 1980), pp. 52–59.

Museum Boymans-van-Beuningen. *Walter De Maria.* Rotterdam, 1988.

Jim Dine

Kirby, Michael. *Happenings: An Illustrated Anthology.* New York, 1966.

Shapiro, David. *Jim Dine: Painting What One Is.* New York, 1981.

Whitney Museum of American Art. *Blam: The Explosion of Pop, Minimalism, and Performance 1958–1964.* New York, 1984.

Jean Dubuffet

Solomon R. Guggenheim Museum. *Jean Dubuffet: A Retrospective.* New York, 1973.

The Museum of Modern Art. *The Work of Jean Dubuffet.* New York, 1962.

Tate Gallery. *Jean Dubuffet: Paintings.* London, 1966.

Dan Flavin

National Gallery of Canada. *Dan Flavin, fluorescent light, etc. from Dan Flavin.* Ottawa, 1969.

Staatliche Kunsthalle Baden-Baden. *new uses for fluorescent light with diagrams, drawings and prints from Dan Flavin.* Baden-Baden, 1989.

Lucio Fontana

Ballo, Guido. *Lucio Fontana.* New York, 1971.

Cotter, Holland. "Fontana's Post-Dada Operatics." *Art in America* 75, no. 3 (March 1987), pp. 80–85.

Solomon R. Guggenheim Museum. *Lucio Fontana, 1899–1968: A Retrospective.* New York, 1977.

Paul Gauguin

Bretell, Richard, Francoise Cachin, et al. *The Art of Paul Gauguin.* Washington, D.C., 1988.

Solomon-Godeau, Abigail. "Going Native." *Art in America* 77, no. 7 (July 1989), pp. 118–29.

Varnedoe, Kirk. "Gauguin." In *"Primitivism" in 20th Century Art: Affinity of the Tribal and the Modern.* Vol. 1. Ed. William Rubin. New York, 1984, pp. 179–209.

Alberto Giacometti

Hirshhorn Museum and Sculpture Garden. *Alberto Giacometti 1901–1966.* Washington, D.C., 1988.

Krauss, Rosalind. "Giacometti." In *"Primitivism" in 20th-Century Art: Affinity of the Tribal and the Modern.* Vol. 2. Ed. William Rubin. New York, 1984, pp. 503–33.

Lord, James. *Giacometti: A Biography.* New York, 1985.

Gilbert and George

The Baltimore Museum of Art. *Gilbert and George.* Baltimore, 1984.

Collaboration Gilbert and George. *Parkett*, no. 14 (Dec. 1987), pp. 24–83.

Jahn, Wolf. *The Art of Gilbert and George, or: an Aesthetic of Existence.* London, 1989.

Ratcliff, C. *Gilbert and George: The Complete Pictures, 1971–1985.* New York, 1986.

Natalia Goncharova

Bowlt, John E., ed. and trans. *Russian Art of the Avant-Garde: Theory and Criticism 1902–1934*. New York, 1976.

Chamot, Mary. *Goncharova: Stage Designs and Paintings*. London, 1979.

Dabrowski, Magdalena. "The Formation and Development of Rayonism." *Art Journal* 34, no. 3 (spring 1975), pp. 200–7.

Gray, Camilla. Revised by Marian Burleigh-Motley. *The Russian Experiment in Art 1863–1922*. New York, 1986.

Félix González-Torres

Avgikos, Jan. "This is My Body: Félix González-Torres." *Artforum* 29, no. 6 (Feb. 1991), pp. 79–83.

Nikas, Robert. "Félix González-Torres: All the Time in the World." Interview in *Flash Art* 24, no. 161 (Nov./Dec. 1991), pp. 86–89.

Spector, Nancy. "Félix González-Torres." *Galeries Magazine*, no. 42 (April/May 1991), pp. 80–81.

Peter Halley

Halley, Peter. *Collected Essays 1981–1987*. Zurich, 1988.

Miller, John. "Lecture Theatre: Peter Halley's Geometry and the Social." *Artscribe International*, no. 74 (March/April 1989), pp. 64–65.

Wei, Lilly. "Talking Abstract: Part Two." *Art in America* 75, no. 12 (Dec. 1987), pp. 120, 171.

Eva Hesse

Barrette, Bill. *Eva Hesse: Sculpture*. New York, 1989.

Lippard, Lucy. *Eva Hesse*. New York, 1976.

Nemser, Cindy. "An Interview with Eva Hesse." *Artforum* 8, no. 9 (May 1970), pp. 59–63.

Hans Hofmann

Goodman, Cynthia. *Hans Hofmann*. New York, 1986.

Greenberg, Clement. *Hans Hofmann*. Paris, 1961.

Hofmann, Hans. *Search for the Real and other Essays*. Ed. Sarah T. Weeks and Barlett Hays, Jr. Andover, 1948.

Jaffe, Irma B. "A Conversation with Hans Hofmann." *Artforum* 9, no. 5 (Jan. 1971), pp. 34–39.

Jenny Holzer

Evans, Steven. "Not All About Death." *Artscribe International*, no. 76 (summer 1989), pp. 57–59.

Ferguson, Bruce. "Wordsmith: An Interview with Jenny Holzer." *Art in America* 74, no. 12 (Dec. 1986), pp. 108–15.

Foster, Hal. "Subversive Signs." *Art in America* 70, no. 11 (Nov. 1982), pp. 88–92.

Waldman, Diane. *Jenny Holzer*. New York, 1989.

Vasily Kandinsky

Barnett, Vivian Endicott. "Kandinsky and Science: The Introduction of Biological Images in the Paris Period." In *Kandinsky in Paris: 1934–1944*. New York, 1985, pp. 61–87.

―――. *Kandinsky at the Guggenheim*. New York, 1983.

Derouet, Christian. "Kandinsky in Paris: 1934–1944." In *Kandinsky in Paris: 1934–1944*. New York, 1985, pp. 12–60.

Lindsay, Kenneth C., and Peter Vergo, eds. *Kandinsky: Complete Writings on Art*. 2 vols. Boston, 1982.

Long, Rose-Carol Washton. *Kandinsky: The Development of an Abstract Style*. Oxford, 1980.

Ellsworth Kelly

Coplans, John. *Ellsworth Kelly*. New York, 1973.

Anselm Kiefer

Rosenthal, Mark. *Anselm Kiefer*. Chicago and Philadelphia, 1987.

Schjeldahl, Peter. "Anselm Kiefer and the Exodus of the Jews." *Art and Text*, no. 19 (Oct.–Dec. 1985), pp. 5–11.

Ernst Ludwig Kirchner

Gordon, D. E. *Ernst Ludwig Kirchner*. Cambridge, Mass., 1968.

Paul Klee

Aichele, K. Porter. "Paul Klee's Operatic Themes and Variations." *The Art Bulletin* 68, no. 3 (Sept. 1986), pp. 450–66.

Kagan, Andrew. *Paul Klee: Art and Music*. Ithaca and London, 1983.

Lanchner, Carolyn, ed. *Paul Klee*. New York, 1987.

Werckmeister, O. K. *The Making of Paul Klee's Career 1914–1920*. Chicago and London, 1989.

Yves Klein

The Jewish Museum. *Yves Klein*. New York, 1967.

McEvilley, Tom, and Nan Rosenthal, eds. *Yves Klein*. Houston, 1982.

Franz Kline

Gaugh, Harry F. *The Vital Gesture: Franz Kline*. New York, 1985.

Kingsley, April. "Franz Kline: Out of Sight, Out of Mind." *Arts Magazine* 60, no. 9 (May 1986), pp. 41–45.

Oskar Kokoschka

Solomon R. Guggenheim Museum. *Oskar Kokoschka*. New York, 1986.

Joseph Kosuth

Hapgood, Susan. "Joseph Kosuth: Language and its (Dis)contents." *Contemporanea* 2, no. 7 (Oct. 1989), pp. 44–49.

Kosuth, Joseph. *Art After Philosophy and After: Collected Writings, 1966–1990*. Ed. Gabriele Guercio. Cambridge, Mass. and London, 1991.

Jannis Kounellis
Moure, Gloria, ed. *Kounellis*. New York, 1990.

Museum of Contemporary Art. *Jannis Kounellis*. Chicago, 1986.

Barbara Kruger
Owens, Craig. "The Medusa Effect, or, The Specular Ruse." *Art in America* 72, no. 1 (Jan. 1984), pp. 97–105.

Squiers, Carol. "Diversionary (Syn)tactics: Barbara Kruger Has Her Way with Words." *Artnews* 86, no. 2 (Feb. 1987), pp. 76–85.

Wifredo Lam
Day, Holliday T., and Suzanne Garrigues. "Wifredo Lam 1902–1982." In *Art of the Fantastic: Latin America, 1920–1987*. Indianapolis, 1987, pp. 103–6

Fouchet, Max-Pol. *Wifredo Lam*. New York and Barcelona, 1976.

Sims, Lowery. "Wilfredo Lam: Transpositions of the Surrealist Proposition in the Post–World War II Era." *Arts Magazine* 60, no. 4 (Dec. 1985), pp. 21–25.

Yau, John. "Please Wait by the Coatroom: Wifredo Lam in the Museum of Modern Art." *Arts Magazine* 63, no. 4 (Dec. 1988), pp. 56–59.

Fernand Léger
Green, Christopher. *Léger and the Avant-Garde*. New Haven and London, 1976.

Whitechapel Art Gallery. *Fernand Léger: The Later Years*. London, 1988.

Roy Lichtenstein
Alloway, Lawrence. *Lichtenstein*. New York, 1983.

Coplans, John, ed. *Roy Lichtenstein*. New York, 1972.

Swenson, G. R. "What Is Pop Art?: Answers from 8 Painters, Part I." *Artnews* 62, no. 3 (Nov. 1963), pp. 24–27.

Waldman, Diane. *Roy Lichtenstein*. New York, 1971.

Richard Long
Fuchs, R. H. *Richard Long*. New York, 1986.

Kazimir Malevich
National Gallery of Art. *Kazimir Malevich 1878–1935*. Washington, D.C., 1990.

Edouard Manet
Cachin, Françoise, Charles S. Moffett, and Juliet Wilson Bareau. *Manet: 1832–1883*. New York, 1983.

Clark, T. J. *The Painting of Modern Life: Paris in the Art of Manet and His Followers*. New York, 1985.

Hanson, Anne Coffin. *Manet and the Modern Tradition*. New Haven and London, 1977.

Robert Mangold

De Wilde, Edy, and Alexander van Grevenstein. *Robert Mangold: Schilderijen/Paintings 1964–1982*. Amsterdam, 1982.

Gruen, John. "Robert Mangold: A Maker of Images—Nothing More and Nothing Less." *Artnews* 86, no. 6 (summer 1987), pp. 132–38.

Solomon R. Guggenheim Museum. *Robert Mangold*. New York, 1971.

Franz Marc

Levine, Frederick S. *The Apocalyptic Vision: The Art of Franz Marc as German Expressionism*. New York, 1979.

Rosenthal, Mark. *Franz Marc*. Munich, 1989.

Selz, Peter. *German Expressionist Painting*. Berkeley, 1957.

Brice Marden

Poirier, Maurice. "Color-Coded Mysteries." *Artnews* 84, no. 1 (Jan. 1985), pp. 52–61.

Shearer, Linda. "Brice Marden's Paintings." In *Brice Marden*. New York, 1975, pp. 9–27.

Smith, Roberta. "Brice Marden." In *Brice Marden: Paintings, Drawings and Prints 1975–90*. London, 1981, pp. 45–53.

Agnes Martin

Alloway, Lawrence. "Agnes Martin." In *Agnes Martin*. Philadelphia, 1973, pp. 9–12.

Ashton, Dore. "Agnes Martin and . . . " In *Agnes Martin: Paintings and Drawings*. London, 1977, pp. 7–14.

Henri Matisse

Cowart, Jack, and Dominique Fourcade. *Henri Matisse: The Early Years in Nice, 1916–1930*. New York and Washington, D.C., 1986.

Flam, Jack D. *Matisse on Art*. New York, 1978.

———. *Matisse: The Man and His Art, 1869–1918*. Ithaca and London, 1986.

Schneider, Pierre. *Matisse*. Trans. Michael Taylor and Bridget S. Romer. Paris and New York, 1984.

Mario Merz

Celant, Germano. *The Knot: Arte Povera at P. S. 1*. Long Island City, New York, 1985.

———. *Mario Merz*. New York, 1989.

Tisdall, Caroline. "'Materia': The Context of Arte Povera." In *Italian Art of the 20th Century*. London, 1989.

Joan Miró

Dupin, Jacques. *Joan Miró: Life and Work*. Trans. Norbert Guterman. New York, 1962.

Solomon R. Guggenheim Museum. *Joan Miró: A Retrospective*. New York, 1987.

Rowell, Margit, ed. *Joan Miró: Selected Writings and Interviews*. Trans. Paul Auster and Patricia Mathews. Boston, 1986.

———, and Rosalind Krauss. *Joan Miró: Magnetic Fields*. New York, 1972.

Rubin, William S. *Miró in the Collection of The Museum of Modern Art*. New York, 1973.

Weelen, Guy. *Miró*. Trans. Robert Erich Wolf. New York, 1989.

Amedeo Modigliani

Hall, Douglas. *Modigliani*. Rev. ed. Oxford, 1984.

Hobhouse, Janet. "Amedeo Modigliani." In *The Bride Stripped Bare: The Artist and the Female Nude in the Twentieth Century*. New York, 1988, pp. 135–66.

Sichel, Pierre. *Modigliani*. New York, 1967.

László Moholy-Nagy

Caton, Joseph Harris. *The Utopian Vision of Moholy-Nagy*. Ann Arbor, 1984.

Kostelanetz, Richard, ed. *Moholy-Nagy: An Anthology*. 2nd rev. ed. New York, 1991.

Moholy-Nagy, László. *Vision in Motion*. Chicago, 1947.

Piet Mondrian

Bois, Yve-Alain. "The De Stijl Idea" and "*Piet Mondrian*, New York City." In *Painting as Model*. Cambridge, Mass., 1990, pp. 101–22, 157–83.

Carmean, E. A., Jr. *Mondrian: The Diamond Compositions*. Washington, D.C., 1979.

Cheetham, Mark A. "The Mechanisms of Purity I: Mondrian" and "Purity as Aesthetic Ideology." In *The Rhetoric of Purity: Essentialist Theory and the Advent of Abstract Painting*. Cambridge, England and New York, 1991, pp. 40–64, 102ff.

Solomon R. Guggenheim Museum. *Piet Mondrian, 1872–1944: Centennial Exhibition*. New York, 1971.

Krauss, Rosalind E. "Grids." In *The Originality of the Avant-Garde and Other Modernist Myths*. Cambridge, Mass., 1985, pp. 8–22.

Mondrian, Piet. *The New Art—The New Life: The Collected Writings of Piet Mondrian*. Ed. and trans. Harry Holtzman and Martin S. James. Boston, 1986.

Seuphor, Michel. *Piet Mondrian: His Life and Work*. New York, 1956.

Robert Morris

Berger, Maurice. *Labyrinths: Robert Morris, Minimalism, and the 1960s.* New York, 1989.

The Corcoran Gallery of Art. *Robert Morris.* Washington, D.C., 1969.

Grey Art Gallery and Study Center. *Robert Morris: The Felt Works.* New York, 1989.

Morris, Robert. "Anti Form." *Artforum* 6 (April 1968), pp. 33–35.

Robert Motherwell

Carmean, E. A., Jr. "Robert Motherwell's Spanish Elegies." *Arts Magazine* 50, no. 10 (June 1976), pp. 94–97.

Flam, Jack. *Motherwell.* New York, 1991.

Gaugh, Harry F. "Elegy for an Exhibition." *Artnews* 85, no. 3 (March 1985), pp. 71–75.

Mattison, Robert Saltonstall. *Robert Motherwell: The Formative Years.* Ann Arbor, 1987.

Bruce Nauman

Richardson, Brenda. *Bruce Nauman: Neons.* Baltimore, 1982.

Tucker, Marcia. "pheNAUMANology." *Artforum* 9, no. 4 (Dec. 1970), pp. 38–44.

van Bruggen, Coosje. *Bruce Nauman.* New York, 1988.

Louise Nevelson

Glimcher, Arnold B. *Louise Nevelson.* New York, 1972.

Nevelson, Louise. *Dawns + Dusks: Louise Nevelson, taped conversations with Diana MacKown.* New York, 1976.

Wilson, Laurie. *Louise Nevelson: Iconography and Sources.* New York, 1981.

Isamu Noguchi

Grove, Nancy, and Diane Botnick. *The Sculpture of Isamu Noguchi, 1924–1979, A Catalogue.* New York and London, 1980.

Noguchi, Isamu. *The Isamu Noguchi Garden Museum.* New York, 1987.

Claes Oldenburg

Celant, Germano, Claes Oldenburg, and Coosje van Bruggen. *A Bottle of Notes and Some Voyages.* Sunderland and Leeds, 1988.

Rose, Barbara. *Claes Oldenburg.* New York, 1976.

van Bruggen, Coosje. *Claes Oldenburg.* Frankfurt, 1991.

Francis Picabia

Borràs, Maria Lluisa. *Picabia.* New York, 1985.

Camfield, William A. *Francis Picabia, His Art, Life and Times.* Princeton and New York, 1979.

The Museum of Modern Art. *The Machine as Seen at the End of the Mechanical Age.* New York, 1968.

Pablo Picasso

Barr, Alfred H., Jr. *Picasso: Fifty Years of His Art*. New York, 1946.

Blunt, Anthony, and Phoebe Pool. *Picasso, The Formative Years, A Study of His Sources*. New York, 1962.

Boeck, Wilhelm, and Jaime Sabartés. *Picasso*. New York, 1955.

Golding, John. *Cubism: A History and an Analysis 1907–1914*. New York, 1959.

Jaffé, Hans L. C. *Pablo Picasso*. New York, 1964.

Penrose, Roland. *Picasso: His Life and Work*. London, 1958.

————, and John Golding, eds. *Picasso in Retrospect*. New York, 1973.

Rosenblum, Robert. *Cubism and Twentieth-Century Art*. New York, 1961.

Schwarz, Herbert T. *Picasso and Marie-Thérèse Walter, 1925–1927*. Sillery, Quebec, 1988.

Camille Pissarro

Brettell, Richard. "Pissarro, Cézanne, and the School of Pontoise." In *A Day in the Country, Impressionism and the French Landscape*. Los Angeles, 1984.

Hayward Gallery. *Camille Pissarro 1830–1903*. London, 1980.

Lloyd, Christopher, ed. *Studies on Camille Pissarro*. London and New York, 1986.

Michelangelo Pistoletto

Celant, Germano. *Michelangelo Pistoletto: Division and Multiplication of the Mirror*. Long Island City, New York, 1988.

Poli, Francesco. "Reflections Unlimited." *Contemporanea* 2, no. 9 (Dec. 1989), pp. 40–49.

Schwabsky, Barry. "Pistoletto Through the Looking Glass: A Conversation on the Art of Subtraction." *Arts Magazine* 63, no. 4 (Dec. 1988), pp. 36–41.

Jackson Pollock

Clark, Timothy J. "Jackson Pollock's Abstraction." In *Reconstructing Modernism: Art in New York, Paris, and Montreal 1945–1964*. Ed. Serge Guilbaut. Cambridge, Mass. and London, 1990, pp. 172–238.

Landau, Ellen G. *Jackson Pollock*. New York, 1989.

O'Connor, Francis V., and Eugene Victor Thaw, eds. *Jackson Pollock: A Catalogue Raisonné of Paintings, Drawings and Other Works*. 4 vols. New Haven and London, 1978.

Liubov Popova

The Museum of Modern Art. *Liubov Popova*. New York, 1991.

Sarabianov, Dimitri, and Natalia Adaskina. *Liubov Popova*. Paris, 1989.

Martin Puryear
Benezra, Neal. *Martin Puryear.* New York, 1991.

Brenson, Michael. "Maverick Sculptor Makes Good." *The New York Times Magazine.* Nov. 1, 1987, pp. 84, 88–89.

Davies, Hugh M., and Helaine Posner. *Martin Puryear.* Amherst, 1984.

King, Elaine. *Martin Puryear: Beyond Style, The Power of the Simple.* Pittsburgh, 1987.

Princenthal, Nancy. "Intuition's Disciplinarian." *Art in America* 78, no. 1 (Jan. 1990), pp. 130–37, 181.

Robert Rauschenberg
Feinstein, Roni. *Robert Rauschenberg: The Silkscreen Paintings 1962–64.* New York, 1990.

Kotz, Mary Lynn. *Rauschenberg: Art and Life.* New York, 1990.

National Collection of Fine Arts, Smithsonian Institution. *Robert Rauschenberg.* Washington, D.C., 1976.

Rose, Barbara. *An Interview with Robert Rauschenberg.* New York, 1987.

Faith Ringgold
Fine Arts Museum of Long Island. *Faith Ringgold: A Twenty-Five Year Survey.* New York, 1990.

Gouma-Peterson, Thalia. "Faith Ringgold's Narrative Quilts." *Arts Magazine* 61, no. 5 (Jan. 1987), pp. 64–69.

Ringgold, Faith. *Tar Beach.* New York, 1991.

Mark Rothko
Chave, Anna C. *Mark Rothko: Subjects in Abstraction.* New Haven and London, 1989.

Rosenblum, Robert. "Abstract Expressionism." In *Modern Painting and the Northern Romantic Tradition: Friedrich to Rothko.* New York, 1975, pp. 195–218.

Tate Gallery. *Mark Rothko: 1903–1970.* London, 1987.

Waldman, Diane. *Mark Rothko, 1903–1970: A Retrospective.* New York, 1978.

Henri Rousseau
The Museum of Modern Art. *Henri Rousseau.* Boston, 1988.

Shattuck, Roger. *The Banquet Years.* New York, 1968.

Robert Ryman
Dia Art Foundation. *Robert Ryman.* New York, 1988.

Grimes, Nancy. "White Magic." *Artnews* 85, no. 6 (summer 1986), pp. 86–92.

Stedelijk Museum. *Robert Ryman.* Amsterdam, 1974.

Whitechapel Art Gallery. *Robert Ryman.* London, 1974.

Egon Schiele
Comini, Alessandra. *Egon Schiele's Portraits*. Berkeley and London, 1990.

Kallir, Jane. *Egon Schiele: The Complete Works*. New York, 1990.

Julian Schnabel
Adams, Brooks. "I Hate to Think: The New Paintings of Julian Schnabel." *Parkett*, no. 18 (Dec. 1988), pp. 110–22.

Ammann, Jean-Christophe, Diego Cortez, et al. *Julian Schnabel: Reconocimientos, The Recognitions Paintings*. Seville, 1988.

Kurt Schwitters
Elderfield, John. *Kurt Schwitters*. New York, 1985.

Nill, Annegreth. "Weimar Politics and the Theme of Love in Kurt Schwitters' *Das Bäumerbild*." *Dada-Surrealism*, no. 13 (1984), pp. 17–36.

Richard Serra
Güse, Ernst-Gerhard, ed. *Richard Serra*. New York, 1987.

The Museum of Modern Art. *Richard Serra: Sculpture*. New York, 1986.

Georges Seurat
Broude, Norma, ed. *Seurat in Perspective*. Englewood Cliffs, N. J., 1978.

Herbert, Robert L. "City vs. Country: The Rural Image in French Painting from Millet to Gauguin." *Artforum* 8, no. 6 (Feb. 1970), pp. 44–55.

Rewald, John. *Georges Seurat*. New York, 1990.

Thomson, Richard. *Seurat*. Oxford, 1985.

Gino Severini
Apollonio, Umbro, ed. *Futurist Manifestos*. Trans. Robert Brain, et al. New York, 1973.

Lukach, Joan M. "A Study of Gino Severini's Writings and Paintings of 1916–17, based on his 1917 exhibition in New York City." *Critica d'Arte* 20, no. 39 (Nov.–Dec. 1974).

Perloff, Marjorie. *The Futurist Moment: Avant-Garde, Avant Guerre, and the Language of Rupture*. Chicago, 1986.

David Smith
Carmean, E. A., Jr. *David Smith*. Washington, D.C., 1982.

Krauss, Rosalind E. *Terminal Iron Works: The Sculpture of David Smith*. Cambridge, Mass., 1971.

Smith, David. *David Smith by David Smith*. Ed. Cleve Gray. New York, 1972.

Wilkin, Karen. *David Smith*. New York, 1984.

Haim Steinbach

C. A. P. C. Musée d'Art Contemporain de Bordeaux. *Haim Steinbach: Recent Works*. Bordeaux, 1989.

The Museum of Contemporary Art, Los Angeles. *A Forest of Signs: Art in the Crisis of Representation*. Los Angeles, 1989.

Frank Stella

Fried, Michael. "Art and Objecthood." *Artforum* 5, no. 10 (summer 1967).

Rosenblum, Robert. *Frank Stella*. Harmondsworth and Baltimore, 1971.

Rubin, William S. *Frank Stella*. New York, 1970.

Antoni Tàpies

Agustí, Anna. *Tàpies: The Complete Works, Volume 1: 1943–1960*. Barcelona, 1989. *Volume 2: 1961–1968*. Barcelona, 1990.

Cembalest, Robin. "Master of Matter." *Artnews* 89, no. 6 (summer 1990), pp. 142–47.

Tàpies, Antoni. *Antoni Tàpies: Selected Essays*. Trans. Antoni Kerrigan. Eindhoven, 1986.

Cy Twombly

Schmidt, Katharina. *Cy Twombly*. Houston, 1989.

Szeemann, Harald, ed. *Cy Twombly: Paintings, Works on Paper, Sculpture*. Munich, 1987.

Whitney Museum of American Art. *Cy Twombly: Paintings and Drawings 1954–1977*. New York, 1979.

Vincent van Gogh

The Complete Letters of Vincent Van Gogh. 3 vols. Greenwich, Conn., 1958.

Pickvance, Ronald. *Van Gogh in Saint-Rémy and Auvers*. New York, 1986.

Rewald, John. *Post-Impressionism: From Van Gogh to Gauguin*. 3rd rev. ed. New York, 1978.

Andy Warhol

Crow, Thomas. "Saturday Disasters: Trace and Reference in Early Warhol." In *Reconstructing Modernism: Art in New York, Paris, and Montreal 1945–1964*. Ed. Serge Guilbaut. Cambridge, Mass. and London, 1990, pp. 311–26.

McShine, Kynaston, ed. *Andy Warhol: A Retrospective*. New York, 1989.

Stich, Sidra. *Made in U.S.A.* Berkeley, 1987.

Gilberto Zorio

Celant, Germano. *The Knot: Arte Povera at P. S. 1*. Long Island City, New York, 1985.

———. *Gilberto Zorio*. Eindhoven, 1987.

Glossary of Terms

Starting dates for styles and art movements are given.

Abstract Expressionism (New York, ca. 1940). The designation Abstract Expressionism encompasses a wide variety of postwar American painting through which the U.S. first became the center of the avant-garde. Critic Clement Greenberg, a major proponent of the New York School (another name for American artists working in this manner), preferred the term Painterly abstraction in order to describe the formal qualities of this painting: its lack of figuration and loose brushwork. The related term Action Painting was coined by critic Harold Rosenberg to refer to the gestural act of painting, which he considered the artist's unconscious outpouring or enactment of some personal drama. The expressive aspect of this art has been linked to the subjective heroism of earlier forms of Expressionism as well as to the Surrealist technique of automatic writing. The influence of Surrealists and other artists who fled Europe for New York in the late 1930s and the 1940s was integral to the development of Abstract Expressionism.

In the late 1940s and early 1950s Jackson Pollock, considered the foremost Abstract Expressionist, placed his canvases on the floor to pour, drip, and splatter paint onto them and to work on them from all sides, which set him apart from the tradition of vertical easel painting. Other painters who worked in gestural modes were William Baziotes, Willem de Kooning, Arshile Gorky, Adolph Gottlieb, Philip Guston, Franz Kline, and Robert Motherwell. Another component of the Abstract Expressionist school used large planes of color, often to evoke invisible spiritual states. These Color-field painters include Barnett Newman and Mark Rothko. Their lead was followed by Helen Frankenthaler, Morris Louis, and others who poured thin acrylic stains onto unsized canvases in order to make color an inherent part of their paintings. The term Abstract Expressionism has also been applied to the work of sculptors such as Herbert Ferber and David Hare.

Art Brut (raw art; France, ca. 1950). The term Art Brut was first used by the painter Jean Dubuffet to refer to a range of art forms outside the conventional dictates of the art world. He amassed a large collection of graffiti art and art made by the mentally ill, prisoners, children, and other naive (untrained) artists, whose raw or innocent vision and directness of technique he admired. In turn, he sought to emulate these qualities in his own work, and in 1948 he established a society to encourage the study of Art Brut. This kind of art has also been referred to as "outsider art"; that designation has been applied to Dubuffet's own work and that of Adolf Wölfli and others.

Arte Povera (poor or impoverished art; Italy, mid-1960s). The term Arte Povera was first used by Italian art critic Germano Celant to describe a broad category of art being produced by an international cross section of artists in the late 1960s through the 1970s, although it is now generally used to apply only to Italian art of this period. Celant related street theater and other antielitist, "poor" forms of expression and protest to this artistic style; the term "poor" also referred to the humble, often ephemeral materials employed and the anti-institutional quality that originally pervaded this art. Arte Povera usually incorporates organic and industrial materials in ways that reveal the conflicts between the natural and the man-made. Through sculpture, assemblage, and performance, Arte Povera artists became engaged in subjective investigations of the relationships between life and art and between seeing and thinking. They include Giovanni Anselmo, Alighiero E Boetti, Luciano Fabro, Jannis Kounellis, Mario Merz, Marisa Merz, Giulio Paolini, Giuseppe Penone, Michelangelo Pistoletto, and Gilberto Zorio.

Art Informel ("unformed" art; Europe, 1950s). In 1952 French writer Michel Tapié authored the book *Un Art autre* (*Art of Another Kind*) and organized an exhibition of the same name, which included paintings by Karel Appel, Camille Bryen, Alberto Burri, Jean Dubuffet, Jean Fautrier, Ruth Francken, Willem de Kooning, Jean-Paul Riopelle, and Wols, among other artists. Tapié was trying to define a tendency in postwar European painting that he saw as a radical break with all traditional notions of order and composition—including those of Modernism—in a movement toward something wholly "other." He used the term Art Informel (from the French *informe*, meaning unformed or formless) to refer to the antigeometric, antinaturalistic, and nonfigurative formal preoccupations of these artists, stressing their pursuit of spontaneity, looseness of form, and the irrational.

Art Informel tends toward the gestural and expressive, with repetitive calligraphic marks and anticompositional formats related to Abstract Expressionism, which is often considered its American equivalent. It eventually took root in France, Germany, Italy, Japan, and Spain, and was known in its various manifestations as Gesture Painting, Lyrical Abstraction, Matter Art, and Tachisme (from the French *tache*, meaning a spot or stain). Artists who became associated with Art Informel include Enrico Donati, Lucio Fontana, Asger Jorn, Emil Schumacher, Kazuo Shiraga, Antoni Tàpies, and Jiro Yoshihara.

Bauhaus (Germany, 1919). The Bauhaus was founded in Weimar in 1919 as a state-sponsored school of art, architecture, and design. Architect Walter Gropius served as its director until 1928. The school's curriculum was organized on the principle that the crafts were united with the arts on an equal footing (as they had been in medieval times), on the guild system of workshop training under the tutelage of "masters," and on the ideas concerning the relationship of art to society developed by the German industrial-design association Deutscher Werkbund, which was greatly influenced by the Arts and Crafts movements in England, Austria, and the Netherlands. The Bauhaus's utopian aims included raising the quality of everyday life through the production of buildings, design objects, and art works according to an aesthetic of modernity and universality. Lyonel Feininger, Vasily Kandinsky, Paul Klee, and Oskar Schlemmer were among the first "masters" or teachers at the school. The addition of such artists as László Moholy-Nagy and Josef Albers to the faculty in 1923 and after reinforced a shift away from Expressionism and toward the functional and technology-based aesthetics of Constructivism and De Stijl. The school was forced to relocate to Dessau in 1925. In April 1933, when conditions imposed by the Nazis made continued operation impossible, the faculty decided to close the Bauhaus, and several of its professors, including Albers, Gropius, and Ludwig Mies van der Rohe, emigrated to the U.S., where they assumed important teaching posts. In 1937 the New Bauhaus opened in Chicago under the direction of Moholy-Nagy.

Conceptual Art (New York and London, ca. 1966). Conceptual Art is based on the notion that the essence of art is an idea, or concept, and may exist distinct from and in the absence of an object as its representation. It has also been called Idea Art, Post-Object Art, and Dematerialized Art because it often assumes the form of a proposition (i.e., a document of the artist's thinking) or a photographic document of an event. Conceptual Art practices emerged at a time when the authority of the art institution and the preciousness of the unique aesthetic object were being widely challenged by artists and critics. Conceptual artists interrogated the possibilities of art-as-idea or art-as-knowledge, and to those ends explored linguistic, mathematical, and process-oriented dimensions of thought and aesthetics, as well as invisible systems, structures, and processes. Artists such as Joseph Kosuth and members of the Art & Language group wrote theoretical essays that questioned the ways in which art has conventionally acquired meaning. In some cases such texts served as the art works themselves. Other figures associated with Conceptual Art include Mel Bochner, Hanne Darboven, Agnes Denes, Jan Dibbets, Hans Haacke, On Kawara, Les Levine, Sol LeWitt, and Lawrence Weiner.

Constructivism (Russia, ca. 1918). Vladimir Tatlin and some of his colleagues, such as Ivan Puni, Ivan Kliun, and Lev Bruni, influenced by Pablo Picasso's Cubist sculptures, began to make abstract, nonutilitarian constructions in Russia in the years just before the 1917 revolution. This aesthetic, allied with a geometric vocabulary based on Kazimir Malevich's Suprematism, developed into a rational, materialist, utilitarian approach to socially committed art, led by Tatlin and Aleksandr Rodchenko. After the revolution many Constructivist artists were placed in important pedagogical and administrative positions, where they advocated a culture based on new principles in art, design, typography, and architecture. In attempting to link art with industry, technology, and the ideals of a classless society through the production of socially useful objects, they developed the notion of the artist-as-engineer. The First Constructivist Art Exhibition was held in Moscow in 1921. Artists affiliated with this group included Aleksei Gan, Konstantin Medunetsky, Georgy and Vladimir Stenberg, and Varvara Stepanova, among others. The Constructivists also included another group—led by Vasily Kandinsky together with Naum Gabo and his brother Antoine Pevsner—who shared Malevich's commitment to art as a primarily spiritual activity. Other important Constructivist artists were Aleksandra Ekster and Olga Rozanova and, in Germany, László Moholy-Nagy.

Cubism (France, ca. 1907). Georges Braque and Pablo Picasso originated the style known as Cubism, one of the most internationally influential innovations of 20th-century art. Other practitioners of Cubism in its varied forms include painters Albert Gleizes, Juan Gris, Fernand Léger, Jean Metzinger, and (in his early work) Piet Mondrian, and sculptors Alexander Archipenko, Henri Laurens, and Jacques Lipchitz. The advent of this style marked a rupture with the European traditions, traceable to the Renaissance, of pictorial illusionism and the organization of compositional space in terms of linear perspective. Its initial phase (ca. 1908–12), known as Analytic Cubism (referring to the "analysis" or "breaking down" of form and space), developed under the influence of Paul Cézanne's and Georges Seurat's formal innovations.

The Cubists fragmented objects and pictorial space into semitransparent, overlapping, faceted planes of color, thought by some to show the spatial shift from different perspectives within the same time and space and to emphasize the canvas's real two-dimensional flatness instead of conveying the illusory appearance of depth.

With Analytic Cubism, Braque's and Picasso's attempts to depict the conceptual planes of figures and objects in space developed into an austere, depersonalized pictorial style. They at first employed a limited palette of ochers, browns, greens, grays, and blacks, which were considered less expressive than a full range of color, and in 1911 began experimenting with simulated textures, shadows, and modern stenciled typography. The elements within Cubist compositions often inverted the devices of artistic illusionism as if mocking the codelike qualities of two-dimensional representation. In 1912, as part of their exploration of the ambiguities of real and representational space, they adopted the technique of *papier collé* (from the French *coller*, meaning to paste or glue), wherein overlapping and fragmented pieces of newspaper, wallpaper, tickets, cigarette wrappers, and other detritus were arranged, altered, and adhered to the ground of paper or canvas, disrupting Modernism's inviolate picture plane. By 1913 Analytic Cubism was succeeded by Synthetic Cubism, in which the "analysis" of objects was abandoned and replaced by "constructing" or "synthesizing" them through the overlapping of larger, more discrete forms that seemed as if they might have been cut and pasted to the canvas. This new form of Cubism, which featured brighter colors, ornamental patterns, undulating lines, and rounded as well as jagged shapes, was common into the 1930s.

Dada (New York and Western Europe, ca. 1915). One of the first large-scale movements to translate art into provocative action, Dada produced some of the most antibourgeois, antirational, anarchic, playful works to come out of this century. It began in 1916 in Zurich's Cabaret Voltaire, where expatriate artists, poets, and writers gathered in refuge from World War I. Dada started as an indictment of the bourgeois values responsible for the horrors of the war, and assumed many forms, including outrageous performances, festivals, readings, erotic mechanomorphic art, nonsensical chance-generated poetry, found objects, and political satire in photomontage. Over several years it developed in New York as well as many European cities—primarily Zurich, Berlin, Cologne, Paris, and Hannover—through the activities of such artists and writers as Jean Arp, Hugo Ball, Marcel Duchamp, Max Ernst, George Grosz, Raoul Hausmann, John Heartfield, Hannah Höch, Man Ray, Francis Picabia, Kurt Schwitters, and Tristan Tzara.

De Stijl (the style; Holland, 1917). The Dutch review *De Stijl* was founded in 1917 by Theo van Doesburg, and the name has come to represent the common aims and utopian vision of a loose affiliation of Dutch and international artists and architects. The central figures of De Stijl—van Doesburg and Piet Mondrian—strove for a universal form that would correspond to their spiritual vision. Neo-Plasticism (meaning "a new plastic art") was the term adopted by Mondrian to describe the qualities that De Stijl artists endeavored to achieve in their work. The essential idea underlying De Stijl's radical utopian program was the creation of a universal aesthetic language based in part on a rejection of the decorative excesses of Art Nouveau in favor of a simple, logical style that emphasized construction and function, one that would be appropriate for every aspect of modern life. It was posited on the fundamental principle of the geometry of the straight line, the square, and the rectangle, combined with a strong asymmetricality; the predominant use of pure primary colors with black and white; and the relationship between positive and negative elements in an arrangement of non-objective forms and lines. Some scholars have considered the philosophical grounds of De Stijl in terms of theosophical spiritualism, while others view it in relation to Hegel's philosophy of the dialectic. Other artists affiliated with De Stijl include Vilmos Huszár, J. J. P. Oud, Gerrit Rietveld, Bart van der Leck, and Georges Vantongerloo.

Expressionism (primarily Germany, and Austria, first decade of 20th century). The very elastic concept of Expressionism refers to art that emphasizes the extreme expressive properties of pictorial form in order to explore subjective emotions and inner psychological truths. Although much influenced by the work of Vincent van Gogh, Paul Gauguin, and Edvard Munch, the artists who pioneered Expressionism departed even further from traditional notions of recording the appearance of reality than had the Post-Impressionists or the Symbolists. They were also influenced by Henri Matisse and the other Fauves, the Cubists, African and Oceanic art, and the folk art of Germany and Russia. In conjunction with poets, dramatists, and other writers, they championed idealist values and freedom from the constricting forces and repressive materialism of bourgeois society. One prominent Expressionist group, Die Brücke (The Bridge), which was active as a group from 1905 to 1913, included founders Fritz Bleyl, Erich Heckel, Ernst Ludwig Kirchner, and Karl Schmidt-Rottluff as well as Otto Müller, Emil Nolde (for a brief period), and Max Pechstein. Members of Die Brücke conveyed pictorially the Modernist themes of alienation, anxiety, and social fragmentation. They employed emotion-charged images, a "primitive" simplification of form, a deliberate crudeness of figuration, agitated brushwork, and powerful, often violent juxtapositions of intense color.

Artists involved in the more stylistically diverse Der Blaue Reiter (The Blue Rider), founded in 1911 in Munich by Vasily Kandinsky, Franz Marc, and Gabriele Münter, sought to convey spiritual states through the abstraction of forms. Alexej Jawlensky and August Macke were associated with the group, and many others participated in the Blue Rider exhibitions. Other important Expressionists in Germany were Käthe Kollwitz and Paula Modersohn-Becker, and in Austria Oskar Kokoschka and Egon Schiele.

Fauvism (France, ca. 1905). The Fauves (wild beasts) were so-named in a statement made by French art critic Louis Vauxcelles in reaction to a group of their paintings at the 1905 Salon d'Automne (Autumn Salon). Although their subject matter was conventional—mostly landscape and still life—the way they painted was radical for the time, favoring nonassociative and often jarring juxtapositions of luminous color patches interspersed with exposed portions of canvas, and brushwork accentuated by broad strokes. Under the influence of Paul Cézanne's art and the Divisionist technique developed by Georges Seurat and his followers, the Fauve painters pursued the expression of sensations before nature in terms of pure color. Fauvism included Georges Braque, Charles Camoin, André Derain, Maurice de Vlaminck, Raoul Dufy,

Othon Friesz, Henri Charles Manguin, Albert Marquet, Henri Matisse, and Kees van Dongen.

Fluxus (U.S. and Europe, ca. 1961). Fluxus has been described as an attitude and a style, subversive in its casual, spontaneous quality that challenges institutionally framed understandings of art. It developed as a loose affiliation of artists who gathered around the central figure of George Maciunas. Like the Situationists, their primary goal was to upset bourgeois routine in life and in art. Fluxus experiments explored connections between the visual arts, poetry, music, dance, theater, and the more radical forms of performance, such as actions, often combining them in guerrilla theater and street spectacles. The elements of chance and humor so prominent in Marcel Duchamp's visual experiments and John Cage's musical compositions played important roles in the Fluxus approach to art making. Major figures associated with Fluxus in the U.S. and Europe include Joseph Beuys, George Brecht, Walter De Maria, Dick Higgins, Ray Johnson, Alison Knowles, Charlotte Moorman, Yoko Ono, Nam June Paik, Ben Vautier, Wolf Vostell, Robert Watts, Robert Whitman, and La Monte Young.

Futurism (Italy, 1908). In a stylistic idiom that integrated some of the techniques of Cubism and Divisionism, the Futurists glorified the energy and speed of modern life together with the dynamism and violence of the new technological society. In their manifestos, art, poetry, and theatrical events, they celebrated motor cars, airplanes, machine guns, and other phenomena that they associated with modernity; they denounced moralism and feminism, as well as museums and libraries, which they considered static institutions of an obsolete culture. The Futurists sought to represent the experience of the modern metropolis—namely, the overstimulation of the individual's sensorium—by portraying multiple phases of motion simultaneously and by showing the interpenetration of objects and their environment through the superimposition of different chromatic planes. Artists and poets affiliated with Futurism include Giacomo Balla, Umberto Boccioni, Carlo Carrà, Filippo Tommaso Marinetti (the movement's founder), Luigi Russolo, and Gino Severini. Balla led a second generation of Italian Futurists, including Fortunato Depero, Gerardo Dottori, and Enrico Prampolini, in the 1920s and 1930s.

Almost concomitantly with Italian Futurism, a Russian version of Futurism developed under the leadership of Kazimir Malevich, who described most of his work from 1912 to 1915 as "Cubo-Futurist." This Cubist fragmentation of space allied to the Futurist simultaneity of shifting forms was also taken up briefly by Liubov Popova and other Russian artists. Futurism, however, was more prevalent among Russia's poets than its painters.

Happenings (U.S. and Europe, 1959). The term Happening was coined by New York artist Allan Kaprow in 1959 as a name for the antinarrative theatrical pieces that he and such artists as Jim Dine, Red Grooms, Dick Higgins, Claes Oldenburg, and Robert Whitman staged in studios, galleries, and offbeat locations, usually with direct audience involvement. These multimedia performance events radically altered the conventional role of audience members, who, in the tradition of Antonin Artaud's Theater of Cruelty, were assaulted by an array of auditory, visual, and physical phenomena. Composed out of the absurdities and banalities of everyday life and filtered through the gestural vocabulary of Abstract Expressionism, these spectacles incorporated junk materials, found and manipulated objects, and live or electronic music, sometimes in elaborate constructed environments intended to break down the boundaries between art and life. They explored the objectification of mundane movements and play-related activities, as well as the depersonalization of their participants.

Hard-edge painting (U.S., late 1950s). The term Hard-edge painting was coined in 1959 by art historian Jules Langsner to characterize the nonfigurative work of four artists from California in an exhibition called *Four Abstract Classicists*. The term then gained broader currency after British critic Lawrence Alloway used it to describe contemporary American geometric abstract painting featuring an "economy of form," "fullness of color," "neatness of surface," and the nonrelational, allover arrangement of forms on the canvas. This style of geometric abstraction refers back to the work of Josef Albers and Piet Mondrian. Artists associated with Hard-edge painting include Al Held, Ellsworth Kelly, Alexander Liberman, Brice Marden, Kenneth Noland, Ad Reinhardt, and Jack Youngerman.

Impressionism (France, ca. 1870s). The Impressionists were a group of painters who, in general, departed from the traditional pursuit of reproducing an illusion of real space in paintings of academic subjects, choosing instead to exploit the possibilities of paint to explore the fleeting effects of nature and the vagaries of visual sensation in, for the most part, rapidly executed works. Among the several dozen painters who participated in this loosely defined group—most of whom are unknown today—were Mary Cassatt, Paul Cézanne, Edgar Degas, Claude Monet, Berthe Morisot, Camille Pissarro, and Pierre Auguste Renoir. These artists were associated principally through their group exhibitions (although some, like Cézanne, never showed their work in the so-called Impressionist exhibitions) and were perceived by some critics of the time as sharing certain stylistic devices, such as employing loose brushwork to produce the illusion of the artist's spontaneous recording of natural light on the canvas and rejecting the practice of chiaroscuro (modeling in light and dark). In their pursuit of modernity, some of them borrowed formal devices used in photography and Japanese prints, such as radical foreshortening, cropping, and keyhole or bird's-eye perspective.

The work of the Impressionists was indebted to the Barbizon school of artists active in the 1850s in developing plein-air (out-of-doors) painting, although even the Impressionists who were most celebrated for painting directly from nature, such as Monet, often completed their canvases in the studio. The Impressionists moved away from the Barbizon school's romantic naturalism and themes of rural peasant life to more urban subject matter, especially scenes of Parisian leisure and entertainment, city parks, and suburban landscapes.

Minimalism (New York, 1960s). Minimalism refers to painting or sculpture made with an extreme economy of means and reduced to the essentials of geometric abstraction. It applies to sculptural works by such artists as Carl Andre, Dan Flavin, Donald Judd, Ellsworth Kelly, John McCracken, Robert Morris, Richard Serra, Tony Smith, and Anne Truitt; to the shaped and striped canvases of Frank Stella; and to paintings by Jo Baer, Ellsworth Kelly, Robert Mangold, Brice Marden, Agnes Martin, and Robert Ryman. Minimal Art is generally characterized by precise, hard-edged, unitary geometric forms; rigid planes of color—usually cool hues or commercially mixed colors, or sometimes just a single color; nonhierarchical, mathematically regular compositions, often based on a grid; the reduction to pure self-referential form, emptied of all external references; and an anonymous surface appearance, without any gestural inflection. As a result of these formal attributes, this art has also been referred to as ABC Art, Cool Art, Imageless Pop, Literalist Art, Object Art, and Primary Structure Art. Minimal Art shares Pop art's rejection of the artistic subjectivity and heroic gesture of Abstract Expressionism. In Minimal Art what is important is the phenomenological basis of the viewer's experience, how he or she perceives the internal relationships among the parts of the work and of the parts to the whole, as in the *gestalt* aspect of Morris's sculpture. The repetition of forms in Minimal sculpture serves to emphasize the subtle differences in the perception of those forms in space and time as the spectator's viewpoint shifts in time and space.

Neo-Dada (international, 1950s). The term Neo-Dada, first popularized in a group of articles by Barbara Rose in the early 1960s, has been applied to a wide variety of artistic works, including the pre-Pop "combines" and assemblages of Robert Rauschenberg and Jasper Johns, Happenings, Fluxus, Pop art, Junk Art, and Nouveau Réalisme, as well as other Conceptual and experimental art forms. The unifying element of Neo-Dada art is its reinvestigation of Dada's irony and its use of found objects and/or banal activities as instruments of social and aesthetic critique.

Neo-Expressionism (New York, Italy, and West Germany, late 1970s). Rejecting the restrictions against imagery and gestural treatment set by their Minimalist and Conceptual teachers and contemporaries, the Neo-Expressionists revived the formal elements of German Expressionism and Abstract Expressionism, often on a heroic scale. As the "new" Expressionism this style reiterated the subjectivism associated with the earlier forms, marked by flamboyant textural brushwork and distorted figures. In their work the Neo-Expressionists took up a variety of cultural-mythological, nationalist-historical, erotic, and "primitivizing" themes. Some critics welcomed this art for its return to the personal and its lifting of what had become aesthetic taboos; others criticized its aura of nostalgia and its depoliticized, ahistorical tendencies. Georg Baselitz, Sandro Chia, Francesco Clemente, Enzo Cucchi, Jörg Immendorff, Anselm Kiefer, Markus Lüpertz, A. R. Penck, and Julian Schnabel are among the primary figures of Neo-Expressionism.

Neue Sachlichkeit (new objectivity; Germany, late 1910s). The term Neue Sachlichkeit was first used by museum director Gustav Hartlaub in 1923 in preparation for an exhibition of recent paintings that he said were grounded in the depiction of reality. The artists themselves were not organized in a formal group and worked in many locales. Two major trends were identified under Neue Sachlichkeit. The so-called Verists, including Otto Dix and George Grosz, aggressively attacked and satirized the evils of society and those in power and demonstrated in harsh terms the devastating effects of World War I and the economic climate upon individuals. Max Beckmann was connected with these artists. A second term, Magic Realists, has been applied to diverse artists, including Heinrich Maria Davringhausen, Alexander Kanoldt, Christian Schad, and Georg Schrimpf, whose works were said to counteract in a positive fashion the aggression and subjectivity of German Expressionist art. They employed a controlled manner and naturalistic coloring in painting unpeopled city views, seemingly airless spaces, escapist themes, portraits, and family scenes. Neue Sachlichkeit was replaced by the conservative style prescribed by the Nazis.

Nouveau Réalisme (new realism; Paris, late 1950s). In 1960 French art critic Pierre Restany first used the term Nouveau Réalisme in a manifesto for an exhibition at the Galleria Apollinaire in Milan. In this exhibition he brought together art works created through the appropriation of ordinary materials and objects by artists such as Arman, César, Christo, Niki de Saint-Phalle, François Dufrêne, Raymond Hains, Yves Klein, Mimmo Rotella, Daniel Spoerri, Jean Tinguely, and Jacques de la Villeglé, among others. Like the Dadaists and the Surrealists, these artists performed archaeological excavations of everyday life; their works ranged from torn and lacerated posters, wrapped objects, and accumulations of found objects to assemblages of junk materials and urban detritus (automobile parts, fabrics, rope, dishes, etc.). As a result of its vernacular bias, Nouveau Réalisme is often considered a counterpart to Neo-Dada and Pop art.

Orphism (France, ca. 1912). In 1912 the poet Guillaume Apollinaire applied the French term *Orphisme* to the visionary and lyrical paintings of Robert Delaunay, relating them to Orpheus, a poet and musician in Greek mythology. It also applies to the paintings of Sonia Terk Delaunay and is often mentioned in connection with František Kupka and a group of then-contemporary American and Canadian artists, called Synchromists, who painted according to a system of "color harmonies" that equated hues to musical pitches. The term Orphic Cubism is sometimes used instead of Orphism because of Robert Delaunay's roots in a Cubist style. Departing from the limited palette of Georges Braque's and Pablo Picasso's initial phase of Cubism, the Delaunays' paintings are full of brightly colored circular forms, the color combinations of which are based on the "law of simultaneous contrast of colors," developed in the 19th century by French chemist Michel-Eugène Chevreul; Chevreul's theories had already influenced painters such as Eugène Delacroix and Georges Seurat.

Pop art (Great Britain and U.S., 1950s). Pop art was pioneered in London in the mid-1950s by Richard Hamilton and Eduardo Paolozzi (members of the Independent Group), and in the 1960s by Peter Blake, Patrick Caulfield, David Hockney, Allen Jones, and Peter Phillips. It was supported by such critics as Lawrence Alloway and Reyner Banham. In the early 1960s Pop art took off in the U.S., exemplified by the work of Jim Dine, Robert Indiana, Roy Lichtenstein, Claes Oldenburg, Mel Ramos, James Rosenquist, Ed Ruscha, Andy Warhol, and Tom Wesselmann. With its roots in Dada—and the immediate precedent of Jasper Johns's Neo-Dada adaptations of such things as beer cans and the American flag—Pop art explored the image world of popular culture, from which its name derives. Basing their techniques, style, and imagery on certain aspects of mass reproduction, the media, and consumer society, these artists took inspiration from advertising, pulp magazines, billboards, movies, television, comic strips, and shop windows. These images, presented with (and sometimes transformed by) humor, wit, and irony, can be seen as both a celebration and a critique of popular culture. In the early 1960s German artists Konrad Lueg, Sigmar Polke, and Gerhard Richter explored a Pop-related style, which they called Capitalist Realism.

Post-Impressionism (France, ca. 1880s). For an exhibition in 1910–11 British art critics Roger Fry and Desmond MacCarthy classified the art of Paul Cézanne, Paul Gauguin, Georges Seurat, and Vincent van Gogh (and in a second exhibition in 1912, early works by Henri Matisse and Pablo Picasso) under the somewhat clumsy rubric of Post-Impressionism. The Post-Impressionists were seen as being less interested than the Impressionists in recording the shifting patterns of nature, placing fresh emphasis on the "subjective" effects of objects rather than the scientific reproduction of visible phenomena. The artists were thought to embrace the idea of art as a process of formal design with purely expressive aims.

Post-painterly abstraction (U.S. and Canada, mid-1950s). The term Post-painterly abstraction was coined by critic Clement Greenberg in conjunction with an exhibition of the same name at the Los Angeles County Museum of Art in 1964, featuring contemporary American and Canadian artists. In his essay for the catalogue Greenberg distinguished between Painterly abstraction—his preferred designation for what others have called Abstract Expressionism—and the artistic work that it precipitated by such artists as Gene Davis, Paul Feeley, John Ferren, Sam Francis, Helen Frankenthaler, Alfred Jensen, Morris Louis, Jules Olitski, Frank Stella, and others. Some of these artists continued the painterly, loose facture of color and contour pursued by Jackson Pollock and Willem de Kooning, while others moved toward a more hard-edged style. What they shared, according to Greenberg, was the kind of linear clarity and physical openness of design that had begun with Painterly abstraction and continued in its wake, as well as a new tendency to stress contrasts of pure hues, and a rejection of the tactile application of paint in favor of staining the canvas with diluted paint. Often they also sought a flat, anonymous style of execution.

Primitivism (Western Europe, late 19th century). "Primitivism" is less an aesthetic movement than a sensibility or cultural attitude that has informed diverse aspects of Modern art. It refers to Modern art that alludes to specific stylistic elements of tribal objects and other non-Western art forms. With roots in late-19th-century Romanticism's fascination with foreign civilizations and distant lands, particularly with what were considered to be naive, less-developed cultures, it also designates the "primitive" as a myth of paradise lost for late-19th- and 20th-century culture. Behind this captivation with the "other" was a belief in the intrinsic goodness of all humankind, a conviction inspired by French philosopher Jean-Jacques Rousseau's notion of the Noble Savage. At the same time, however, industrialized Western culture evoked the "primitive" as a sign on which to map what it had socially and psychologically repressed: desire and sexual abandon. The problematic nature of "primitivism" can be illustrated by the example of Paul Gauguin, who spurned his own culture to join that of an "uncivilized" yet more "ingenuous" people. Although he sought spiritual inspiration in Tahiti, he showed a more earthy preoccupation with Tahitian women, often depicting them nude. This eroticization of the "primitive" was amplified in the work of the German Expressionist group Die Brücke and in Pablo Picasso's proto-Cubist paintings, particularly *Les Demoiselles d'Avignon* (1907).

The influence of tribal fetishes on Modern painters and sculptors, such as Constantin Brancusi, Alberto Giacometti, Henri Matisse, and Picasso, has been the subject of much art-historical and critical debate. While the formal impact of ritual objects on these artists is undeniable, recent attempts to locate affinities between the "primitive" and the Modern have been perceived as suspect because they evince a certain ethnocentrism. Moreover, the usage of the word "primitive" to describe cultures and creations outside of the European tradition can be seen to be degrading. For this reason, "primitivism" and "primitive" appear within quotation marks in this book.

Process Art (U.S. and Europe, mid-1960s). Process Art emphasizes the "process" of making art (rather than any predetermined composition or plan) and the concepts of change and transience, as elaborated in the work of such artists as Lynda Benglis, Eva Hesse, Robert Morris, Bruce Nauman, Alan Saret, Richard Serra, Robert Smithson, and Keith Sonnier. Their interest in process and the properties of materials as determining factors has precedents in the Abstract Expressionists' use of unconventional methods such as dripping and staining. In a ground-breaking essay and exhibition in 1968, Morris posited the notion of "anti-form" as a basis for making art works in terms of process and time rather than as static and enduring icons, which he associated with "object-type" art. Morris stressed this new art's de-emphasis of order through nonrigid materials, pioneered by Claes Oldenburg, and the manipulation of those materials through the processes of gravity, stacking, piling, and hanging.

Process artists were involved in issues attendant to the body, random occurrences, improvisation, and the liberating qualities of nontraditional materials such as wax, felt, and latex. Using these, they created eccentric forms in erratic or irregular arrangements produced by actions such as cutting, hanging, and dropping, or organic processes such as growth, condensation, freezing, or decomposition.

Purism (France, 1918). Purism is the aesthetic approach that was advocated and practiced by Charles-Edouard Jeanneret (later called Le Corbusier) and Amédée Ozenfant. Jeanneret and Ozenfant first described the principles of Purism in 1918 in a small book entitled *Après le cubisme* (*After Cubism*). They sought to eliminate the picturesque, decorative aspects of Cubism that had become prevalent in painting after 1914 in favor of an art that stressed mathematical order, purity, and logic. To achieve this sense of fundamental order they systematized their expression of visual phenomena into a precise arrangement of modern, impersonal, "universal" forms, especially images of simple machine-made objects from everyday life. Jeanneret and Ozenfant shared with Fernand Léger an enthusiasm for the beauty of the machine aesthetic and precisely delineated forms, but they went even further in reducing such elements to a simplified geometry and combining them to produce compositions of unruffled harmony. Purism's movement away from the radical vocabulary of the preceding decade can be seen as part of a pervasive desire for a "return to order" after World War I and the consequent widespread neoclassical tendency among European artists of the period.

Site-specific Art/Environmental Art (pioneered in U.S., and international, mid-1960s). Site-specific or Environmental Art refers to an artist's intervention in a specific locale, creating a work that is integrated with its surroundings and that explores its relationship to the topography of its locale, whether indoors or out, urban, desert, marine, or otherwise. In its largest sense it applies to a work made by an artist in the landscape, either by radically manipulating the terrain in a remote area to produce an "earthwork" (such as Robert Smithson's *Spiral Jetty*) or by creating ephemeral or removable tableaux along particular pathways so that the terrain is not permanently altered (Richard Long's circles or lines of stones, Christo's fabric walls or umbrellas). Other artists known for such work include Walter De Maria, Michael Heizer, Nancy Holt, Mary Miss, Robert Morris, Dennis Oppenheim, and James Turrell. The term also applies to an environmental installation or sculpture created especially for a particular gallery space or public site, by such artists as Joseph Beuys, Daniel Buren, Dan Flavin, Joseph Kosuth, Jannis Kounellis, Mario Merz, Claes Oldenburg, and many others. No matter which approach an artist takes, Site-specific Art is meant to become part of its locale, and to restructure the viewer's conceptual and perceptual experience of that locale through the artist's intervention.

Situationism (Western Europe, ca. 1957). In Italy in 1957 a group of artists, filmmakers, architects, and intellectuals from the avant-garde groups Lettriste Internationale and the International Movement for an Imaginist Bauhaus forged an alliance called the Internationale Situationiste (IS). The IS condemned the deterioration of culture brought about by the pernicious effects of corporate capitalism—especially its role in turning people into passive consumers of media-created spectacle—and formed the highly theoretical movement of Situationism to counteract it. Extracting elements from Dada and Surrealism, the theater of Bertolt Brecht, and the writings of Comte de Lautréamont, Situationists invented new kinds of art works and performance intended to critique, disrupt, and change conventional Western bourgeois society. The IS developed notions of psychogeography and unitary town planning, emphasizing the effects of environment on the emotions and behavior of individuals. Their concept of the *dérive* (drifting), a "transient passage" through territory ordinarily untraversed, was related to Surrealist excursions through Paris and unearthing the uncanny in chance encounters, while their technique of *détournement* consisted in the alteration of pre-existing aesthetic material, often based on refiguring the relationship between image and text (for example, in comics or film).

Situationists in the 1960s turned increasingly to political organizing and theoretical writing; Guy Debord, an IS leader, codified Situationist cultural and political theory in his 1967 book *Society of the Spectacle*. In May 1968, during the student uprisings in Paris, Situationist ideas proliferated in the form of street posters, graffiti, and cartoons. Among the members of the IS are Michèle Bernstein, Nieuwenhuys Constant, Asger Jorn, Attila Kotányi, Giuseppe Pinot-Gallizio, the Spur Group, Raoul Vaneigem, and René-Donatien Viénet.

Suprematism (Russia, ca. 1914). Around 1914, after two years of painting in a Cubo-Futurist style, Russian artist Kazimir Malevich began to work in an abstract style, which he called Suprematism. For Malevich, the guiding principle of Suprematism was "the supremacy of pure sensation in creative art," best represented by the square, which he considered the most elementary, basic, and thus supreme formal element; but he increasingly combined the square with the circle, other geometric shapes, and even curved lines. He began by limiting himself in his Suprematist paintings to black, white, gray, and red, but he expanded his palette as his compositions became more complex. Malevich, like other artists of his time, believed that the external world could no longer serve as the basis for art, which had, instead, to explore pure non-objective abstraction in the search for visual analogues to experience, both conscious and unconscious. As he wrote in 1915, "Nothing is real except sensation . . . the sensation of non-objectivity." He first showed his Suprematist works at *0.10: The Last Futurist Exhibition* in St. Petersburg in December 1915. The exhibition, which included a broad sampling of then-current tendencies in Russian avant-garde painting, has become famous for inaugurating the two directions that would largely govern artistic production in Russia (including architecture, graphic design, theater, and the decorative arts) for the next seven years: Suprematism, and the closely related (although more socially oriented) movement Constructivism. Other artists affiliated with Suprematism include Ilya Chashnik, Ivan Kliun, El Lissitzky, Liubov Popova, Ivan Puni, Aleksandr Rodchenko, Olga Rozanova, Nikolai Suetin, and Nadezhda Udaltsova.

Surrealism (primarily France, ca. 1924). Surrealism, which had many international manifestations and which began as a literary movement before developing into an artistic one, was pioneered in France under the leadership of André Breton in the 1920s. Breton's circle of poets and artists was deeply influenced by Comte de Lautréamont's vision of unexpected poetic combinations of objects. In their visual and written work the Surrealists explored Sigmund Freud's notions of the dream-work and the uncanny, stressing the relationship of the unconscious to lived reality and using techniques of psychic automatism as a way of tapping into the unconscious and detaching themselves from habitual thought processes. They were inspired by the poetry of Stéphane Mallarmé and Arthur Rimbaud, the writing of Guillaume Apollinaire (from whom the notion of surreality derived), Symbolism, Giorgio de Chirico's metaphysical painting, and then-current notions of ethnography. Advocating an art of pure imagination, Surrealists deployed the imagery of hysteria, "primitive" art, hallucinatory experiences, and phenomena associated with the radically "other" to effect a revolution in everyday consciousness based on a critique of rationalist thought. This critique, also posed by Georges Bataille and the dissident Surrealists, took the form of disturbing images and juxtapositions to disrupt stable, conventional notions of form. Through the influence of Joan Miró's paintings and Jean Arp's sculptures and reliefs, the abstract realm of biomorphic forms also became a primary element in much Surrealist work. Artists affiliated with Surrealism include Hans Bellmer, Salvador Dalí, Max Ernst, Alberto Giacometti, Frida Kahlo, Paul Klee, Wifredo Lam, Dora Maar, René Magritte, Man Ray, André Masson, Matta, Meret Oppenheim, Pablo Picasso, Yves Tanguy, and Dorothea Tanning, among others.

The Solomon R. Guggenheim Foundation

Honorary Trustees in Perpetuity
Solomon R. Guggenheim
Justin K. Thannhauser
Peggy Guggenheim

Chairman
Peter Lawson-Johnston

President
Ronald O. Perelman

Vice-Presidents
Robert M. Gardiner
Wendy L-J. McNeil

Vice-President and Treasurer
Stephen C. Swid

Director
Thomas Krens

Secretary
Edward F. Rover

Honorary Trustee
Claude Pompidou

Trustee, Ex Officio
Jacques E. Lennon

Director Emeritus
Thomas M. Messer

Trustees
Giovanni Agnelli
Jon Imanol Azua Mendia
Edgar Bronfman, Jr.
The Right Honorable Earl Castle Stewart
Mary Sharp Cronson
Carlo De Benedetti
Daniel Filipacchi
Robert M. Gardiner
Rainer Heubach
Barbara Jonas
David H. Koch
Thomas Krens
Peter Lawson-Johnston
Rolf-Dieter Leister
Peter B. Lewis
Natalie Lieberman
Wendy L-J. McNeil
Edward H. Meyer
Ronald O. Perelman
Michael M. Rea
Richard A. Rifkind
Denise Saul
Rudolph B. Schulhof
Terry Semel
James B. Sherwood
Raja Sidawi
Seymour Slive
Stephen C. Swid
John S. Wadsworth, Jr.
Jürgen Weber
Cornel West
Michael F. Wettach
John Wilmerding
William T. Ylvisaker